POLITICS AND THE NEW CHALLENGE OF MIGRATION

This volume provides a comprehensive overview of the social psychology of conflict rooted in human evolution, with a particular focus on migration and its challenges in a globalised world. It examines theories for how conflict emerges between cultural, social and political groups striving to advance their own interests and agendas and considers their impact on democratic systems that guarantee human rights and freedoms. Building on the study of social psychological tendencies and motivations, including human needs for identity and affiliation, new empirical procedures are introduced for bridging cultural, social and political divides that encourage students, scholars and policymakers to consider reconciliatory strategies for conflict resolution. By examining political leanings and tendencies for activism and democratic engagement, this book articulates the ethical and political moral grounds guiding decision-making in inter-group and inter-cultural relations and challenges readers to reflect on their moral standpoints.

GORDON SAMMUT is Professor of Social Psychology at the University of Malta. He is former editor of *Papers on Social Representations* and associate editor of *Peace and Conflict: Journal of Peace Psychology*. His previous publications include *The Psychology of Social Influence* (Cambridge University Press, 2020) and *The Cambridge Handbook of Social Representations* (Cambridge University Press, 2015).

The Progressive Psychology Book Series

This book is part of the Cambridge University Press book series, Progressive Psychology, edited by Fathali M. Moghaddam. As the science of human behaviour, psychology is uniquely positioned and equipped to try to help us make more progress toward peaceful, fair and constructive human relationships. However, the enormous resources of psychology have not been adequately or effectively harnessed for this task. The goal of this book series is to engage psychological science in the service of achieving more democratic societies, towards providing equal opportunities for all. The volumes in the series contribute in new and unique ways to highlight how psychological science can contribute to making justice a more central theme in health care, education, the legal system and business, combatting the psychological consequences of poverty, ending discrimination and prejudice, better understanding the failure of revolutions and limits on political plasticity and moving societies to more openness. Of course, these topics have been discussed before in scattered and *ad hoc* ways by psychologists, but now they are addressed as part of a systematic and cohesive series on Progressive Psychology.

POLITICS AND THE NEW CHALLENGE OF MIGRATION

Bridging Cultural, Social and Political Divides

GORDON SAMMUT

University of Malta

CAMBRIDGE
UNIVERSITY PRESS

Shaftesbury Road, Cambridge CB2 8EA, United Kingdom

One Liberty Plaza, 20th Floor, New York, NY 10006, USA

477 Williamstown Road, Port Melbourne, VIC 3207, Australia

314–321, 3rd Floor, Plot 3, Splendor Forum, Jasola District Centre, New Delhi – 110025, India

103 Penang Road, #05-06/07, Visioncrest Commercial, Singapore 238467

Cambridge University Press is part of Cambridge University Press & Assessment, a department of the University of Cambridge.

We share the University's mission to contribute to society through the pursuit of education, learning and research at the highest international levels of excellence.

www.cambridge.org
Information on this title: www.cambridge.org/9781009285087

DOI: 10.1017/9781009285094

© Gordon Sammut 2025

This publication is in copyright. Subject to statutory exception and to the provisions of relevant collective licensing agreements, no reproduction of any part may take place without the written permission of Cambridge University Press & Assessment.

When citing this work, please include a reference to the DOI 10.1017/9781009285094

First published 2025

Cover image: Vlatko Gasparic / Moment / Getty Images

A catalogue record for this publication is available from the British Library

A Cataloging-in-Publication data record for this book is available from the Library of Congress

ISBN 978-1-009-28508-7 Hardback
ISBN 978-1-009-28507-0 Paperback

Cambridge University Press & Assessment has no responsibility for the persistence or accuracy of URLs for external or third-party internet websites referred to in this publication and does not guarantee that any content on such websites is, or will remain, accurate or appropriate.

For EU product safety concerns, contact us at Calle de José Abascal, 56, 1°, 28003 Madrid, Spain, or email eugpsr@cambridge.org

To my dear father Joe (1952–2021), who taught me the value of seeing things from the other side

Contents

List of Figures		*page* viii
List of Tables		ix
Acknowledgements		x
1	In Search of the Promised Land	1
2	The Social Contract	12
3	Social Cognition	24
4	Social Identity	39
5	The Public Sphere	52
6	Multiculturalism and Competing Policies	67
7	The Populist Backlash	81
8	Democracy: The Impossible Dream	96
9	Building a Bridge over Babylon: Patching up Discord	112
10	Ethics–Politics Morality: What's Good for the Goose Is Not Good for the Gander	129
11	The Dark Side of Politics: Who Dares Wins	149
Appendix		171
References		179
Index		192

Figures

4.1	Minimal group matrices	page 46
6.1	Acculturation expectations and social capital	79
7.1	Attunement triangle	88
9.1	Maltese and Arabs views towards integration	124
9.2	Maltese views towards integration and Arab views of Maltese views	125
9.3	Arab views towards integration and Maltese views of Arab views	126
10.1	The ethics–politics moral compass	144
11.1	The political tug-of-war	166
A.1	Argumentation structure: too contrasting	171
A.2	Argumentation structure: no discrimination	171
A.3	Argumentation structure: contact can be good	172
A.4	Argumentation structure: impose ways of life	172
A.5	Argumentation structure: multiple faiths make for a strong society	173
A.6	Argumentation structure: better to engage than isolate	173
A.7	Argumentation structure: better if Maltese and Arabs avoid each other	174
A.8	Argumentation structure: keep cultural practices private to get along	174
A.9	Argumentation structure: racism makes sense	174
A.10	Argumentation structure: Maltese and Arabs can definitely get along	175
A.11	Argumentation structure: religious and cultural differences can be problematic	175
A.12	Argumentation structure: similarities can help us get along	175

Tables

7.1	Vignettes used to identify closed-minded, open-minded and dialogical views on integration	*page* 90
7.2	Distribution of views on integration in 2010 and 2019	91
10.1	Intuitive belief theories	140
11.1	Everyday extremism themes and actions	154
11.2	Ranked everyday extremism items	156
11.3	Everyday extremism incremental behavioural scale	157
11.4	Everyday extremism scale responses for Malta	163

Acknowledgements

This work has been long in the making, and many have assisted me along the way. I thank everyone who lent a helping hand or a listening ear throughout the journey. I would especially like to thank the series editor, Prof. Fathali M. Moghaddam, for constructive support and believing in this project from the start. I would also like to extend special thanks to my two doctoral tutees, Dr. Rebekah Mifsud and Dr. Luke Joseph Buhagiar, for delving into the study of psychology with me. I further thank Prof. Noellie Brockdorff and Prof. Saviour Formosa for their scholarly engagement with my work and for granting me exile in their departments knowing I have very little to contribute to their programmes. Their support restored my sanity and allowed me to keep going forwards. I thank Prof. Martin Bauer and Dr. Mohammad Sartawi for the opportunity to study culture of science; Prof. Kesi Mahendran, Prof Umut Korkut and Prof Xenia Chryssochoou for the opportunity to study everyday extremism; and Prof. Sergio Salvatore for the opportunity to study symbolic universes. Thanks also to Chris, Dhanuja and Liz from the Cambridge University Press office for their constructive support in flogging this manuscript into shape.

The work reported in this volume has benefitted from a number of research grants. I thank the University of Malta Research Council for grants R97-31-397, PSYRP03-01 and PSYRP03-02; the European Commission for Horizon 2020 grant no. 649436 and Horizon Europe grant no. 101095170; the LSE Middle East Centre for funding our work on science culture through the LSE–Kuwait programme; and The Malta Ministry for Home Affairs and National Security for funding the National Safety and Security Monitor.

It is fair to note that, whilst some events are best left to the trash can of history, this work would also not have been possible without the numerous spanners in the work cast my way by colleagues whose agendas reflect other than scholarly pursuits. Whilst they have caused me much anguish and personal suffering, and for this I am most certainly not grateful, it is only fair for me to acknowledge that without the aggravation they caused me, the questions concerning underhanded political manoeuvring and strategising which I take up in this volume would never have dawned on me.

Finally, I thank my wife Claire, my daughters Aanah and Nina, my mother Mary, my brothers Keith and Warren and their families and my City of London pub mates for their support and amusement, without which my enthusiasm for this volume would have fizzled out a long time ago.

CHAPTER 1

In Search of the Promised Land

For the Lord your God is bringing you into a good land – a land with brooks, streams, and deep springs gushing out into the valleys and hills;

a land with wheat and barley, vines and fig trees, pomegranates, olive oil and honey;

a land where bread will not be scarce and you will lack nothing; a land where the rocks are iron and you can dig copper out of the hills
Deuteronomy 7-9

On 31 December 2019, the WHO Country Office in China was informed of a number of patients in the city of Wuhan who had demonstrated an affliction with pneumonia of unknown aetiology. A week later, on 7 January 2020, Chinese authorities identified the causal agent of the condition as a new type of coronavirus: COVID-19 (WHO, 2020). In the months that followed, the COVID-19 virus spread wildly across the globe, quickly rising to pandemic proportions and claiming millions of lives worldwide. In an effort to curb the spread of the virus, nations worldwide went into lockdown, closing off borders and ports and instructing their populations to stay at home unless absolutely necessary. Children found themselves home-schooled, adults worked through teleconferencing and elders found themselves isolated at home. Those who were required to travel faced obligatory quarantines and significant costs.

And yet, in the midst of this global calamity, the Internal Displacement Monitoring Centre (IDMC) in Geneva reported that around 40.5 million new displacements took place during 2020 – the highest figure in a decade! (Internal Displacement Monitoring Centre, 2021). At the point when world leaders decided we should lock ourselves at home and took measures to force us to do so, more people actually moved than at any other time in history. Following a dip in 2021 with another 38 million displacements, 2022 pushed the number of internally displaced to another record level of 60 million movements in a year as a result of the Russo-Ukrainian conflict.

Another 46 million people were internally displaced the following year in 2023, bringing the current total number of displaced people worldwide to a staggering 75.9 million people. And that figure represents only those who were forced to move due to conflict or natural disasters. It does not include legitimate inter-state migration in the United States, the EU, Russia, China, or anywhere else. In this light, it is more than fair to conclude that migration is an endemic characteristic of the human species.

And yet, migration remains a perennial concern everywhere. With a raging pandemic for which humanity did not have a working vaccine, European citizens in 2020 reported being more concerned about immigration than health (Eurobarometer 93, European Union, 2020)! During the same period, the United States halved the number of green cards it issued in 2020 compared to the previous year, and in 2021 admitted the lowest number of refugees since Congress passed the Refugee Act in 1980 (Pew Research Center, 2022: pewresearch.org, 26 April 2022). In Britain, immigration was a primary motive for Brexit (Britain's exit from the European Union) (Andreouli, Greenland & Figgou, 2020). The political aftermath of this historical event saw millions of Europeans lose their freedom of movement to the United Kingdom and vice-versa for British citizens in the EU. Ironically, the problem was only compounded as Britain now struggles with irregular migration across the Channel. Europe itself has not been spared the immigration controversy either. A new pact on migration and asylum published by the European Commission (2020) famously saw Home Affairs Commissioner Ylva Johansson claim that 'No one will be satisfied' [with the pact in the end] (EU Observer, 2020). This is due largely to disagreements over burden sharing (i.e. the proportional distribution of asylum-seeking immigrants amongst European member states).

The EU lacks a coordinated response mechanism for dealing with asylum seekers. Whilst European citizens enjoy unrestricted freedom of movement across member states, this is not the same for asylum seekers, whose movement is limited to the country in which asylum is granted. Member states along the EU's border have long lobbied for burden sharing, claiming that the pull factor of Fortress Europe results in a disproportionate burden on their infrastructure due to the high volume of claims for asylum. EU support to border states facing this predicament is typically of a financial nature, such that very little national relocation actually takes place between member states as relocation is based on a voluntary procedure. The disproportionate burden of migration between European member states remains a matter of dispute due to the fact that the management of immigration remains a national competence not a European one.

Over the years, thousands of African migrants have swamped the islands of Lampedusa, Malta and Lesbos to make it to European territory, traversing the Mediterranean Sea on perilous boat journeys that have claimed countless immigrant lives. The extent of this recurrent crisis is palpable. To give some catastrophic examples, in May 2021, Spain deployed its troops to Ceuta when over 8,000 migrants, including 1,500 minors, crossed from Morocco over a mere two days. And in September 2023, over 8,000 migrants landed in Lampedusa over 24 hours, prompting visits by Italian prime minister Giorgia Meloni as well as European Commission president Ursula Von Der Leyen. Many more make or attempt the crossing on a regular basis – some make it, many don't.

National responses to such crises are hardly welcoming. In June 2021, Denmark passed a controversial bill allowing it to relocate asylum seekers offshore and outside the EU whilst their applications are reviewed. This was intended to prevent failed asylum seekers from gaining a foothold in the country. In Japan, the very same procedure was withdrawn only after the death of a young Sri Lankan woman in an immigrant detention facility. Less than a year later, the UK announced a deal with Rwanda to process asylum seekers on its behalf, following a 240 per cent increase in migrants crossing the Channel over the previous 12 months. The Rwanda plan was challenged in court and scrapped following a change of government in 2024. Giorgia Meloni faced the very same situation in Italy, after financing an asylum processing centre in Albania to the tune of millions of euros.

It gets worse. In 2023, Belgium suspended asylum for single male asylum seekers, arguing that its reception facilities were too stretched and that it therefore would prioritise families, women and children. In 2024, Poland suspended asylum rights to prevent Russia from 'weaponising' immigration to destabilise the European bloc, following its conflict with Ukraine. And, at the time of writing, European countries have suspended asylum applications for Syrians across the EU following the overthrow of President Assad in December 2024.

These examples are but a snippet of the vast and myriad immigration issues worldwide, from the United States' concern with the permeability of its border with Mexico, to China's controversial handling of its Uighur community, the European Union's €6 billion deal with Turkey to curb illegal migration to Europe from war-ravaged Syria, and countless other immigration issues that regularly dominate the news headlines around the world. Migration remains a critical concern everywhere, so much so that it has come to dominate the political landscape.

In Europe, anti-immigration sentiment has fuelled a rising tide of far-right electoral successes. In 2022, Giorgia Meloni became the first female to occupy a prime ministerial position in Italy after her party became the most voted party in the election and she the most voted for candidate. In 2024, Austria's far-right Freedom Party attracted the highest number of votes in elections held in September of that year over any other party. In European Parliament elections held during the same year, Germany's far-right Alternative for Germany (AfD) beat the Chancellor's centre-left party to second place whilst France's National Rally pulled a similar feat to beat the President's Renaissance party. All campaigned on anti-immigration tickets. Perhaps the biggest election story of 2024 is Donald Trump's re-election to the White House in the United States. In a similar vein, Trump promised mass deportations of undocumented migrants, on which he refused to put a 'price tag' (i.e. commit to a budget).

But why is this so? As human beings, we all trace our origins to the African savannah, from which our ancestors roamed in search of fertile pastures. This means that we are all progeny of migrants who ventured from their place of origin in search of a better land. Even on a personal level, many of us have at the very least wondered what life would be like if we packed our bags and moved elsewhere – someplace where the grass seems greener. Not only do we, on a daily basis, use and consume goods that originate elsewhere, we also travel for vacations to other countries, where we spend time taking in different cultures and cuisines and marvelling at different lifestyles for recreational purposes. And we probably all know someone who's moved elsewhere – for love, for study, for work or for fun. Given the pervasiveness of human mobility and trade across the globe, one necessarily wonders, why is migration such a politically charged problem?

The Psychology of Migration

The effort to answer this question will guide our exploration of various topics across the chapters of this volume, as we weigh the social sciences literature in an attempt to understand xenophobia well enough to overcome it. For the moment, we turn the question on its head and wonder why people migrate at all in the first place, given the fact that migration is such an ominous endeavour. Think about this for yourself. Have you ever wondered what life would be like elsewhere? If you could move anywhere, where would you go? And why would you go there? What are the attributes you find enticing?

Now assume you strike lucky and a golden opportunity presents itself for you to actually move. Assume you decide to go ahead with it. What would you leave behind that you will miss? What would you leave behind that you won't (miss)? What do you think your life will be like as an immigrant? Will you be treated the same as locals? Better? Worse? These are questions that every immigrant faces. They underlie the Push–Pull theory of migration (Van Hear, Bakewell & Long, 2018), which posits that the act of migration is a tricky balance that hinges on a knife's edge about features we find attractive and others we do not. Migration depends on where the scales tip – whether what we do not like here is stronger than what we do not like about somewhere else, and whether what we like about somewhere else is stronger than what we like here. The former are termed push factors, the latter are pull factors.

It is worth noting that the variable which underlies this theory is, in fact, a psychological variable of a subjective nature. That is, migration involves an individual appreciation of what is considered to be good enough and not good enough about more than one locale, that is, the one an individual is moving *from* and the other locale the individual is moving *to*. The appraisal will include matters such as the educational system, the health care system, job opportunities, national security, the weather, in other words, something in one's environment that becomes salient to the individual concerned which might be satisfactory for some but wholly unacceptable for some others. The former will be happy to stay; the latter will seek opportunities to move. In psychology, such disparities are called *individual differences*. These might not have much to do with actual, objective differences.

For instance, the health care system might be a salient issue prodding some people to move to another country. One could determine, on the basis of objective criteria, that the health care system in one country is indeed better than in another. For instance, it might provide for a wider range of treatments, or it might generally be more successful or more responsive, and so on. But how much better does it need to be for individuals to move and leave everything else behind them, including what they value about their own lives in their current dwellings, such as friends and family? We can all agree that natural calamities and conditions of war may justify such an enterprise, although even with regards to extremely adverse circumstances some will argue that it is necessary for people to stay and help rebuild, or fight, and so on. The point here is how bad does bad need to be for one to decide to pack up and go? This is where individual differences arise.

What is bad enough for some might not be quite all that bad for others. Conversely, what might be great for some might be barely good enough for others. The point about migration is that it is primarily and fundamentally a psychological act. Its objective manifestation, in terms of how many people move, from where to where else and using what means, rests on its subjective psychological nature in terms of why and when individual migrants decide to pack up and go. This entire volume is addressed at this psychological dimension. If effective solutions are to be devised, they need to cater to the psychological features of the migration phenomenon that include immigrants, hosts, and the relations that are established between them. Consequently, our starting point in this volume is to pose the psychological question of why, specifically, do *some* people migrate when others do not?

To Move or Not to Move

In their seminal work on herding economies, Cohen and Nisbett (1994, 1997) claim that a 'culture of honour' lies behind the highly disparate homicide rates between northern and southern states in the United States. Nisbett and Cohen (1996) argue that southern states in the United States developed a 'culture of honour' due to their being settled by herding communities originating from Scotland and Ireland who demonstrated different tendencies from roaming communities that settled in the north. The latter ventured across US plains in search of grazing pastures for their cowherds. Settled southern communities were thus faced with the need to protect their territory and possessions from roaming cowboys. Protection, therefore, became key to economic survival. A cultural feature thus took root in southern states that saw farmers nurture and protect a reputation of zero tolerance to trespassing as a matter of honour, which was defended by force if necessary. Failure to do so would have left farmers vulnerable to pillaging cowboys, who would simply have moved on to the next territory when resources were sufficiently depleted, leaving desolated farmers in their wake. The settlers' only seeming option was to repel herders' exploitation by making sure that costs outweighed benefits. There is, in essence, no higher cost than human life, so settler communities fell back on this option out of necessity. This is how, in certain states, it became common practice to resort to violent means more readily than in others. The cultural features that took root justifying such drastic measures, centuries down the line, remain in circulation and are argued to lead to differential homicide rates between northern and southern US states.

Cohen and Nisbett go on to suggest that the hunter–gatherer adaptation in the human species, which saw our ancestors roam the African savannah in search of nutrition as well as establish communities to return to following hunting expeditions, led to distinct cultural specialisations further down the ancestral line. These were propagated by social institutions, such that some individuals came to benefit from roaming in search of booty whilst others reaped the benefits of settling and farming to satisfy their needs. The Hunter and the Gatherer, therefore, appear to be two distinct potentialities that inhere in human nature and that could, in certain circumstances, be invoked in mutually opposing ways. That is, in given circumstances, some may opt to stay and tend to local matters whilst others may pack up and leave in search of better opportunities. This basic tendency marks the ebb and flow of migration, both in a phylogenetic evolutionary sense as well as in a geopolitical sense. Those who stay when the situation is dire will need to defend their accomplishments from migrants who come over when the situation is improved. If they do not, they will open themselves up to transient marauders in search of greener pastures. Conversely, those who move go on to potentially acquire coveted resources that are no longer available in their place of origin. At times, survival may well depend on getting out in the nick of time, such as in cases of war. Both strategies may lead to survival and are, therefore, equally adaptive in an evolutionary sense.

Social theorists have long queried the factors that stimulate people to move. The Push–Pull theory of migration, as we have seen, claims that these factors fall into two classes: (a) unfavourable living conditions that urge people to move on, such as conflict and natural disasters and (b) attractive living conditions elsewhere, such as good job opportunities, health care, education and other quality-of-life criteria. The former are deemed *push* factors, whilst the latter are deemed *pull* factors. Both act on the migrant simultaneously, determining when to leave and where to go. Entailed in this decision is a psychological belief that things will be better elsewhere, which may not necessarily be true. Such a belief may be a mere social representation. That is, one may find after getting to New York that the streets are not *really* paved in gold. One might also find that, whilst there are resources aplenty, locals are less than willing to share them with outsiders. Metaphorically speaking, the drawbridge may remain drawn, and the only opportunities extended to immigrants might be exploitative ones. Be this as it may, the psychological forces acting on the potential migrant involve a relative dissatisfaction with the current situation rooted in everyday life experiences, along with expectations of an anticipated future based in social representations of an imaginary locale. This experience is captured in the common aphorism: *the grass is greener on the other side*, denoting false expectations of a better alternative that is bound to disappoint and thus not worth the trouble.

Indeed, experiences of migration are all too commonly fraught with frustration. On the one hand, host communities may prove to be less than welcoming. They may be protective of their stock and the ways of life they nurtured over the years. These might include cultural practices that are somewhat inconsequential in material terms but that might nevertheless be vested with psychological value, such as cultural attire, spiritual convictions, and so on. Yet, like settlers guarding against herders in Cohen and Nisbett's analysis, hosts may resist immigration and the consequent changes it precipitates in demographic and cultural terms. They might argue that suddenly there are a lot more of them than us, or that here we do things differently. These strategies ostracise immigrants and mark them out as 'other' than local. Moreover, hosts have strategies at their disposal which immigrants lack by virtue of their deficient legal status.

For instance, locals may guard their citizenship in a number of ways. They may put in place arduous points-based immigration visas or require hefty investment of capital for golden visas, intended to attract only those immigrants whose skills and wealth benefit the receiving country. They may also put quotas on the reception of refugees and seek to redistribute immigrants claiming asylum to other countries using international exchange programmes based on socio-economic and political criteria. Asylum seekers may also be placed in definite or indefinite detention camps whilst they await a decision on their fate, which may well be prolonged and which will not necessarily be favourable in the end. Furthermore, those who are allowed in are commonly met with an expectation of assimilation (Berry, 2011; Sammut, 2011), requiring them to confine their own cultural inclinations to the private domain whilst adopting the host culture's ways of life as their own in public (Moghaddam, 2008; Buhagiar, Sammut, Rochira & Salvatore, 2018).

On their part, faced with institutional, social and psychological barriers to integration, many migrants suffer frustrated expectations regarding their new life and the realistic possibilities that accrue from their immigrant status, including a stigmatising perception of themselves as 'Other' in the eyes of their beholders (Howarth, Wagner, Magnusson & Sammut, 2014).

This positions them as second-class citizens irrespective of their personal features (Sammut & Bauer, 2021). In such circumstances, migrants are motivated to band together in communities that offer both support in navigating an alien cultural environment and solace in recognising one's personal inclinations as valued attributes. In other words, migrant communities offer their members *bonding* social capital (Sammut, 2011), but risk ghettoization if jettisoned by hosts. Whilst many studies have demonstrated the benefits of migrant integration (Berry et al., 2023), these can only accrue when host societies offer institutionalised opportunities for *bridging* social capital (Sammut, 2011) that allow migrants to integrate and contribute to the host society in their own right. The populist movements that have swept many Western democracies over the past decade and propelled many an anti-immigrant politician to power are testament to the fact that the successful integration of cultural diversity remains easier said than done (Kaufmann, 2019).

Overview

Short of giving up and accepting enmity as the default inter-cultural strategy, we need to consider the psychological underpinnings of immigration as fundamental to any attempt at promoting positive migrant–host relations. These, admittedly, do not necessarily unfold of their own accord. Immigration may provide enriching outcomes, but not necessarily and certainly not always and everywhere. For this reason, a carefully managed approach is required to avoid a spiral of conflict in the face of diversity regarding claims over 'the way we do things around here' (Sammut, Bezzina & Sartawi, 2015). To design such a carefully managed approach, we need to take stock of human nature and the psychological inclinations individuals demonstrate, even if these are not what one might wish them to be. Moreover, we will need to consider sociality as a fundamental condition in the human species. It does not help anyone to forget our evolved phylogenetic heritage whilst chasing some moral ideal.

We must bear in mind that migration entails the establishment of social relations between migrants and hosts and that these are key to positive outcomes quite aside from the subjective characteristics of either taken singly. In other words, our solutions need to be social-psychological, without foregrounding one at the expense of the other. In this spirit, this volume paves the way to designing and implementing empirically based solutions that satisfy mutual aspirations in ways that do not frustrate psychological inclinations. The catch is that solutions need to be open-ended with a future trajectory that has not yet been mapped by any party. This comes from the admission that those trajectories already mapped out, either by migrants or by hosts, lead demonstrably to conflicting outcomes. This much we already know. The challenge, therefore, is in charting another and different course in which migration opens up opportunities for mutual enrichment. This volume presents a methodology for doing this based on human nature in its social psychological manifestation, as opposed to any other foundation however ideal.

In Chapter 2, we start our excursion by considering the social contract (Moghaddam, 2008). The chapter starts by reviewing some major philosophical traditions concerning this notion before reviewing the Tragedy of the Commons and Realistic Conflict Theory, both of which shed light on the evolutionary benefits of self-interest and lead us to acknowledge that selfishness, in certain circumstances, leads to material benefits. Chapter 3 delves into the psychological underpinnings of these social manifestations. It reviews a host of cognitive biases and heuristics that generate xenophobic reactions but that are nevertheless part and parcel of the human psychological predicament. Chapter 4 focuses on how social cognition serves the achievement of social identities that bind individuals with some but that also demarcate them from others. Chapter 5 proceeds to outline how these identities rest on social representations that are generated by social groups in pursuit of collective projects that satisfy group as well as personal interests. These, however, clash with competing projects in diversified public spheres marked by contrasting identities, diversified interests and power relations of a political nature.

Chapter 6 considers the political implications of managing such contrasts through policy and legislation. It reviews the tension between assimilationist and integrationist policies that promote bonding and bridging social capital. Chapter 7 considers the political implications of such policies on hosts. It reviews works on closed-mindedness, right-wing authoritarianism and social dominance, that is, psychological tendencies that fuel the populist backlash. Chapter 8 looks at democratic systems and practices, which are assumed to be able to weather the diversity storm, but which often fall short of the mark. It further considers what is needed to actualise democracy in everyday life. Chapter 9 introduces the PASS method for building a bridge over inter-group and inter-cultural differences, given all the difficulties and caveats reviewed in previous chapters. It deconstructs conflict in a manner that serves conciliatory aspirations that hold over the inter-group/inter-cultural divide. Chapter 10 examines the role and range of grand theories that motivate collaboration in the human species, but which also distinguish some from others as well as pitch some interests against others. These are summarised in the ethics-politics moral compass presented in this chapter, that is argued to serve in taking a bearing of social relations. Finally, Chapter 11 considers the political dynamics of social relations in terms of what to do and how far to go in pushing forward our agenda on the one hand, and in managing opposition stemming from alternatives on the other.

Overall, this volume provides a focus on the psychology of migration, its political consequences, and the challenges to social order it poses in a manner that is faithful to what we know about human nature. The book does more than take stock of disciplinary progress and findings. After considering both tendencies for conflict and potential for reconciliation, the book advances an empirically based solution for bridging cultural, social and political divides in practice. Whilst policy arguments tend either to overlook the psychological tendencies that incline human beings to social exclusion and to conflict with different others, or the possibilities of identifying mutually acceptable strategies that satisfy the requirements of a global village, this volume takes stock of both sides of the migration debate in a way that is not antithetical to human psychology.

The empirical solution advanced in this book is innovative as well as demonstrably realistic. It is thus preferable to the naïve optimism or cynical pessimism that mark the policy divide. Building on a deep understanding of human psychology based on decades of research traditions concerned with inter-group relations and cultural conflict, this volume steers clear of a one-size-fits-all strategy for inter-group contact in favour of an ecologically valid reconciliatory *method*. This serves to fashion strategies for bridging cultural divides in the settings in which these have instantiated and where they need to be implemented, drawing on realities on the ground that incorporate both migrant perspectives as well as those of hosts. In this way, empirically based solutions can be identified that serve mutual interests and that are acceptable and demonstrably justifiable for all sides. Rather than fabricate solutions that satisfy no one, to echo the European Commissioner's predicament, this volume invites readers to empirically explore possibilities concerning a future that is not yet envisioned and that in this way stands to satisfy the common aspirations of all.

CHAPTER 2

The Social Contract

In Chapter 1, we touched upon Cohen and Nisbett's (1994, 1997) analysis of culture of honour that prevails in southern American states. A culture of honour is held to lie behind disparities in homicide rates between northern and southern US states. According to Nisbet and Cohen (1996), this culture of honour can be traced back to settling herding economies in southern states, which banded together to repel cowboy gangs by force. Cowboys at the time roamed the prairies in search of grazing pastures for their herds. It almost goes without saying that Cohen and Nisbett's analysis is not intended as psychologically deterministic. In other words, it does not mean to say that every individual born in northern states grew up to be a marauding cowboy and, in similar fashion, every bloke growing up in southern states grew up to be a sentinel farmer. It also does not mean to say that every cowboy was a thief and every farmer a trigger-happy vigilante. There are, obviously, individual differences across the board.

In essence, however, Cohen and Nisbett's work nevertheless speaks to cultural tendencies that take root given geo-political circumstances, which might become precursory conditions for particular behavioural practices that help resolve certain ecological challenges. Viewed in another way, it makes sense for those who come to occupy agriculturally fertile land to stay put and grow produce. It also makes sense for those who occupy barren land to look for opportunities further afield. Naturally, those who produce must guard their property and harvest from those whose property produces less crop and who therefore opt for growing livestock. It all makes sense; it cannot be the other way around and it cannot be otherwise. That is, it cannot be that cowboys need to guard from farmers. And it cannot be that farmers do not guard – if they harvest excessive produce which can be sold for profit, they will need to protect it or it will simply be swooped up by marauders.

It also goes without saying that, routinely, such divergent interests are resolved quite easily through trade. That is, cowboys purchase (rent) grazing crop for their livestock from farmers at a mutually agreed upon fee. The issue of divergent needs is basically resolved through a mutual agreement that caters to the interests of cowboys seeking to fatten their herds as well as to the interests of farmers seeking recompose for excess produce. There is an equilibrated price that satisfies the interests of both sellers and purchasers, and this is no different from when we purchase anything ourselves today, from sandwiches to sneakers, motor vehicles, houses and everything else.

In this way, Cohen and Nisbett's analysis leads to a consideration of cultural tendencies that aspire to resolve *violations* of this kind, that is, what to do when purchasers do not oblige and avail themselves of the goods anyway. Obviously, in such cases, the social contract between purchaser and seller breaks down, leaving sellers to pick up the pieces and purchasers (or thieves) to reap the spoils. Nowadays, we go to court to seek enforcement of contracts. Before our judicial institutions worked as well as they do now (for all their faults) people were left with less civilised options. Even now, Gambetta (1993) makes the compelling case that the continued existence for the Mafia in Sicily is down to the malfunctioning of the state. That is, when the state does not fulfil its obligations to citizens, citizens find other ways to make do (see Marinaci, Venuleo, Infurna & Di Maria, 2025). Organised crime is one such solution.

Unless security and protection are assured, sellers become inclined to protect their interests by force directly themselves. In many ways, this also happens today with the recruitment of private security at entertainment establishments, for instance, or bodyguards to protect the rich and famous. In these cases, reputation helps. If the seller (or bouncer) has a reputation for violence, would-be thieves might not even try, knowing that the spoils may end up being too costly anyway – you pay with your life! To go back to Cohen and Nisbett, thieving cowboys would have been inclined to move on and prey upon someone else with a softer reputation. As regards sellers, the best way to build a strong reputation is to be firm and fair, always, no exception. In other words, it does not matter how big the violation might have been. Or how small. The point is that no violation, big or small, is tolerated and every violation, big or small, is to be defended at all costs. Tolerating violations is not a matter of price or profit, it is a matter of honour. And there is no price on honour – you either have it or you don't. Consequently, a culture of honour stands to take root in trading locations where sellers have a lot to lose, where they are not sufficiently protected through formal institutions and where a strong reputation might save the day. This could be the southern United States with its fertile prairies, or it could be a gold souk in the Middle East, a maritime harbour in the Mediterranean or a trading enclave along the Silk Road. Underlying culture of honour everywhere is a *social contract* that is implicated in all forms of social relations. And it especially comes into play in matters of migration.

The Social Contract

'No man is an island', wrote the Dean of St Paul's Cathedral, John Donne, in his famous meditation in 1624. According to Donne, a community made up of distinct individuals is nevertheless a single body – individuals are parts of a whole and they cannot exist independently on their own. Consequently, a loss of any member of a community is a personal loss for all other members: 'never send to know for whom the bell tolls, it tolls for thee', meaning funeral bells are a community call addressed at members who are still living. Donne in this way pre-empted social contract theorists whose point of departure is shared with Donne, that is, human beings are not solitary beings but live naturally in a state of communion with their fellows. Aristotle is credited with being the first to point out humanity's irreducibly social nature: 'Man is by nature a social animal', he wrote in *Politics*; anyone who isn't is either beast or god.

What about Robinson Crusoe? Daniel Defoe's mythical character spent 28 years castaway on a remote island following shipwreck. But he did not live alone. He had Friday, his mortal companion. And in the end, he was rescued and returned to civilisation. Also, he was a fictional figure. Human beings have not evolved to live on their own. Let us consider a trivial imaginary example. Envision a duel, one against one. It is unclear what the duel is about. Something, however, is clearly at stake and the individuals involved in the duel are arguing about it. They are both willing to fight and possibly die for the sake of it. Duels of honour actually took place in Western societies until the mid-nineteenth century (not that long ago!). They were arranged instances of combat using matched weapons and were fought mostly with swords, although sometimes pistols were used. And they typically revolved around notions of honour. The aim was not so much to kill the opponent as to demonstrate one's honour by being willing to die for the cause. Eventually, they were replaced by public institutions. So human beings don't really duel anymore. But in a fight of one against one, clearly the strongest man (or woman, duels were fought by both genders) wins. Each party starts with a 50 per cent chance of winning but emerges out of it either a winner with 100 per cent of the stake or a loser with a 0 per cent return. In this sense, duels are do or die – literally.

But duels, even in history, represent an exceptional form of combat. In other situations involving forceful adversity, a combatant may increase his odds by soliciting assistance from another. Imagine a situation where the disagreement between two parties (e.g. a cowboy and a farmer) sees one of them recruit an ally to assist (e.g. a neighbouring farmer). In this case, the situation of two against one[1] means that the party of two has increased their odds of overcoming the single party to acquire a decreased share of the spoils.[2] Sure, the single party may still triumph if sufficiently skilful and astute, but he goes into combat with decreased odds of victory. Now imagine the party of two recruits yet another ally, becoming a party of three. The odds of winning are increased further. With a party of four, victory is assured no matter how skilful or astute the single adversary – on his own he is sure to be overwhelmed. Each member of the party thus acquires 25 per cent of the spoils, against the 100 per cent had they gone into combat alone (and won). But they now do so with certainty of winning. To get the coveted net 100 per cent return at stake in the original fight, all the party needs to do is fight four times in succession, each time against a party of one. In this case, the party will face four instances of combat in which it has 100 per cent chance of winning a 25 per cent stake for each of its members every time. Repetition alone will secure the resources each individual combatant was personally after, with no risk of losing ever. Obviously, in such a turn of events, the single party facing certain defeat will also likely solicit assistance, promising in his turn the sharing of spoils in case of victory. And so it goes. In a nutshell, human beings increase their strength by communion with others.

This state of affairs, which is but a fictional example, represents what social contract theorists have called the state of nature. This state is merely a rhetorical device, meaning that it did not correspond to any particular moment in our species' evolutionary history when these events actually took place in reality. There was no single moment of revelation when the fact of coalition dawned on some human specimen who then went on the rampage with his mates accumulating untold resources (Seabright, Stieglitz & Van der Straeten, 2021). But, as an exemplative illustration, it serves by way of contrast with the gradual establishment of formal institutions that

---

[1] 66 per cent vs 33 per cent.
[2] 100 per cent of the spoils divided amongst a party of two = 50 per cent each. Therefore, 66 per cent chance of winning 50 per cent of the adversary's spoils.

serve the purpose of government, the management of collective resources and the provision of security by regulating naturally occurring social interaction. This is what political philosophers have termed 'the social contract'. Hobbes (1651) and Rousseau (1762) are two of the most well-known social contract theorists (Moghaddam, 2008), although others such as Locke (1690), Rawls (1971) and more recently Shafik (2022) have developed aspects of the social contract further, particularly in light of the various rights and duties entailed in contemporary cosmopolitan publics.

At its most basic, however, social contract theory assumes that human beings are ill-equipped to survive on their own when relying solely on their individual capabilities and resources. Physically, they are not adequately equipped to ward off groups of assailants (e.g. a wolf pack) or large predators (e.g. a bear) whose paths they might have crossed (Tooby & DeVore, 1987). Humans maximise their capabilities by consorting with others. To do this, they consent to respect each other and face common enemies together. This agreement then enables them to seek prey larger than themselves and bring it down through collaborative action. Tomasello and Carpenter (2007) have argued that shared intentionality, that is facing circumstances together with a common purpose, is what has given the human species its adaptive edge. Consequently, by fighting for their common interests together, human beings never have to fight alone. In this way, survival necessitates individuals to establish functional social relations. They can then buy into collective schemes that secure and distribute resources amongst the party to ensure the survival of all. In political terms, this remains the way contemporary Western democracies function. In evolutionary terms, the social contract represents the leap from private to collective security arrangements. Its consequence, amongst other things, is the establishment of formal institutions that serve to guard contractual agreements and obligations. In other words, law and order.

Such an arrangement also provides for the conditions needed to establish division of labour. In this way, those who are best skilled at hunting can hunt for all, whilst those who are better skilled at foraging can also do so for all. The hunter finds shelter on his[3] return, whilst those who stayed home to forage are nevertheless assured alimentation upon the hunters' return. This is the hunter–gatherer adaptation that has secured our evolutionary survival. Since then, over evolutionary history, division of labour has led us towards incredibly high levels of specialisation across all domains

---

[3] In the environment for evolutionary adaptation, it was more commonly men who hunted or fought.

of human activity. Teams of differently skilled specialists are implicated not only in the provision of our security, but also in every other domain of activity, such as education, health care, transport, trade and so on.

Even in a single domain, the level of specialism involved in our contemporary era is astounding. Take, for example, the matter of security, which both Hobbes and Rousseau claim as the primary motif underpinning the social contract. Security concerns in our times are the province of the military on the one hand (external affairs) and the police on the other (internal affairs). In turn, the military is divided into three large-scale entities, that is, army, navy and air force. The police, on the other hand, are complemented by the courts on the one hand and correctional services on the other. Each of these organisations is further segmented along specialist lines. The courts, for example, can be divided into criminal and civil jurisdictions, as well as the courts of first instance and the courts of appeal. Court proceedings require the involvement of judges or magistrates to adjudicate cases, possibly civilians as jury, lawyers representing different parties, registrars and other court officials, court experts, and so on.

No single person has full knowledge of the entire system, but each plays their role on the assumption that everyone else will do likewise. That is, in essence, the social contract. In the process the court registrar, in undertaking her duties, is not actively worried about having to knead dough to make bread for a sandwich which she intends to consume for lunch, any more than she is actively worried about whether the train to take her home will run, whether electricity will be produced to power her home appliances, whether the media will put on some entertainment display for her recreation this evening, whether the school teacher will follow the national curriculum in educating her children today and so on. The social contract provides a basis for reciprocation such that you do one thing, I do another and we both benefit from this accord.

Seabright, Stieglitz and Van der Straeten (2021) explain the evolutionary implications of the social contract. According to the authors, selfish and contentious people do not fare well in evolutionary terms as they are incapable of cohering with others and, without the ability to cohere, nothing can be achieved or effected. Any tribe that came into competition with another tribe during our phylogenetic past would have benefited from the inclusion of a great number of courageous members amongst its ranks, as well as sympathetic and faithful members who would have warned each other of danger, rushed to each other's defence as one and helped ingroup members in times of need. Such tribes were better able to compete and would have thus had better chances to prevail over tribes with more selfish dispositions.

In this way, social and moral qualities would have diffused across the human gene pool, as Darwin (1871) himself observed. Cosmides and Tooby (1989) further note that social exchange, that is, the ability for individuals to cooperate with others for mutual benefit, is a pervasive aspect of all human cultures and manifests in many different forms, such as gift giving, favours between friends and acquaintances, barter and trade and so on. The adaptation of social exchange is not particular to the human species either. It is found in other primate species, such as chimpanzees and bonobos, as well as other non-primate species, such as bats. According to Seabright, Stieglitz and Van der Straeten (2021), the fact that hunter–gatherer groups traded and inter-married with other groups indicates inter-group relations between human coalitions that were not necessarily, or at least not always, hostile. They alternated between collaboration and hostility in response to situational demands.

Over time, therefore, human beings have evolved tendencies towards sociality. That is, they thrive in groups and their wellbeing deteriorates in isolation. Outcasts are thus motivated to leave the group they do not belong to and from which they are rejected, to search for affiliation with other groups that offer inclusion, even if at the price of competition or conflict with the former party (Sammut & Bauer, 2021). This strategy ensures that individuals do not isolate themselves completely, which is risky in evolutionary terms as we have seen. Rather, they seek affiliation with different others with whom they can belong. Social exchange facilitates this process through reciprocity. In tandem with others, individuals participate in coalitions that compete for scarce resources against other coalitions.

This point, however, raises two critical issues. First, as Buller (2005) argues, the evolution of reciprocal altruism creates selection for cheats, that is, those who do not reciprocate but who take advantage of others' altruistic tendencies by accepting the benefits of altruism without providing a benefit in return. The evolution of cheats, in turn, creates selection pressures for the ability to detect cheats. Secondly, the hunter–gatherer adaptation precipitated surplus and trade as some were able to secure more alimentation than needed for consumption. Excess could, thus, be traded for goods and services produced by others elsewhere. This means to say that trade ought to have defused the need for inter-group competition due to generation of tradeable surplus. Basically, what is in short supply in one place is produced in surplus somewhere else and trade ought to have equilibrated supply and demand, circumventing the need for hostilities.

In essence, with the advent of inter-group trade, resources were no longer scarce. We proceed to deal with these two issues in turn.

The Tragedy of the Commons

Let us do another thought experiment. Imagine you form part of a small cooperative in some old village where a small number of herdsmen are raising livestock for themselves and their families. They take turns letting their livestock graze a stretch of prairies that lie adjacent to the village. In fact, this is why the village was established in this location in the first place. A sheriff runs the village and provides law and order. A number of shops are set up for providing goods and services villagers need but the local economy depends, by and large, on the production and consumption of livestock by the cooperative. The prairies are big enough to provide grazing pasture for the village's herdsmen, who do not rear more livestock than necessary due to the strains of the labour involved. One day, a long-lost cousin returns to the village and asks to acquire one of your lamb – he wishes to take it and sell it in another village, far away and at a higher price than what he's paying you for it. In other words, you face the prospect of profit from export. You cannot afford to do this now as you need all the livestock you have reared for this season. However, you agree to the transaction for the next season. All you need to do now is rear one extra sheep until the time your cousin returns to pick it up. Perhaps he has also left a deposit to cover any costs involved. So, you think: why not? – the pasture is big enough to serve all the herdsmen's stock and one more. By raising an extra lamb, you gain a profit for yourself once the transaction is completed whilst hurting no one. Naturally, you agree to the trade.

Over the next year, other tradesmen ride into the village striking export deals with you and with the other herdsmen. Each time, you as well as each of the others think: why not, an extra lamb won't hurt? And so it goes. Each herdsman keeps adding to their stock until such point where an extra lamb does hurt, that is, the pasture can no longer serve this many sheep. What one eats, they take away from another. Pretty soon, someone's profit will become somebody else's loss, due to the fact that grazing the prairies is no longer sustainable. The sheer volume of sheep the villagers are now grazing, for their own consumption as well as for export, needs more than the prairies are capable of offering. And so it goes, the self-interest pursued by one has become a problem for all.

At this point, strict rules for the use of common prairies are adopted by the villagers so that each can take their turn. They agree that they should have equal opportunity to profit from the increased demand for lamb coming from overseas. Now imagine you are grazing your sheep according to the common agreement. It just so happens that the herdsman following you is a little late, for some reason. You have an opportunity to let your sheep graze just slightly longer. Maybe you proceed with taking your sheep off the pasture just a little bit more slowly than usual. Your sheep will graze just that little bit longer. At the end of the season, your sheep are now just slightly fatter than they would have been had your fellow villager not turned up late for her duties. But the prairie is now a finite resource. The extra weight your sheep are showing contrasts with the weight of others' sheep, which are relatively skinnier. Naturally, your sheep command a higher price and, consequently, pay a higher return for your labour than others'. Herein lies the 'Tragedy of the Commons'. As Hardin put it: 'Each man is locked into a system that compels him to increase his herd without limit – in a world that is limited. Ruin is the destination toward which all men rush, each pursuing his own best interest' (Hardin, 1968, p. 1244). In other words, as human beings, we profit (a) from pursuing our own self-interest and (b) from cheating when it comes to the fulfilment of our obligations.

This little thinking exercise makes clear that the Tragedy of the Commons throws a spanner in the works of cooperative activity. Whilst no real village can be assumed to have undergone this simplistic development of trade and export during their history, it is nevertheless clear that cooperation itself gives rise to new challenges. On the one hand, if one decides against cooperation and opts to go it alone, one is left with the prospect of being overcome by an overwhelming external coalition. On the other hand, if one decides for cooperation, one is left with the possibility that an undetected internal cheat (such as someone who can exploit a legal or financial loophole) gains an undue advantage, leaving oneself relatively worse off. Cheating transpires thus as a corollary of cooperation. Without cooperation, the opportunity to cheat does not arise. But without cooperation we perish, so detracting cheats becomes an imperative societal concern.

And this is basically what politics is all about, that is, (a) what laws to put in place that will regulate who can do what, (b) how much do members need to pay (in taxes) to achieve 'a' and (c) what are the costs and punishments for violating 'a'. Institutions, therefore, provide some remedy to the Tragedy of the Commons, not least by punishing or expelling (e.g. jailing) those who exploit the commons unduly. This is why we agree to measures that ensure we pay our taxes (however begrudgingly) and why we agree to respect private property. In Hardin's (1968) terms, we institute 'coercive devices to escape the horror of the commons'

(p. 1247). The Tragedy of the Commons thus sets the stage for the emergence of private property. If you want your sheep to thrive, you would do well to own the land on which they graze rather than rely on publicly available resources, which are sure to be pillaged at some point. And the more land you own, the more sheep you can have, the more profits you make, and so on. You then obviously need to pay more for security, to keep the marauding cowboys from grazing their own livestock on your land. And you also need to pay for lawyers to go after those who try to cheat you out of your legitimate earnings. And on it goes. In any case, laws and institutions serve to protect the social contract that enables cooperation between what are essentially self-interested parties.

Conclusion

We have seen how human beings have evolved an ability to cooperate for mutual benefit, as Cosmides and Tooby (1989) note. But we have also seen that human beings have also evolved an ability to cheat. In ancestral times, those who cheated successfully gained an adaptive advantage and this tendency has passed on in our phylogenetic lineage. Stroebe and Frey (1982) argue that research shows that whenever a public good is provided under conditions of non-excludability of consumption (i.e. publicly consumable goods, as opposed to private goods whose consumption is protected at law), it tempts group members to profit from the activities of others without making a fair contribution themselves. We are, therefore, inclined to freeride if we can, by pitching in less than our due. Consequently, human beings have also evolved social psychological mechanisms to deal with cheats.

The benefits of identifying and weeding out cheats are directly proportional to the losses of overlooking them. In this way, both cheating and detecting cheats are adaptive strategies in their own right. This is a critical point in understanding the complexity of social relations, particularly when they go wrong. For this reason, reputation and the consequences of it being tarnished are an unequivocal deterrent to cheating. The proverb that there is no honour amongst thieves speaks directly to this state of affairs. A thief is someone who has taken possession of property unduly, and this is not an honourable thing to do. One cannot, therefore, rely on honour when dealing with those who are manifestly dishonourable. We see this in everyday terms, such as when applying for a job and submitting one's curriculum vitae, along with supporting references and police conduct. What are references if not respectable people who can attest to your reputation? Think about the prospect of gaining employment if you have to explain a gap in your CV with 'time spent in prison for a criminal offense', as opposed to something else like 'traveling' or 'stay-at-home parent'. In such a case, the odds are clearly not stacked in your favour, however charitable or kind-hearted your would-be employers might be. Cosmides and Tooby (1989) further argue that the possibility of communicating cheating potential through reputation may have allowed far more reliable systems of cooperation to evolve amongst humans than other species who are unable to communicate such information about specific individuals amongst them.

Chapter 3 reviews a number of socio-cognitive inclinations that humans have evolved to deal with the reality of cheats. Presently, it is worth noting that immigrants unwittingly hit this alarm bell in host populations. This does not mean to say that immigrants are cheats. It means to say that some members of society will regard them as cheats due to the fact that they benefit from social arrangements that accrue from other people's accumulated efforts, possibly over a number of generations. Objections to immigration are commonly tied to arguments concerning population sizes and available resources (Sammut et al., 2018). Citizens who are settled down in their native societies perceive benefits to their citizenship that they will assume also appeal to others who wish to join their ranks. For instance, in my native Malta, many think that immigrants are naturally attracted to the country due to its temperate climate, sunny weather and sandy beaches. Why wouldn't they be? This is part of what the fabulous Mediterranean lifestyle is all about! Locals thus understand why others might wish to move there to enjoy these elements, but they are concerned that should they keep doing so the situation might become unsustainable and there just will not be enough to go round, however well-meaning everybody is (Sammut et al., 2018). In other words, they are worried that the commons will degenerate into a tragedy (many claim it already has) and that population increases will make life as they know it impossible.

Naturally, immigrants also participate in public life; they use public parks, public roads, public transport, public health care, social care, education, security and any other service their host society deems fit to extend to its own citizens. They lack, however, a history of contributions to the commons that have made those very services possible. Their claims, like anybody else's, put additional strain on a limited and potentially already-stretched collective system. At some point, if this keeps recurring, the system might collapse. Like the herdsmen whose sheep are skinnier than everyone else's, some are concerned that, due to the inevitable tragedy of the commons, they are/will themselves suffer when others take without having duly given. And those who take without giving are, in psychological terms, cheats (Cosmides & Tooby, 1989). Immigrants, that is, those who have been lured here through managed migration processes (e.g. skills-based visas) or who have come over unsolicited, are regarded as unsustainable at best or de facto cheats at worst.

CHAPTER 3

Social Cognition

What do 'Madoff', the 'Wolf of Wall Street', the 'Tinder Swindler' and 'Inventing Anna' have in common? Other than all of them being blockbuster productions aired by Netflix, they all depict a fraudster as the main character who swindled victims out of their money to fund obscenely extravagant lifestyles that, truth be told, have a definite allure. Champagne and caviar, private jets, supercars, superyachts, designer clothes and jewellery – there's worse things to complain about in life! Many of us would concede that none of these goods necessarily make us happy or are necessarily worth working hard for. Most of the time, average is good enough to satisfy most needs without having to swindle anyone out of their life savings and risk life imprisonment for doing so. We recognise that, in developed countries, the difference between the haves and the have-nots has given way to that between the haves and the have-mores, meaning that many are able to live healthy and comfortable lifestyles that fulfil most of their needs if not all of their wants (James, 2007). But, as Jordan Belfort puts it in the Wolf of Wall Street: 'at least as a rich man, when I have to face my problems, I show up in the back of a limo, wearing a $2,000 suit and a $40,000 gold "f" watch'. I personally see what he means! It is worth bearing in mind, however, that in the end reality caught up with all three fraudsters and they all ended up behind bars. That is because, as we have seen in Chapter 2, societies put in place regulations and institutions to capture and punish cheats. But these blockbuster productions drive a key point home: cheats that go undetected do really well! The problem with cheating, of course, is getting caught.

To be fair, there is also something to be said about the morality side of things. Not everyone who stands to not get caught cheating would cheat, because the act of defrauding another person is morally reprehensible in its own right. But we still understand that some people might not be so morally upright and that, given an opportunity, they would cheat us for their own personal profit. So, we put passwords on our computers and smartphones so that no one can access our possessions even if they're stolen. Our banks put in place security measures to ensure that it is us making purchases and we, in our turn, insure our goods to protect their value from theft. We are all very aware that cheats lurk amongst us and we all willingly succumb to institutional efforts to deter them. In evolutionary terms, we understand how cheating is adaptive, insofar as it results in accumulation of resources that grant the successful cheat an advantage over others, however undue.

Conversely, we understand how the ability to detect cheats is also adaptive, as this helps weed out those who claim more than their fair share. As Cosmides and Tooby (1989) have pointed out, the evolution of collaboration is hampered by the evolution of cheating, such that indiscriminate collaboration turns out to be an unstable strategy. On the other hand, the evolution of collaboration is possible only alongside a strategy that retaliates against cheats. There are two points in this insight that we need to unpack. First, to retaliate against cheats we need to be able to identify them. The question arises, how do we identify cheats? The second point is that collaboration is a discriminatory exercise. We don't collaborate with just anyone – they could be cheats! We, therefore, collaborate with some and, by implication, compete with others. This begs the question; how do we choose with whom to collaborate and with whom to compete? In this chapter we unpack the first of these questions and proceed to address the second more fully in Chapter 4.

Theory of Mind

Imagine you are on your way to college, walking briskly to make class on time. A street seller jumps out from nowhere and lands right in front of you, blocking your path. As you try to squeeze past as courteously as you can, the seller offers you a mobile phone package that sounds like an outright bargain. They are offering a free cell phone with a one-year monthly-fee contract that gives you double the calling time, double the texts, and double the data that other providers presently offer. You hesitate and ask yourself: Is this deal too good to be true? The street seller informs you that this is a limited time deal and the offer is only available until close of business today. You remember an insight from your undergraduate psychology courses, that is, scarcity is one of the core principles of persuasion (Sammut & Bauer, 2021)! This is a strategy that sellers use to make purchasers believe that the product being sold is valuable and scarce, and that if they do not make an immediate purchase someone else will grab the deal instead. For fear of missing out, would be purchasers are incentivised to cut short the search for alternatives and bag the bargain. The 'scarce' offer then turns out to be not so scarce after all, and the deal is extended to other purchasers due to 'high demand' or some other sensational bundle is offered instead with the same pretext.

Back to our story – with this memory now alive in your head, you grow suspicious and you think it best to return tomorrow to check if this deal or a similar one is on offer. In essence, you first want to test whether the street seller is trustworthy or whether they're a cheat. If you find that they are trustworthy, you will make your purchase then, not now. You reason that you need to think things through and you need to be sure that you are not being duped into purchasing a cell phone contract that might not be as good as it seems, in the middle of the street on your way to class. You understand that the seller might be telling you things you wish to hear to entice you to make the purchase. You understand that people might say things that are not entirely true and you do not wish to be cheated. So, you thank the seller politely, tell her you intend to return another time, and get back on your way.

The above encounter is based on real events. It actually happened to me during my postgraduate study days in London. Much as I hate to admit it, the bargain was real and it was no longer on offer the following day, as the salesperson had indeed pointed out. I kicked myself for missing out every time I ran out of free minutes or data on the much less attractive contract I signed up for only a short while later. The morale of this story, however, is not that knowledge of the principles of persuasion works against you in the end (!). The real morale of the story is that we understand that human beings could hold false beliefs that are consequential in social relations. We do not, therefore, take what others say at face value. Rather, we probe and scrutinise what they say to ensure that we are not being misled.

Evolutionary and developmental scientists have investigated the cognitive ability by which humans come to understand that people can hold false beliefs. Perner, Leekam and Wimmer (1987) claim that this ability seems to emerge around the age of four. In a cleverly designed experiment, which they called The Smarties Test, the investigators showed a 'Smarties' tube to children and asked them what they thought was inside the tube. Naturally, the children replied that they thought the tube was full of smarties. They then proceeded to open the tube and show children that, in reality, the tube was full of pencils. After they closed the tube, the researchers once again asked children what they thought was inside the tube. The children duly replied that the tube was full of pencils. The children had by now seen the pencils inside the tube and were aware that there were no goodies to be had.

The researchers then asked them what they originally thought was inside the tube. Four-year-old children understood that they had previously held a mistaken belief that the tube was full of smarties. Three-year-olds, however, were prone to revise their answers and say they originally thought the tube was full of pencils. In another variation to the experiment, the researchers called in another child from outside into the room where the experiment was held and asked children already present what this child would think was inside the tube. Three-year-olds replied that the child would think pencils were inside the tube, whilst four-year-olds answered correctly that the child would mistakenly think the tube was full of smarties, just like they had done themselves earlier.

The Smarties Test is a study that falls under the false-belief paradigm (Topaloglu, 2019). This topic of inquiry examines the human ability to detect and relate with false beliefs. As noted, this ability seems to emerge around the age of four. This is also the time around which 'Theory of Mind' seemingly emerges in human cognition. Theory of Mind refers to the ability to recognise that other humans have mental states just like we do, and that these could be different from our own. That is, if I am feeling happy right now, this does not mean that anyone I am interacting with is also happy, as human beings hold individually distinct mental states. Moreover, we do not have direct access to others' mental states. They must be inferred from our social interactions. This is why Theory of Mind is a 'theory' in the subjective sense. We can never really prove that others have mental states, as we do not have direct access to them in the same way we do, for instance, physical features. Given we ourselves have mental states, however, we can reasonably assume that others do too and that these work for them in a similar way that ours do for us.

In social interaction, we therefore infer these mental states so that we can tailor our interactions accordingly. In this way, we understand that people at a funeral might not be up for a joke and we refrain from sharing any that crop into our head during the ceremony. Similarly, we understand that individuals partying at a clubbing venue may not be favourably inclined to discuss the intricate ethics of nudge theory. In other words, we use our own mental states to make assumptions about those of others and proceed to interact accordingly.

Theory of Mind is a rather complex cognitive operation (Westra & Carruthers, 2017). It necessitates (a) that the subject understands that others can hold different beliefs or mental states than one's own; (b) that these beliefs or mental states can be inferred during the course of social interaction; (c) that others can also infer our own beliefs or mental states during social interaction; (d) that we could act in a way that leads others to infer the wrong belief or state than we actually hold; (e) that others could similarly mislead us into making the wrong inferences about their true beliefs or mental states; and (f) that others have the same capability and disposition to mask their own false-beliefs and to uncover those held by others during social interaction as we do. For this reason, Theory of Mind has been postulated as an evolved psychological mechanism for detecting cheating (Whiten & Byrne, 1988). It relies on the interpretation of verbal and non-verbal communication cues to conjecture a cognitive representation of others' cognitive states on the basis of one's own cognitive experiences. In this way, it relies on a process of introspective projection (Sammut, Mifsud & Brockdorff, 2021a) that enables us to practice mind-reading during social interaction. In this manner, we try to determine when and how to act in ways that serve our interests whilst managing other people's expectations and reactions at the same time.

Prejudice and Stereotyping

It is worth noting that our inferences about other people's mental states, that is, our theory of mind, might actually be mistaken. As the street seller example discussed in the previous section demonstrates, we could infer suspicious intent that, however, has no material basis in reality. Conversely, we might infer good intentions mistakenly and open ourselves up to exploitation. That is to say, our theory of mind is essentially prejudiced. It is our best guess of other people's intent given the limited information we have at our disposal concerning the verbal and non-verbal behaviour they manifest and our own inclinations and behaviour in similar circumstances. It is prejudiced in the sense that we exercise judgment of other people's intentions before we have full knowledge of the transaction. Etymologically, prejudice refers to a judgment exercise undertaken in the absence of full knowledge or disclosure. Theory of mind is prejudiced insofar as it enables us to reach conclusions regarding whether to trust or not trust others we meet in everyday life (Tomasello, 2014).

Aside from non-verbal communication and behavioural cues, we also use other cognitive shortcuts, like appearance and physical features, to make judgments about others. We make inferences about other people on the basis of our perception of cues they demonstrate that we hold are indicative of something we despise or value. For instance, we perceive a bearded, dark-skinned male wearing traditional Arab clothing and we assume he could well be a dangerous fundamentalist Muslim. Potentially, not definitively, but possibly. Or probably. Or, we perceive a young, attractive, blonde female and we assume she is sweet and approachable. Not certainly, but likely.

Prejudice, in simple terms, is an attitude we level at someone on the basis of what we hold to be indicative features. Think of skin colour and the racism levelled at black people on a daily basis all over the world. But think also about our perception of features such as baldness, tattoos, gender, age, accessories, clothing, obesity, muscle tone and so on. Each of these features could tell us something about the individual demonstrating it. Not every perceptible feature is held to indicate something. For instance, features such as a length of nose, or size of ears, or colour of fingernails, and many other features hold no currency in social relations at all. They are not held to indicate anything particular about that person. But other features do!

The crucial thing about prejudice is that we do not judge one another on the basis of individual characteristics; we do so on the basis of features we associate with the entire class who demonstrate them. Rupert Brown (1995) defines prejudice as the holding of derogatory attitudes or beliefs about others accompanied by the expression of negative affect, hostility or discriminatory behaviour towards members of a group on account of their membership of that group (p. 8). Brown's definition is faithful to the ABC model of prejudice, incorporating (a) attitudes, (b) behaviours and (c) cognitions relative to other people. It is worth noting that prejudice can also be positive, such as when we assume, for instance, that people who bear the title 'professor' must be very smart (I can assure you, not always!). Most of the time, however, we refer to prejudice when it involves derogatory attributions levelled to others on the basis of potentially superfluous features.

The manifestation of prejudice rests on the individual expression of stereotypes. Stereotypes are widely held simplistic beliefs about a social group and its members. They represent what we consider others to be like – as members of a social group, not individually speaking. For instance, Arab Muslims are commonly regarded as fundamentalist, dangerous, amenable to terrorism and incapable of integration (Buhagiar et al., 2018). Clearly, not every Arab is Muslim and not every Muslim is Arab. More importantly, not every Arab-Muslim is a closeted terrorist any more than every Black man is a thug, every White girl a slut and every Catholic Priest a paedophile.

The point about stereotypes, though, is that they provide an association between perceptible features and expected outcomes that, whilst evidently hypothetical at a personal level (the individual might or might not fulfil the stereotype), is nevertheless popularly endorsed for the group by another group. Consequently, inter-personal interactions between human beings often take the form of inter-group relations. Individuals draw on stereotypes of others that are shared within their own groups to typify members of another group and act accordingly. In simple terms, stereotypes are akin to mental templates that particular individuals could deviate from but that are held to be more or less accurate (Lippmann, 1922). In other words, our mate Ahmed might well be a lovely chap, but generally speaking one should be wary of Arabs because some of them are known to have committed terrorist acts against us and, before we get to know them well individually, we should exercise caution. So common sense goes.

Evidently, prejudice gets in the way of positive and harmonious relations. Imagine yourself in an opposite situation, that is, meeting someone new who keeps you at arms' length because they believe you look like the dangerous type, or the stupid type, or the unhygienic type, or the bullying type and so on. Being on the receiving end of prejudice is most certainly not a pleasant experience. We tend to avoid relations that make us feel unpleasant and this is how prejudice gets in the way of things. But prejudice on the basis of stereotypes serves broader relational functions. In particular, it conforms to the smoke detector principle (Nesse, 2019). This represents the idea that a particular characteristic might be indicative of something else that might warrant a protective response to avert danger.

To go back to our example, imagine taking a bus for a short ride which, in reality, you could have walked. At one point, a bearded Arab-looking, middle-aged male wearing a kurta and carrying a seemingly packed backpack boards the bus you are on, whispering to himself but within earshot: 'Allahu Akbar'. Sure, this individual might well be the nicest person you have ever met. For all you know, he could be a surgeon on a day off, a community officer devoted to peace, a loving and religious family man and so on. But he could also be a terrorist on the loose! And just like a smoke detector alarm rings at the detection of smoke, not necessarily fire, stereotyped prejudice alerts us to a potential threat that might not be entirely real, but that should not be overlooked. Best to act – by getting off the bus – just in case.

We do realise that such actions might be false alarms. We know that smoke alarms may ring when our bacon rind has been fried too crispy. But when we hear a smoke alarm go off, we err on the side of caution and assume that smoke generally or potentially indicates fire, and if there is indeed a fire underway it is best to be safe and exit the building. There is certainly no harm in that! If we turn out to be wrong, we would have experienced a minor inconvenience but we live to tell the tale; if we are right, however, our prejudice might just save our skin.

Our common sense frames the issue in two proverbs: (i) There is no smoke without a fire and (ii) Better safe than sorry. In this way, prejudice is a frugal way of interacting that saves cognitive time and effort, and this is also adaptive. Instead of using our time to try to determine whether the Arab looking fellow with the backpack is a well to do gentleman or otherwise, we direct our energies towards more profitable pursuits. Fiske and Taylor (2008) proposed the cognitive miser theory to account for the fact that human beings routinely rely on attributional biases and heuristics to manage their cognitive load. Gigerenzer et al. (1999) have provided evidence that such cognitive heuristics make us behave in more efficient and more profitable ways. They showed, for instance, that naïve investors outperformed stockbrokers by relying on a familiarity heuristic to invest in blue-chip companies whilst overlooking small caps with better fundamentals. In social relations, however, prejudice leads to stigmatisation as individuals come to be connoted with attributes that misrepresent them and that label them in negative ways before they are genuinely evaluated on the basis of who they really are as individuals.

Cognitive Heuristics

It should be clear by now that our innate mental faculties do not work as accurately as we might hope. For example, when we perceive some feature of the outside world, we relate with it in 'objective' terms. This means to say that we assign properties to the object in itself rather than to our own perceptions of it. We say the armchair is blue, not that we perceive the armchair to be blue whilst also allowing for the possibility that the chair might be perceived in a different colour by someone else (which would be true for a colour-blind person, like me!).

Basically, we attribute elements to entities we perceive, assuming that our subjective perceptions of them are faithful representations of the objective features of the object itself. And most of the time, this works perfectly well because others perceive objects in the same way that we do – unless there is some physical impediment (like colour-blindness) which explains the discrepancy. Sometimes, however, our attributions do not say anything about the object. Rather they reveal something about us and the stereotypes we privately endorse. These, in essence, are due to systematic biases and heuristics that have evolved in our social cognition and that lead us to make useful – not accurate – representations that aid our survival. Again, note that these could well be mistaken! But mistaken representations might still be useful if they predispose us to act in survival enhancing ways. This is the crucial point about socio-cognitive biases.

Think about someone sitting at a desk who smells fire then hears a fire alarm go off. It would be reasonable to conclude, in those circumstances, that a fire might well be underway and that one should proceed immediately out of the building towards safety. Whilst we all recognise that the perceptions involved could have been due to a burnt-up slice of toast in the kitchen, we would still expect the individual to stick to the fire drill and proceed to safety. The perception may have been faulty, but that is not the issue right now. The same is true for other socio-cognitive processes. We assume that the shadow we saw in the foliage could be a snake, so we avoid stepping on it even though it could have been a twig. When it comes to our sensorial perceptions, as we have seen, the smoke detector principle has served our species well over our evolutionary history, even though it might have led to innumerable false positives. The point here is that the bottom line of our mortal existence is not how accurate our cognition is but how useful it turns out to be in evolutionary terms. That is, does it lead us to make choices that facilitate our survival? Insofar as false positives push us to seek safety every time, we never really pay a price for not being accurate. We simply survive to tell the tale, misperceptions, misunderstandings and all.

Cognitive biases and heuristics are not limited to the perception of safety features alone but extend to every domain of our cognition including perceptions of other people and their ways. Hirschfeld (1998) has noted how humans tend to typify different others in terms of biological features that are held to constitute racialised 'essences'. In this way, we believe ourselves to know what 'Asians' are essentially like, what 'Russians' are essentially like, what 'Africans', 'Europeans', 'Eastern Europeans', are essentially like, and so on and so forth for any human sub-group we can distinguish from ourselves on the basis of some physical feature (e.g. shape of the eyes, colour of skin, etc.). According to Hirschfeld, this cognitive tendency leads directly to the social construction of race.

It is worth noting that all human 'races' pertain to the same species (homo sapiens) and are not racially distinct in biological terms in the same way that, for example, different canine species are from each other, or in the way that equidae (donkeys, horses, zebras, etc.) are biologically distinguishable from each other. Race, in the human case, is a social not a biological construct. The differences between humans are, therefore, more akin to differences between white and tan horses than they are between horses and zebras, to make the point clear. Be that as it may, we nevertheless identify different human races based on perceptible biological differences that mask what we deem to be essential features of those races for all intents and purposes (Wagner, Holz & Kashima, 2009).

Buhagiar and colleagues (2018) further note that, when no biological differences are perceptible between groups, essentialisation might also proceed along cultural lines. In their study, Maltese respondents essentialised Muslim Arabs as potentially violent even at the best of times, due to the fact that Muslim Arabs were held to have been socialised into a violent culture. Consequently, Muslim Arabs were deemed as essentially capable of violence to a higher extent than their European counterparts even if they were law-abiding citizens – their potential for violence was merely dormant and could be triggered by unexpected events. The Maltese thus justify prejudice and discrimination of Arab Muslims on the grounds of culturally imbued essences.

Biological and cultural essentialism serves to demarcate human groups from each other and typify groups in simplistic and stereotypical ways. As we have seen, this leads to prejudice. Moreover, a range of other biases are at work in human cognition to regulate our interactions with others who we perceive to be different from us. We use two reciprocal biases to preserve our ways and the sense we have of who we are and how we differ from them. On the one hand, we rely on the confirmation bias to zone in on information that supports our beliefs, our thinking, our values, attitudes and general preconceptions (Mercier & Sperber, 2011). In other words, our starting point in social relations is that we are right, and we are always on the lookout for new information that proves us to be so (even when we're not!).

On the other hand, we are prone to a naïve realism bias (Ross & Ward, 1996) by which we assume our beliefs and perceptions to be objectively right and other people's discrepant views to be subjectively wrong, therefore biased or misinformed. We reason that, if others who think differently from us were as objective in their thinking as we ourselves have been in ours, then their conclusions would agree with ours so, to the extent that they do not, they have necessarily not been equally objective and reasonable. Once our thinking is rooted in naïve realism, we proceed to dish out an attribution of ignorance (Sammut & Sartawi, 2012) to others' discrepant views that enables us to disengage and, in the process, avoid critically examining the unchallenged veracity of our own ways.

By virtue of these socio-cognitive biases, critical challenges are difficult to mount from the outside as they are easily dismissed. The evident consequence of this cognitive inclination is the preservation of our own ways and the common sense that underpins them. Any contradictory view from the outside is either sense that is not common or, more likely, simple nonsense (Sammut & Bauer, 2021). Either way, it threatens the hegemony of our own beliefs and practices. The only viable challenge is one that emanates from within. Even here, however, our cognitive biases err on the side of preserving the ingroup status. Marques, Yzerbyt and Leyens (1988) identified a 'black sheep effect' in human cognition, where ingroup dissenters are ostracised and treated more harshly than outgroup dissenters. Sammut, Bezzina and Sartawi (2015) report that ingroup members made higher attributions of knowledge and lower attributions of ignorance to an outgroup member with whom they disagreed than they did an ingroup member with whom they also disagreed. That is to say, the contrarian outgroup member does not know, whilst the contrarian ingroup member should know better and for this reason deserves to be treated more harshly.

Xenophobia

The cognitive biases and heuristics we use in social relations point in one direction: that of preserving our ways and our ingroup status as superior relative to others. The benefits of such thinking are obvious: you stick with what you know because what you know, you know to be right. By contrast, what you do not know is obviously not known to be right (if it were, we would know), so it must be wrong and there's no virtue in joining the ranks of those who are wrong. Right is on our side. The end result is therefore group cohesion. Our social cognition errs on the side of group preservation and protecting the familiar, regardless of whether we are right or wrong. Social cognition, therefore, is an adaptation at the service of group cohesion. It helps us preserve a world we know how to navigate.

Different others threaten us even if they do nothing at all. Their being different, on its own, indicates an alternative way of doing things according to which we might not be as right. That is, if they are right in their own ways, we might be wrong by the same token. Different others force this possibility upon us, which threatens us in an existential sense. If taken seriously, the possibility ought to spur some form of engagement to determine which option might be right or better. Whilst this is laudable in a scientific sense, it could definitely serve to dismantle the group if its own beliefs and values are shunned in favour of those of others. The biases in our social cognition ensure we do not head down this route. Rather, we essentialise and dismiss the alternative and rally even more strongly around our own. We engage with others on this basis, to educate them about the truth and sensibility of our own cultural ways and to correct their mistaken understanding about the correctness of theirs (Sammut & Sartawi, 2012). In other words, the social relations that ensue are not at par but an exercise of dominance where parties try to correct each other's ignorance.

At this point, let us retrace our steps slightly back to the social contract theories we reviewed in Chapter 2. We have seen that, even if communal life entails the possibility of the tragedy of the commons, the social contract remains a preferable option to an asocial existence, for there is strength in numbers. What we have seen in this chapter so far is that human social cognition nudges us to retain our group membership even by sidestepping the possibility of examining errors in our own ways when we perceive others doing things differently from us. Perhaps there is a better way of cooking fish and chips; a better way of making wine; a better system of government than democracy; and a different heavenly setup than what we know. When we dismiss the alternative, as we so readily do, we also dismiss the possibility that we learn where we could be wrong in these and other ways. But this is not the only way we are threatened by different others.

Stephan and Renfro (2002) argue that social relations with other groups are threatening to ingroup members in two ways. First, an outgroup may pose *realistic threats* to the ingroup that involve competition over limited material resources. Many individuals who oppose the integration of immigrants do so on the basis of what they perceive to be a limited national pot of resources that cannot possibly cater to migrant influxes as there simply is not enough to go around. The more one shares, the less one has for their personal use and if there is not enough surplus, something will have to give. Sammut et al. (2018) have shown, for instance, that Maltese arguments resisting integration of migrants commonly draw on the small size of the country, the already high population density and the strain on infrastructure. Participants claimed that there simply is not enough space in Malta to accommodate immigrants and that, if the trend of receiving migrants were to continue, this would jeopardise the wellbeing of locals due to a deterioration in public services such as health, education, energy, transport and social security, amongst others. Participants went to great lengths to argue that they would be very happy and very willing to help if they could and that Malta must do its utmost to help save lives in the Mediterranean, but not at the expense of the well-being of the local population. In their eyes, the net effect of sustained immigration would be that everybody would end up worse off in the end, immigrants and locals included.

Realistic threat was originally proposed by Campbell (1965), who argued that inter-group relations involve incompatible goals and competition over limited resources. Even if there might be enough to go round on a global level, the fact of the matter is that wealth is concentrated in the hands of the few and individuals who find themselves in inter-group relations must contend with the material costs involved in accommodating others. The argument is reminiscent of the Tragedy of the Commons, which we reviewed in Chapter 2. To extend the analogy, an equilibrated group of herdsmen with sufficient grazing land for their flock are basically threatened by the prospect of allowing additional herdsmen to join their ranks for fear that the resources available might no longer suffice to sustain all flocks, to the detriment of all.

A second type of threat that marks inter-group relations is *symbolic threat* (Stephan & Stephan, 2000; Stephan & Renfro, 2002). This has to do with the stock of values, beliefs and attitudes that regulate social relations in a collective in everyday life. The introduction of different others to the collective stands also to introduce new beliefs and practices that might stand at odds with those espoused by the local population and that might be neither desired nor valued. Some individuals might certainly value difference for its own sake. Others, however, do not and retain their own ways as customary in their locales. As Sammut and Bauer (2021) note, different others threaten a community's sense of common sense, that is, that things are done in a certain way and that the way things are done makes sense. Alternatives, therefore, either do not make sense or make sense that is not common. Either way, accommodating such differences threatens the common sense already established; it either becomes less common or it potentially no longer makes much sense.

When it comes to symbolic threat, some beliefs and practices may not be very controversial. For example, the opening of a restaurant serving a different type of cuisine that originates in some other part of the world may prove largely unproblematic and might be potentially welcome. Other beliefs and practice, however, might prove more contentious. In Sammut et al.'s (2018) study, for instance, respondents objected to the integration of Muslim migrants to Maltese society on the basis of how they [Muslims] treat women and homosexuals. Respondents claimed that they pride themselves in their country's liberal stance on both of these issues and they feared that an increased proportion of Muslims in their midst might challenge this reality. Some also pointed out that part of Malta's allure is its preponderance of Catholic churches and traditions, and that the Maltese had no part in showcasing other group's ways if these did not represent the Maltese character. Some respondents, for instance, voiced their opposition to the building of new mosques and the promotion of oppressive female attire such as hijabs and burkinis, on this basis.

There are indeed even more pronounced challenges in inter-group relations of this kind that pertain to the symbolic order. Think, for example, of the practice of polygamy. This is not institutionalised in many Western countries but is permissible in a number of predominantly Muslim countries. Migrants originating from these countries claiming asylum in the West often face the prospect of having to choose one wife to include in the asylum application as family out of however many wives a husband might actually have in reality in the country of origin. The remaining ones are left to fend for themselves, including any children they have with the same husband due to the fact that the country's legal system might not cater to males having more than one wife at a given point in time. Consequently, such irregular immigrants might be required to file separate applications with the result that they might be directed to different asylum centres and might well end up hosted, if their claims for asylum are supported, in completely different countries. Remedying this situation by legislating for polygamy might be unacceptable to locals, however, due to the symbolic threat involved.

Similarly, many Western practices are outlawed in other parts of the world on the basis of what locals consider to be good reason. Think, for instance, about prohibitions concerning the consumption of recreational substances, topless and nude bathing, child labour, abortion, homosexual marriage and adoption and so on. In all these cases, the presence of different others threatens the local order by allowing or disallowing practices that flavour cultural ways of life in particular ways.

Taken together, realistic and symbolic threats implicated in the encounter with different others serve to generate prejudice about particular groups as well as heighten inter-group anxiety (Stephan & Stephan, 2000). In this way, they sow the seeds for *xenophobia*. This represents a fundamental fear of other groups that strikes individuals who perceive different others as threatening and which justifies prejudiced attitudes and discriminatory measures to safeguard oneself and one's way of living. This might not be a conscious and deliberated choice. Rather, it might be an instinctive response that follows the perception of a threatening stimulus whether this is truly the case or not. It results, as we have seen, in the banding of coalitions that come together to ward off threats that emanate from the outside and that immigration brings right into one's own backyard.

Conclusion

Diversity is understood by many as a value in its own right. Different people are endowed with different characteristics and these do not necessarily need to be hierarchically sorted as better or worse than one another. It was personal characteristics that led to Seabiscuit's success on the racehorse track in the 1930s, not his brown mane. Similarly, the extent to which individuals may be considered threatening to others, or otherwise, depends on personal dispositions not generalised characteristics.

However, whilst many concede that this is indeed the case, they might nevertheless experience an instinctive discomfort in an encounter with different others. Reactions like these are deeply rooted in our psychological experience and do not require our conscious, reasoned or deliberated choice. So far, we have seen how our evolutionary history predisposes us to band together with others for safety and seek protection with our group from would be marauders. We are able to project our thoughts onto others to guess what their intentions might be, on the basis of thoughts we have ourselves. We understand that, just like us, others might entertain the possibility of cheating for personal profit and we project our introspective reflections onto others' intentions to guard against exploitation. We have also seen how we subscribe to institutionalised rules and regulations that, whilst inconvenient, also confer order and protect us from cheats.

At the heart of our very survival, therefore, is our ability to negotiate ingroup–outgroup relations and the demarcation of friend from foe. In Chapter 4, we will see how our psychological makeup helps us achieve this in a natural way – through the construction of our own identity.

CHAPTER 4

Social Identity

Let's start this chapter with another mental exercise. Imagine you receive an invitation to a party that is being organised by one of your friends. You diarise the event and make sure you get a gift for the host. On the day, you take a cab and go to the party as planned. There's no traffic on the roads today so you get there a little early. You go right in and you see that there are some people around, but you do not recognise anyone you know. People are chatting and laughing and there's a good vibe, so you want to make yourself comfortable. You head over to the bar, get yourself a drink, then stand on the side and gaze around. You occasionally make eye contact with people you are not yet acquainted with, wondering if you could engage someone in conversation or catch a glimpse of any of your friends when they come in. We all understand that, in such circumstances, things might be a little awkward at the start but as soon as the party gets underway people socialise, have fun and get to know each other in the process. There is nothing altogether untoward in what has just been described. So far, so good.

Now let us add one other detail: you are the only adult in the room! This is a children's party and everyone else described above is actually under the age of seven! Basically, you were invited to your friend's son's or daughter's birthday party. What do you think of your behaviour now? In a party like this, would you head to the bar, get a drink, then stand aside waiting to chat someone up? Maybe. Again, there's nothing manifestly wrong in any of this. But the truth is that your demeanour is likely to change quite radically if you went to a children's party and on walking in you saw no adult in sight! You would quite possibly have walked round the venue to check where the adults were before heading to the bar for a drink. If you did chat to any of the children, your topic of conversation would quite likely have been very different than it would have been were the party populated by adults your own age.

Let's extend this exercise a little further. Imagine now that the party was held at a retirement home for your friend's nana's centennial celebration. This time, everyone around could be your grandparent. Would your behaviour, demeanour and style of conversation change as a result of this, relative to the children's party or an adult party? What would you talk about if you were trying to strike up a casual conversation with someone you did not know before in a party like this? Would you talk the same kinds of things to children and the elderly as you do adults? Bear with me just a little bit further. What if you were the only female around in an adult party populated only by men? What if you were the only black, brown, or white skinned person around? What if everyone else was a robed priest? What if everyone else was Muslim? Or transgender? You get where we are going with this.

Nothing in the behavioural description above is manifestly untoward, regardless of who the crowd at the party is and what personal characteristics they demonstrate. What is clear, however, is that our expectations of our own behaviour change between these various categories and the way we respond to one will not be the same as the way we respond to another. We cannot help cognitively categorising people in terms of perceptible traits. And we cannot help tailoring our interactions accordingly. And thank goodness for that – we can be sensitive about proper and improper conversational styles according to specific circumstances. Social categories matter and it is good that they do. It is in terms of social categories that individuals are able to adjust their behaviour to their social circumstances in adaptive ways.

Conversation in social situations, amongst other things, enables people to get to know each other. In the process, individuals discern whether the other party is someone they can relate with. In other words, social conversation provides the setting required for gauging the potential for collaborative activity. As we have seen in Chapters 2 and 3, collaborating with other individuals lies at the heart of our ability to survive – both on an individual basis as well as collectively as a species. In collaborating with similar others, who also share concerns about cheats and marauders, we form social groups to guard against them. We spread gossip or news through social networks about who did what and, on the basis of that, who should or should not be trusted.

Formally, we establish institutions that assume specialised responsibilities that involve scanning our environment for criminal activity – intelligence services. We have developed myriad institutions to deal with myriad issues in the upkeep of law and order. We enact entire communities of members that band together for the fulfilment of these needs; think neighbourhood watch. To do so, communities define membership, identify who belongs and who does not, determine what resources are made available to those who do and what treatment is extended to those who do not, delineate the community's borders, enact security systems for protecting members within the community's jurisdiction, train personnel to execute military operations intended to keep foreigners out, police individual behaviour, enforce the law and administer justice to protect the system from within, and so on and so forth. And, whilst most of these capabilities today are aimed at providing protection from malicious intent on the part of other human beings, we also recognise that our survival as a species over evolutionary time rested on our ancestors' capabilities to similarly collaborate in matters of predation and plunder that also involved other species. Social interaction is what enables us to achieve all of this in communion with others.

A critical capability in ascertaining such positive community relations is the identification of friend from foe. We recognise that some individuals in our environment are friendly and trustworthy. Collaborating with such individuals ensures the satisfaction of mutual goals and interests over time (Sammut, 2011). However, we also recognise that some others are best left to fend for themselves due to their proclivity to take advantage of collective resources for personal gain.

We therefore imbue our institutions with the capacity for social exclusion and proceed to, for example, ban certain individuals from membership in interest groups, deny certain people the rights and resources made available to group members, refuse residence or citizenship permits to foreigners and so on. Such exclusionary mechanisms are to be found across all levels of human organisation, from simple friendship groups to international relations. In certain cases, they may also involve the establishment of total institutions, like prisons or mental asylums, that lock particular individuals away to protect the common good.

Similarly, the practice of exile is a way of 'ejecting' undesirable political fomenters that are held to threaten the social order. This is a very long-standing exercise. Earlier in our evolutionary history, our ancestors would have deemed some people outcasts and proceeded to forcibly kick them out of the city gates. For such individuals, survival prospects were very grim. The feeling of loneliness is arguably an adaptation against self-ostracising tendencies – without a degree of psychological unease when alone, humans would have been inclined towards solitary ventures that did not require any compromise of personal interests in favour of group cohesion (Williams & Nida, 2011). Research has shown that social exclusion activates regions of the brain associated with pain in response to injury (Eisenberger, Lieberman & Williams, 2003). This forces attention to the source of the pain and enables a revision of strategies to resolve the issue. The obvious countermeasure to loneliness is belongingness, which is achieved through group membership and serves to not only strengthen our personal wellbeing but also increases, in evolutionary terms, the entire community's odds for survival.

The demarcation between ingroup and outgroup, therefore, is a critical ingredient in every human system that is either regulated formally through black letter law or informally through cultural norms that invite or deter collaboration. In this chapter, we will look at the psychological underpinnings of such collaborative activity. Specifically, we will look at how the negotiation of our personal and social identities – two sides of the same coin – serves to satisfy our interests (Sammut, 2011) in a way that enables our achievement of the political projects we choose to pursue (Buhagiar & Sammut, 2020).

Personal and Social Identity

The centrality of social categories to identity became evident since the start of early theorising of the concept in the social sciences. Kuhn and McPartland's (1954) Twenty Statements Test, for instance, poses the question 'Who am I?' to survey respondents who are invited to complete the statement 'I am …' up to 20 times. The way people answer this identity question is by providing descriptors that are identifiable as social categories to others. You can try this test out for yourself. For instance, in my case I would list attributes such as 'Father', 'Married, 'Scholar', 'Middle-Aged', 'European', 'Liberal', '[Slightly] Overweight', and so on, to describe my own identity. In your case, or anybody else for that matter, a different configuration of descriptors would be used to describe who you are and how you define yourself.

The jury is still out on how many general characteristics individuals use to describe their own identities. Kuhn (1960) claims that responses to the Twenty Statements Tests can be categorised into five overarching categories, namely Social Group Memberships, Ideological Beliefs, Interests, Ambitions and Self-Evaluations. Rentsch and Heffner (1994) argue that there are eight general categories in identity, not five, as suggested by Kuhn. These include Inter-personal Attributes, Ascribed Characteristics,

Interests and Activities, Existential Aspects, Self-Determination, Internalised Beliefs, Self-Awareness and Social Differentiation. Be that as it may, what the Twenty Statement Test makes clear is that we use categorical descriptions that, in themselves, do not distinguish us in unique terms. Rather, they assign us to social categories that we share with many others. For instance, there is nothing particularly unique in being a 'Father', as in my case. Sure, this distinguishes me from others who would describe themselves as 'Mothers'. It also distinguishes me from those who do not define themselves in terms of having fathered children. Perhaps this might be due to their not having had any offspring, or perhaps the category is not particularly salient for them personally. But being a 'Father' is an attribute I share with many other men on the planet, as is the category of being '[just] slightly overweight', and so on for every other category.

In practice, what distinguishes us from everyone else is the particular constellation of identity markers that defines us in its totality. Identity, in essence, is how we define ourselves – for others. This is a crucial point that is worth underlining. At different points of time in our lives we will identify as a person of a certain kind or another. We might have played tennis when younger, but we have now given up the hobby and we spend our free time circuit training at the gym. We might thus have identified ourselves as tennis enthusiasts in the past but no longer do. The concept of gender fluidity similarly illustrates the malleability of identity categories. An individual might not identify as homosexual or heterosexual, male or female, and so on. Or they might at one point but revise their identification at a later point because they feel this no longer describes who they really are, for whatever reason.

What we identify ourselves as, therefore, is a fundamentally personal issue. You might or might not relate with that yourself – but what categories I experience as categories that define me is a wholly subjective matter. And that configuration of features might well make me characteristically unique. There might be no one else on the planet who shares that same precise constellation with me. The point here is, however, that, even in defining ourselves personally, we mark ourselves out socially. Think about how we use an identity card or passport. We do not use a passport to recognise who we are. We use a passport or identity card to show *others* who we are. In other words, we use social categories to define ourselves for others, in ways that distinguish us from some but that also categorise us with similar others. What this means to say, therefore, is that personal identity and social identity are but two sides of the same coin.

Social Categorisation

Social identity refers to that part of our self-concept that represents the groups we identify with or that we feel we belong to, and the thoughts and feelings we have associated with membership of those groups including our beliefs about what others think about us by virtue of this membership. There are certain groups that we naturally belong to. One's nationality, for instance, is assigned by virtue of where in the world they happen to be born. One could value this group membership, or one could come to despise it and strive to disassociate oneself from it to avoid assuming national attributes that one might not identify with. For instance, many German nationals today would reject any form of identification with the Nazi regime that waged World War II (Liu & Hilton, 2005).

Not all forms of group membership are assigned unvolitionally. For instance, one's political identification is largely a matter of personal choice and may change over a span of a few years. In any case, any form of group membership – voluntary or involuntary – involves value judgments associated with membership held both by oneself as well as by others. For instance, one could identify with the Republican party but feel embarrassed about the Capitol riots. Moreover, one could personally be proud of one's group membership but at the same time be aware of denigrating judgments levelled at one's group by others (Howarth, 2002). Howarth, Wagner, Magnusson and Sammut's (2014) study shows, for instance, how certain individuals only ever realise they possess a recognisable skin colour once they migrate out of their native communities and experience stereotypes levelled at them by others. Many who call out racism and sexism do so precisely on this basis. They resist the derogatory attributions levelled at their group by others who consider themselves superior in categorical, not necessarily individual, terms. Our social identity comprises all of these elements.

In any given situation, our social identity and the perceptions, feelings, attitudes, beliefs and behaviours associated with it might be activated when relating with similar or different others. In this way, inter-personal relations often take the form of inter-group relations. Think of the mental exercise we discussed at the beginning of this chapter. In one situation our gendered social identity might be activated, in another situation our religious social identity, and so on and so forth for the myriad categories we personally identify with (Oakes, 1987). By means of social categorisation, we cognitively represent social categories in ways that describe our group and distinguish it from different others (Turner, Hogg, Oakes, Reicher & Wetherell, 1987).

It goes without saying that these cognitions are stereotypical and may not reflect the genuine attributes of the particular individuals we relate with, even though they might be members of some identifiable group that presumably shares those attributes. Not all Muslims are peaceful in their disposition, and neither are they all prone to extremist violence (Buhagiar, Sammut, Rochira & Salvatore, 2018). Many, however, associate Islam with the potential for violence and use this stereotype to resist integrating Muslims into their society (Sammut et al., 2018). Social categorisation, therefore, is prone to depersonalisation errors that often precipitate misperceptions and misunderstandings in inter-group and inter-cultural situations (Turner, 2010). This said, when social categorisation comes into play in inter-personal relations, it also evokes behavioural norms associated with the prototype of that category (Hogg, 2016).

In essence, social identity theory (Tajfel & Turner, 2004) posits that society is structured into distinct social groups that we cognitively represent as social categories, and that these categories provide us with a template for inter-personal behaviour on the basis of the group memberships we invoke and assign in social relations. Moreover, social identity not only represents perceptible features as markers of group membership, it also includes a definition and evaluation of what membership entails. In other words, social identity categories involve both descriptive (i.e. describe who one is) and prescriptive (i.e. provide a prototypical code of conduct) elements. For example, being a Republican means not only identifying oneself and being identified by others as a sympathiser of the Republican party, it also involves thinking and behaving in characteristically 'Republican' ways (Hochschild, 2016).

Minimal Groups

Social Identity Theory (Tajfel & Turner, 2004) traces its roots to Tajfel's minimal group experiments (Tajfel, Billig, Bundy & Flament, 1971). Tajfel and his colleagues wanted to investigate the minimal conditions that are both necessary and sufficient for individuals to engage in discriminatory inter-group behaviour. In a series of clever experiments, Tajfel proceeded to recruit students and randomly assign them to arbitrary groups. For instance, in one experiment Tajfel asked students to estimate the number of dots projected on a screen. After students gave their responses privately, the experimenters assigned them to either of two groups, that is, the over-estimators (those whose responses were higher than the actual number of dots projected) or the under-estimators (those whose responses were lower than the actual number). In reality, the students' responses did not even matter – they were simply assigned to either of the groups on the basis of a random draw. But they were led to believe that their responses mattered and that other students had erred in a similar way they had. In a subsequent experiment, students were divided on the basis of artistic preferences – Kandinsky or Klee. And in yet another variation students were divided into two groups on the basis of a random toss of a coin which participants actually witnessed.

In all cases, students found themselves in groups during the experiment that had no material bearing outside of it. However, they never got to meet fellow group members. In the second phase of the experiment, students were handed sheets of paper with numeric matrices that required them to assign points to other students (not themselves) whose identity was concealed by means of index numbers but whose group categorisation was revealed on paper. This was the true experiment. Participants were told that the points students received could later be exchanged for cash. Presumably, therefore, the more generous students were in allocating points to other students, the bigger the payoff those other students would get in the end. The trick, however, was that the distribution of points involved an inter-group dimension and whilst the allocation was necessarily pairwise (i.e. vertical allocation) it was not necessarily equitable (see Figure 4.1).

The matrices participants were provided with referenced a pair of students who stood to be allocated points by the participant and whose group membership was revealed, as just detailed. The allocation needed to be pairwise. If the participant got Matrix A, for instance, they had to

Matrix A												
Klee	7	8	9	10	11	12	12	14	15	16	17	18	19
Kandinsky	1	3	5	7	9	11	13	15	17	19	21	23	25

Matrix B												
Klee	18	17	16	15	14	13	12	11	10	9	8	7	6
Kandinsky	5	6	7	8	9	10	11	12	13	14	15	16	17

Figure 4.1   Minimal group matrices

choose what to award to a Klee student, from 7 to 19 points. Whichever number of points they allocated would correspond to a pairwise Kandinsky allocation. For example, if the participant awarded Klee 7 points, Kandinsky would get 1. By contrast, if the participant awarded Klee 19 points, Kandinsky would get 25. As one moves horizontally across the matrix, the points accorded to the other increase and became higher than what is accorded to the fellow student. The matrix has no midpoint, even in Matrix A the allocation tips one way or the other.

Participants could, therefore, opt for giving the indexed students maximum points – meaning the largest possible pay-out. As detailed, this would have meant a higher allocation to the outgroup member. If participants wished to favour members of their own group, they would have to allocate a lower number of points to the pair, meaning a lower monetary pay-out in the end for both (although this would provide a proportionately higher pay-out to ingroup members relative to outgroup members).

The results showed that students opted towards the most equitable strategy that, however, tipped the balance in favour of their own group. This startling finding has since been replicated many times and demonstrates that the mere fact of being categorised as a group member precipitates ingroup discrimination even when categorisation takes place on the basis of arbitrary and irrelevant criteria, when there is no self-interest and when the identities of group members are fully concealed. The expectation that participants would bear in mind their categorisation as students and distinguish themselves from experimenters who would need to cough up monetary pay-outs to students at the end of the experiment did not materialise. Students favoured their own, but not as students contrasting with experimenters. They favoured their assigned ingroup over the outgroup, even if this meant a lower pay-out for all in the end.

Negotiating Identity

Clearly, not every group in society enjoys the same kind of social prestige as every other group. That is to say, some social groups are more highly regarded than others. For instance, disparaging ideas that at some point had or still have currency in social terms include the idea that females are irrational or crazy, that blondes are dumb, that men are logical but emotionally inept, that men are unable to care for children, that old people are senile, that the poor are spendthrifts, that Muslims tend to violence, that gay people are child-molesters, and so on. These ideas result in the development of stigmatised identities that confer shame rather than prestige to the identity holder. Joffe's (1995) study on the social representations of AIDS documented stigmatised identities held by the gay community who felt ashamed of themselves due to media depictions associating the disease with being gay, even amongst individuals who had never experienced sexual intercourse! Racism, sexism, ageism, classism, nationalism and other 'isms' represent relational strategies that put people down on the basis of attributes other than their own personal dispositions.

Goffman (1963) argues that stigmatised identities are spoiled – they carry the stain of the group's stereotype and this conditions the way they are perceived and treated by others (Howarth et al., 2014). In these conditions, individuals find themselves at a disadvantage relative to others who belong to more prestigious and better valued groups. The result of this categorisation process is prejudice and discrimination. For this reason, individuals who find that they belong to stigmatised groups are often motivated to challenge the status quo and revise a system that disadvantages them (Ellemers, 1993; Hogg & Abrams, 1988; Tajfel & Turner, 1979; Taylor & McKirnan, 1984).

In certain circumstances, an individual may simply shed their social identity and trade it for a different one. For instance, if being identifiable as a punk rocker disadvantages the individual when applying for an executive position with a Wall Street firm, the individual may simply shed their punk rocker identity and trade ripped jeans for a pinstripe suit to negotiate a new identity that confers relatively more benefits regardless of personal music preferences. Or, a Republican may become Democrat if it pays her to do so; a Protestant may turn Catholic, a White Sox fan may start rooting for the Cubs, and so on. As we have seen, however, not every attribute can be so easily traded. Skin colour, nationality, biological dispositions, and other attributes may categorise individuals in ways that do not reflect who they really are.

In such circumstances, individuals may be motivated to compete with dominant groups for a fairer representation. Social movements are often intended to challenge stereotypes and revise disparaging group attributes (Milgram & Toch, 1969; Klandermans, 1997, 2003; Tyler & Smith, 1998; Haslam & Reicher, 2012; Sammut & Bauer, 2021). The suffragette movement, for instance, provides a case in point. The movement started a little over 100 years ago in Britain in an effort to gain voting rights for women. It has since expanded to claims for equal pay, family friendly measures at the workplace, gender quotas to revise negative discrimination and so on. In a recent iteration, it incorporates the 'HeForShe' campaign that proposes the idea that it is cool for males to be feminist. Whilst clearly successful in many domains, equality between genders remains a challenge almost everywhere around the world. Other celebrated movements have seen more limited success. Dr King's dream of racial equality remains unrealised, as the 'BlackLivesMatter' (BLM) movement has shown. And still other categories have not mobilised successfully at all – we are yet to witness a granny revolution to fight ageism! The point here is that social identity categories are neither neutral nor immutable. For this reason, they are contested as bearers seek to underline positive attributes that convey positive self-esteem. Howarth's (2002) study of Brixton youth in London shows how remembering the Brixton riots of the 1980s as an event where downtrodden black youth stood up to institutional racism serves to confer positive distinctiveness for one's own group in the place of stigma.

In circumstances where a spoiled identity cannot be traded or shed and where revising its meaning socially is an impossible task, individuals may well internalise the negative attributes and agree with the dominant group about their own inferior status. For instance, in their classical dolls experiment, Clark and Clark (1939) showed how black children socialised in American society develop a preference for white dolls instead of other dolls matching their own skin colour. The effects of colonialism also typically include the internalisation of denigrated identities by subjugated subjects (Fanon, 1965; Gilroy, 2005). Social Dominance Theory (Sidanius & Pratto, 2003) posits that societies are hierarchically structured in relations of dominance and unequal power between distinct groups and that these relations perpetuate themselves over time. For this reason, the negotiation of a distinctive positive identity that confers positive self-esteem may not be as simple and straightforward as declaring oneself to be a person of a certain kind – it also requires that others recognise and legitimate one's self-attributions in unproblematic ways (Abrams & Hogg, 1988; 1990; Crocker & Major, 1989; Crocker & Luhtanen, 1990; Long & Spears, 1997; Rubin & Hewstone, 1998). The negotiation of identity, therefore, is as much a political process as it is a personal one.

The Politics of Identity

We have seen that negotiating a social identity requires recognition by others that one's claims to identity are legitimate (Obradović, Albayrak-Aydemir, Amer, Boza & Kışlıoğlu, 2024). If others do not recognise one's claims as legitimate, political processes ensue. Individuals band together to establish a critical mass that upholds their identity and through which they struggle for recognition (Hill & Wilson, 2003; Bang, 2009; Sammut & Bauer, 2021). Many political movements concern aspirations for self-determination that certain groups claim in distinguishing themselves from other groups. Examples of such political movements abound, from Scotland's longstanding pursuit of independence, Catalonia's efforts for independence from Spain, the Brexit break up from the EU and so on. Underlying all these events is the drive for individuals to distinguish themselves from a higher-order social category that has been imposed on them and with which they do not readily identify. In public life, their actions in pursuit of a defining identity that suits their own sense of self acquires political impetus.

Harris, Pärnamets, Sternisko, Robertson and Van Bavel (2022) note the growing evidence that political identity operates on the pretext of social identity. Clearly, identification with the social category 'Democrat' or 'Republican' is in some ways similar to identification with the categories 'married' or 'single', 'American' or 'European' and so on. In all cases, an individual who identifies with one category necessarily distinguishes themselves from another. Certain categories are imbued with political ramifications and involve a competitive struggle for resources waged against other groups. Political partisanship thus motivates inter-group discrimination and prejudice due to the social identity processes it involves. Lelkes and Westwood (2017) found that Republicans or Democrats, even in tasks that were entirely unrelated to politics, showed a preference for working with a less competent 'Independent' partner than a more competent partner from the opposing party. McConnell, Margalit, Malhotra and Levendusky (2018) found that partisans were willing to forgo financial incentives if doing so would hurt their political opponents. The authors argue that the effect of political partisanship on economic behaviour emulates the effect of religious identity and follows the principles of social identification through social categorisation. Partisans, much like Tajfel and Turner's experimental subjects, are willing to sacrifice self-interest at the altar of positive group distinctiveness.

Political partisanship also influences judgements of moral transgressions. Studies have shown that people punish in-group members less harshly than out-group members for non-cooperative behaviour (Harris et al. 2022), except in cases of unlikeable ingroup members who are treated as traitors and judged more harshly than the outgroup (Sammut, Bezzina & Sartawi, 2015). Marques, Yzerbyt and Leyens (1988) term this 'the black sheep effect'. The tendency to discriminate against outgroup members plays out in political domains. Anduiza, Gallego and Muñoz (2013) report that Spaniards rated a corruption case as more serious when it implicated the opposing party than when it did one's own. Carlson (2015) reports that Ugandans were less likely to blame government for poor-services in their community when they supported rather than when they opposed the incumbent president. What this means to say is that political behaviour influences inter-group behaviour along social identity lines.

It is worth noting that political identification, once forged, also enables collective action in pursuit of political projects (Thomas, Louis & McGarty, 2020). Identities bring people together in search of a common purpose or common interests. The etymology of the term interest is traced back to two Latin terms that represent a state of being together; inter: in between, and esse: being (Sammut, 2011). In other words, it is in every member's interest that the common purpose is advanced. Van Zomeren, Kutlaca and Turner-Zwinkels (2018) demonstrate that collective action is predicted by commitment to groups that effectively mobilise action towards lifting perceived injustices. In Tajfel's (1982) words, collective action is 'efforts by large numbers of people, who define themselves and are defined by others as a group, to solve collectively a problem they feel they have in common, and which is perceived to arise from their relations with other groups' (p. 244).

Conclusion

Individuals who bind together through a shared social identity identify themselves and come to be identified by others as a group in pursuit of a group agenda. The group's agenda constitutes the group's political aims. The pursuit of political action requires a group to formulate a vision of a political project, that is, to represent a more promising future for its members along with an action plan to make it happen (Buhagiar & Sammut, 2020). In the process, the group might need to renegotiate social representations of the issues at stake as well as revise the social relations it is engaged in towards developing a master narrative that fits (Sammut, Tsirogianni & Wagoner, 2012). The grand narrative binds ingroup members together in bonds of identification with the cause. This is how social identity lies at the crux of political action. It follows the principles of social identity rooted in representation (Chryssides et al., 2009) of social categories that legitimate the group and its political aims. It is to the topic of social representation that we now turn.

CHAPTER 5

The Public Sphere

Everyday life presents each one of us with a vast array of choices that need to be managed to ensure good survival prospects and healthy outcomes. As we have seen in Chapter 4, solitary individuals make for poor progenitors. They enjoy poor survival prospects and are vulnerable to psychological distress induced by isolation. In simple terms, isolated individuals are unable to call on assistance in times of need. Human nature has thus evolved a predisposition towards sociality that relies on the emotion of loneliness, which triggers the motivation for establishing social relations with others.

The kind of social relations available to any one individual at a given point in time is determined and constrained by various pragmatic criteria, such as the need for securing alimentation, shelter and so on. Most of us, however, do not wake up in the morning having to face a routine of foraging, scavenging or hunting to ensure nutrition. In contemporary societies, our needs are serviced through engagement in other activities, such as educational or occupational pursuits. These secure our basic needs in a roundabout manner through participation in the economy. Moreover, some of us are lucky enough to not have to worry about such mortal concerns at all, having either accumulated enough wealth to guarantee the satisfaction of basic survival needs for an entire lifetime or having established themselves, by accident or by design, in societies that cater for the provision of basic needs through the welfare state. These might include allowances or subsidies for food, housing, education, healthcare and other benefits.

Yet, individuals who do not face the prospect of starvation on a daily basis still engage in social relations that satisfy their personal interests. They do not sit idle and watch the world go by, as we see other species do when their basic needs are fulfilled. Think of your cat or dog at home after they have been served a meal. What do they do at that point? When have you ever observed a pet at home being industrious during their free time, towards achieving self-fulfilment and self-actualisation? You do not because, having satisfied their needs, animal species rest until the next cycle. Humans, however, do not.

Humans who satisfy their basic needs go on to target higher aspirations. If they do not have any, they make them up by developing new interests. Some go on to study some topic that they find interesting for the sake of acquiring more knowledge about it, even if this might not pay off in monetary terms. Alternatively, many of us spend much of our hard-earned money on hobbies or pastimes that we find pleasurable. Some of us spend their time on artistic pursuits that might not be intended to yield anything other than satisfaction in partaking in the activity itself – painting for the sake of painting, or writing poetry, or singing karaoke at the local club.

Be this as it may, individuals gravitate towards others who share their interests for the purpose of exchanging ideas, practices or products that bring them into some form of association with others. They attend events, like exhibitions or conferences, that serve to bring like-minded people together in a shared and common 'inter-est'. Interests literally constitute ways of *being together* (Sammut, 2011). With reference to legal claims, interests are obligations or rights claimed by some that are effectively recognised by others as dues. Interests, therefore, always involve more than a single party. Contradictory as it may seem, pursuing personal interests is how human beings establish communion with others. The exercise belies the same paradox involved in formulating identity: defining ourselves individually involves identifying ourselves for others. This is the cornerstone of social identity theory, as we have seen in Chapter 4, which presents two notions that are heavily intertwined, that is, the product of the pursuit of our own *personal interests* is a *social identity* that describes who we characteristically are relative to others.

Our interests, therefore, provide the bedrock for the social identities we craft in everyday life. After a hard day's work, some of us head to the pub (in English, the term 'pub' is short for 'public house') to wash away our daily stress by having a drink, listening to music, watching a sporting event or playing a bar game with others who are doing the very same. Others opt to go to the gym and join a spinning class or a yoga class or engage in some sporting event with others who are doing the very same. Even those who head to their private studios to get away from it all will work on producing art to be exhibited to others, or read literary works produced by others, and so on and so forth. Man is a social animal – the kind that pursues interests for re-creational purposes. Again, the term 'recreational' is also interesting. It literally implies an effort to re-create or make something anew. The question that follows is: what do recreational pursuits re-create? The answer is that we re-create who we are – from the person we were when we were doing what we had to do prior to the recreational activity, to the person we *become* when our striving to fulfil our needs has been effectively fulfilled. In other words, we move from one social network to another to re-create the ecosystem of our being-with-others, from a bus driver to a tennis player, from a customer care officer to a wine connoisseur, and so on.

In pursuing our interests, whatever these might be, we necessarily become implicated in social networks that involve others engaging in similar pursuits, as we have seen. Let us refer to this situation as one that involves a group of people pursuing a common project. This might be an occupational project that involves contributing our skills and labour to enable our corporate employer to make profits that serve to earn stakeholders a living. Even if we do not enjoy our occupation, we still get paid so that, in turn, we pay our rent, put food on the table, and so on. Or, it could be a recreational project that involves hooking up with people we know to compete against other people we also know, for example, in a game of bowling that we participate in for sheer entertainment.

The point I am making here is that, in doing anything we do, we join projects that transcend us but that also define us. We become interested parties in the projects we pursue. At work, we strive with others to make more profit; in sport, we seek to win the cup; in faith, we seek redemption or salvation; and so on. Projects are the collective products that accrue from our interested activities. And, whilst these may well be exceedingly remarkable – from building pyramids to landing spacecraft on the moon – the problem with projects is that they clash and compete with other plausible projects put forth by other interested groups in the public domain.

This means to say that the pursuit of some people's interests comes at the direct cost of some other people's interests. If we build a football stadium on a common in our town, we do not build a racetrack, nor do we protect the flora and fauna in the area. All this comes down to the choices we make; in fulfilling one project we necessarily fail to fulfil alternative others. Political conflict is waged precisely over these matters, that is, which (or whose) project will be fulfilled at the expense of which (or whose) alternative project. In matters of migration, such concerns are compounded by the fact that clashes between distinct projects involve social as well as national, cultural, legal, economic, political, and spiritual aspirations.

The projects pursued by migrants when entering a new territory are evidently different from those pursued by locals going about their everyday business. Consequently, the potential for culture clash in migration is exponential. The problem that the migration issue precipitates in our societies is a multilevel problem that has to do with what grand projects we pursue for the future of ourselves and our nation, what interests we legitimate in our social domain, and what kind of people we choose ourselves to be and become. In this chapter, we break down the problem of migration in terms of the social identities that are implicated in it, the social representations we use to fabricate common interests, and the projects we advance at the expense of others.

Social Categories

Let us retrace our steps a little bit at this point. We are born into a world where things are not neutral, they already make sense. We are socialised into navigating an environment that is complicated with objects that regulate our conduct on a collective level (Sammut, Daanen & Sartawi, 2010). So, we learn that black and white stripes on the road are a pedestrian crossing not a zebra artwork design. We learn that if we want to cross the road we walk over the stripes and not five metres up or down from them. We also learn that things in a museum are artistic works being exhibited, so we don't touch them or use them towards obtaining some other purpose.

Not only that, we are also socialised into a world where abstract concepts have meaning. So, psychological sentiments are understandable in terms of the role they play in inter-personal relationships. We understand that Jane and Jill both left their parents and are living together not because they fell out with their respective families but because Jane and Jill love each other. We know what that means and what it entails. Furthermore, we are socialised into a world where some abstract concepts have no materiality at all but their influence rests on the extent to which they are endorsed by a given population. So, we understand that on a Friday Muslims pray at the mosque, on the Sabbath Jews pray at the synagogue and on a Sunday Catholics pray at the church. We know not to go to a mosque on a Friday if we're not Muslim, even though we respect Muslims' choice to do so. And so on for the other categories. But we also know to not go to mass on Friday or Saturday if we are Catholic, because Sunday is when the Catholic community meets. And so on for the other categories here too.

In other words, we are born into a world where social categories are meaningful and exercise an influence on how we conduct ourselves with others. We understand that if we see a crime, we can call on the police to stop it but that we do not have the authority to do so ourselves regardless of whether we are Muslim, Jewish, Catholic, or any other denomination and regardless of whether we agree or disagree that the action involved should or should not be a crime. Similarly, this is relevant for every other social entity, institution or role. The burden of learning what categories mean and how one should relate with them rests on individuals, living and learning their way about the world. The learning process, that takes place developmentally, is what we refer to as socialisation.

This is all well and good but it also raises some scope for contrast. Individuals might have to be socialised into a world with meaningful categories that, to the individual concerned, do not make sense. Let's take the example of gender roles. For a very long time, human societies pursued a more or less strict demarcation in gender roles. In simple terms, males specialised in labour towards securing material provisions whilst females specialised in home care and upbringing. This demarcated specialisation served our ancestors very well over evolutionary time. Men were able to band together and roam to hunt or fight, whilst women stayed behind to care for children and elderly. More recently, women stayed at home to wash, clean, cook and organise family affairs, whilst men spent most of their waking time at the office striving for profits and promotions. This helped them secure the household's income, including for any family members who were not gainfully employed, such as housewives, elders and children.

Whilst this arrangement may have been practical in physical terms – males are generally stronger than females so they can hunt and fight better; women can breastfeed so they can care for children better – it would not have suited everyone in the same way. For instance, one can think of men who are not physically endowed for waging war, or females who are not sensitive enough to care for others. Indeed, there is every reason to believe that many in the past did not identify much with the gender roles assigned to them in this manner. Once domestic appliances proliferated in modern households to alleviate everyday chores, many women with newfound spare time on their hands used this towards joining the labour force and assisting their male counterparts in accumulating additional resources for their households. In other words, they pursued their own interests over resting idle. Conversely, some males raised claims for parenting benefits to enable them to care for their little children instead of their wives. In our time, dual-earner families have become largely the norm in many countries all over the world. Who steps out of the labour market to care for kids in their first years of life up to the point where they can join schooling, that is, whether it is the husband or the wife who takes a parental break, is often a decision that involves weighing up take-home pay and career prospects for both parents. In many places, it is no longer given that the wife is the one to stay at home and care for children.

What this means to say is that not everyone identifies very well with the social categories they find themselves assigned to. Some men do not identify much with masculine attributes just as much as some females do not identify much with feminine attributes. We therefore understand masculinity and femininity to be variable traits that individuals demonstrate independently of their ascribed gender. Some males are more feminine than females and vice-versa. This variable identification applies to any social category we use to classify individuals as specimens of a certain kind. Think of being identified as Muslim due to being born in a Muslim household. Needless to say, not every Muslim child grows up to be a devout Muslim (with all we understand the category entails), just like not every working-class child grows up to be stingy, not every young person is immature and so on. The point here is that the social categories we are assigned to by others may actually not represent us very well at all.

Chapter 4 showed us how individuals unwittingly rely on cues in their environment to identify friend from foe and err on the side of their friends if opportunity arises. These are insights gleaned from Tajfel's minimal group paradigm. Tajfel (1982) claims that individuals use a three-step process to formulate social identities. First, they categorise the world into distinct social types (e.g. male/female; white-collar/blue-collar; Muslim/Christian; Black/Brown/White; etc.). Following this exercise of carving out the social world into different groups, individuals naturally identify with some categories more than they do with others. Once this identification process is fulfilled, individuals then go on to compare categories in an effort to achieve positive distinctiveness for their group that grants them personal self-esteem by virtue of membership in the group.

The individual, therefore, gains personal prestige from collective attributes. For example, I identify myself as male, I recognise in myself attributes of strength and protection, and I feel good about who I am in terms of my masculinity relative to females in my social circle who lack these attributes. Or, I identify myself as female, I recognise in myself attributes of care and concern, and I feel good about who I am in terms of my femininity relative to males in my social circle who lack these attributes. What this means to say is that the value of social categories is relative and some are prized more than others for attributes they supposedly demonstrate or lack, whilst others are devalued on the same criteria. Whether our social identities are valued or vilified depends on the meaning they are assigned in public domains. It goes without saying that particular attributes may be valued in some setting but despised in another. Think of the value of being an educated female in the United States versus Afghanistan under Taliban rule. In essence, human beings are not held by other human beings to be intrinsically worthy in their own right. Their worth is a function of the meaning their attributes connote in public, relative to others.

Let us break this down in simple terms. The self-esteem I am able to personally enjoy accrues out of possessing attributes that are valued by others depending on the social meaning that is assigned to them. In other words, it depends on how my attributes are represented in the public domain I personally inhabit. In certain societies, males are valued for their machismo. A macho man derives prestige from others to the extent he exhibits such traits. In other societies, males are expected to be gentlemen. A male exhibiting machismo in such settings is not very well regarded. It is harder for such a male to acquire a sense of personal esteem when their characteristic behaviour attracts reprisal. Basically, the esteem we are able to acquire for our social identities depends on the social representations of the attributes associated with that identity. To extend the example, what does machismo mean and what social function might machismo fulfil in a certain society? And how is this different from other conceptions of machismo adopted by other groups or other societies? This, in essence, is what social representations research seeks to address.

Social Representations

The notion of social representations was introduced by French social psychologist Serge Moscovici in his studies of the meanings of psychoanalysis in France in the 1960s. Moscovici drew on Durkheim's notion of collective representations, which Durkheim posed to account for the notion of collective consciousness. This involved a shared system of sentiments, beliefs and everyday practices that bound people together in groups and that provided them with common purpose. Without collective representations that objectify elements of the world in line with the group's worldview, there could be no collective consciousness. Moscovici's notion of social representations is a direct affront to Durkheim's assumption of homogeneity in collective beliefs. According to Moscovici, contemporary pluralistic societies allow competing representations of the same objectified elements to circulate and compete in the same public. Consequently, there is not one collective representation giving rise to one collective consciousness. Pluralistic societies are marked by a plurality of *social representations*, each tied to a particular group that seeks to objectify the element in line with its own ideals and aspirations; in other words, its own projects.

To determine whether this was indeed the case, Moscovici studied the social representations of psychoanalysis that proliferated in late twentieth century France. At the time, psychoanalysis was on the rise in France as well as in other countries. Not everyone, however, was similarly predisposed to the practice. Moscovici still posited, in line with Durkheim, that social representations are systemic phenomena that take on a life of their own independent of the individual human minds they inhabit. Moscovici argued that social representations are a phenomenon *sui generis*. Consequently, the study of social representations requires, first and foremost, the identification of social groups that harbour them.

Moscovici (1961) identified three at the time, namely Communists, Catholics and Liberals. Communists seemed largely opposed to the idea of psychoanalysis and elaborated a social representation of it as a tool to subdue the proletariat. Catholics argued that some elements of the practice could be useful and that it was very similar to confession, but that it included some dubious elements and was devoid of spiritual aspirations. Liberals claimed that some individuals could be helped by the practice in ways that other treatment modalities did not address. Moreover, Moscovici noted how the three groups also demonstrated distinct communication methods to advance their own version of the phenomenon. Communists framed psychoanalysis in terms of *propaganda*; Catholics discussed psychoanalysis whilst *propagating* fundamental elements of Catholic dogma; Liberals voiced individual perspectives which *diffused* through the group as a result of a liberal press.

In this way, social representations can be understood as systemic conceptions of objects and events shared across a certain multitude of people that provides members of the group with a blueprint for action. It is worth noting two things at this point. Firstly, social representations are distinguishable from cognitive representations. The former are systemic products, the latter are individual. A good way to understand the difference between the two is by analogy to de Saussure's (1915) distinction of *langue* and *parole*, that is, language and speech. The former is a collective product that is individually manifested. When an individual speaks, the ideas and messages shared in communication are her own. But they can only be understood if the medium of communication is a collective linguistic code. Using a personal code to express ideas eloquently defies comprehension by others who are not versed in the code.

On the other hand, an individual speaking may make a number of linguistic mistakes and errors but is nevertheless understood by others versed in the language used. Indeed, a collection of speakers may all bastardise a common linguistic code but still understand one another perfectly well. Anyone who has attended an international academic symposium has faced the prospect of sense-making using the international language of broken English. Even if no one speaks grammatically correct English in the course of articulating a sequence of private speeches, the common linguistic code of the English language runs right through them. Similarly, individuals may all espouse idiosyncratic representations of some object of common concern. In the process of communication, a social representation emerges that incorporates divergences on the basis of a shared bedrock of meaning. In other words, social representations constitute the underlying common sense that frames particular perspectives on the issue.

The second point that is worth noting is that social representations are crafted by group members in communication to elaborate a common framing of the object in line with the group's raison d'être. One cannot expect Catholics to flock to psychoanalysis instead of confession if it fails to provide absolution of sins. However beneficial in psychological terms, psychoanalysis will not carve a path to heaven. Framed in this way, one can therefore expect Catholics to condone psychoanalysis in instances where it stands to benefit believers in psychological terms. But it obviously needs to be treated with scepticism and should not be allowed to stand for the sacrament of confession. And this is precisely what Moscovici found. In other words, the process of crafting social representations is not neutral. Rather, it is imbued with the group's reason-for-being, that is, the interests group members pursue in coming together.

In social representations terms (Buhagiar & Sammut, 2020), groups formulate social representations of objects and events they encounter in project-serving ways. In other words, individuals form social groups to pursue projects that fulfil their members' interests. To do so, they represent elements in their environment in project-supporting ways. If they did not do so, the project would collapse and interests remain unfulfilled.

Let us consider an example. Imagine I become interested in playing the guitar. I give it a go and find that it is a skill that is harder than I originally thought. To get better at it, I will need to practice. This is better done with others who are also musically inclined and who stand to provide feedback or tuition as needed. So, I join a band. Together we rent a garage and meet every day after work to practice. Playing with the band is now a common project that includes my leaning towards the guitar and all the other group members' leanings towards other instruments. Moreover, to actualise this, we will need to settle on a musical genre that satisfies everybody's interests. The band certainly cannot be an electronic deejay set – there's no option for playing the guitar in that. So, the band needs to formulate a social representation of musical genres in ways that fulfil its own project – it has to justify what it is doing with itself, and this justification needs to be reasonable amongst group members. So, the group might formulate a social representation of rock music as 'proper music' that is worth the effort of mastering traditional musical instruments even though the very same sounds might be produced using a smartphone app. This will not do. Social representations are fashioned to serve group projects that fulfil their members' interests, as detailed.

This trivial example, however, brings another point home. Social representations compete with other social representations in the public domain. My bandmates and I might craft a representation of rock music as authentic, but this might have no currency whatsoever outside of the group. Younger generations, for example, reared on a diet of smartphone apps, might find the prospect laughable. What one group calls authentic music another group might call outdated. A younger generation will fashion its own social representations of rock music and electronic music to fulfil its own interests. It will not do to take another group's social representations lock, stock and barrel, then go on to aspire to novel outcomes. If young people agreed that electronic music was less than authentic, they might end up going to some gig on Saturday night where someone's father has finally come out of the garage after years of after office hours practice with other middle-aged fathers trying to amuse themselves with rock band instruments now that they're all grown up! If this happened, the younger kids would not be going to a rave to intermingle with others their own age, they'd be intermingling with their parents. This will not do either. So, social representations compete against other social representations in project-serving ways. And one can expect as many social representation iterations of the same object or event as there are groups with projects in existence in a given society.

A group might also have to forge social representations of other elements that have nothing to do with the real object, to accommodate its members' practices. For example, the rock band might fabricate a social representation of work that is useful but also stressful, to the extent that it requires recreational activities to cope with the stress it generates, like playing the guitar. It will not do to fabricate a social representation of work as personally fulfilling over a career that spans different roles and different activities. If the members did this, they might change jobs over forming a band. So, social representations involve *systems* of construals that, taken together, serve to justify a project amongst its members, one that competes with other projects by other groups in the public domain.

One final consideration with regards to this example is that groups understand that other groups are involved in self-interested projects in their own right, so they fabricate social representations of those other groups' projects in line with their own project-interested ways. So, the rock band will conclude that the younger generation is not interested in music when going to a rave, they are doing so to socialise with others their own age, to scout for mating partners, or to amuse themselves in ways that have nothing to do with playing good music. That is why their claim to music in inauthentic. On the other hand, as detailed already, the young group will construe a social representation of rock music as an outdated pursuit for dealing with mid-life crises. In an effort to advance their own social representations that actualise their own projects, all groups also represent themselves as well as others and their projects in distinctive terms. We're back to social categories.

Social Influence

Thus far, we have seen how social categories serve to define social identities that are in themselves social representations fashioned by groups in self-interested ways. Accordingly, there might not be a real material basis to certain social categories. Or, in many cases, the observation of some real event or characteristic is interpreted in project-serving ways. This is how social categories are imbued with meaning. But this begs the question: whose meaning imbues which social representations? As Moghaddam (2008) notes, the clash of social representations is a political exercise with material ramifications. No social representation can be fully divorced from the interests it has been shaped to advance. Every social representation serves a project that benefits some at the expense of some others, as we have seen. The study of social representations is crucial in understanding everyday political activity and its effects.

Our overture so far begs a simple question: How do we change disparaging social representations that unfairly denigrate some social identities and that disallow some groups to pursue or achieve their interests? We know very well that some social representations create stigmatised identities. Think of the labelling consequences when individuals are branded as crazy, deviant, fundamentalist, or criminal, on the basis of traits such as skin colour, personal habits, religious affiliation or bodily characteristics. We recognise that these could well be unfair and not at all representative of individual dispositions. But some will argue that there is no smoke without a fire and they will persevere with dishing out stigma for the purpose of actualising their own projects with utter disregard to anybody else's. Again, how can we change this? There seem to be two ways.

Firstly, one could change (or try to change) social representations through forceful means. Guns are a very good way to enforce some projects and disallow others. Think of the return of the Taliban to power in Afghanistan in 2021. Barely one year later, the Taliban government suspended university education for all female students (as expected). This obviously disintegrates the prospect of gender equality in Afghanistan. The project might have to go dormant until circumstances change and the practice is allowed, but until then the social representation of females prescribed by the Taliban through sheer force will prevail.

The problem with violence is that it breeds resentment, which in turn justifies counter-violence, or what dominant groups label as terrorism. Looked at from the side of the oppressed, terrorists are freedom-fighters pursuing the cause, hence their celebration as 'martyrs'. Justification for violence on both sides leads inevitably to a race to the bottom, where warring parties risk annihilating each other as they deploy weapons of mass destruction that are intended to harm the other party more than the other party is able to harm them. The others, however, are thinking exactly the same! So, North Korea pursues nuclear capabilities to deter the nuclear capabilities of the United States should it ever come to that. You don't take a knife to a gunfight! This first option, therefore, seems to be best avoided even though we concede that we need to prepare for any eventuality. Taking a knife to a gunfight would be naïve and were we to do this we would be expecting of others what we are unable to expect of ourselves (i.e. expecting them to subjugate their interests to ours when we are not happy to do the same for them).

Another possibility is to impose conditions for dialogical interaction whilst leaving the guns at the door. Sure, there is always the possibility to return to them later. And the reality of violence certainly stands to influence proceedings. But the idea is to create a space where interlocutors can exercise social influence on each other without fearing losing their heads. This is the idea behind institutions like the United Nations Security Council. Social influence, therefore, is the other method we have for changing social representations.

The study of social influence has waxed and waned over the years. This was in part due to the aspiration to achieve communicative interaction devoid not only of violence but also of social influence. The distinction between genuine communicative action and strategic communication (i.e. social influence) is traced back to Habermas (1991), who outlined four structural conditions for achieving a public sphere where communicative action could manifest. These include (a) unconditional access, (b) freedom of association, assembly and expression, (c) debate over general rules and (d) the formation of public opinion. I know what you're thinking – tell that to the Taliban! Whilst the Habermasian ideals have provided a major impetus to democratisation efforts, they have also been recognised as idealistic. This volume has already shown how human beings are not naturally inclined to respect and observe such idealistic conditions. Quite the contrary, think of the Tragedy of the Commons, which we reviewed in Chapter 2! Realistically, it seems that the best we can do is settle for the less than ideal conditions of social influence. That is, attempt to influence others towards legitimating our project whilst giving others a license to influence us the same way in turn.

In recent years, two modalities of social influence have received a lot of scholarly attention. Firstly, the gentle nudge (Thaler & Sunstein, 2021) provides a blueprint for changing behaviours by making the target behaviour less costly than other alternatives. Do you wish to lose weight? Then have plenty of fruits and vegetables around the home so that when you are tempted to snack you pick a healthy option. Lock chocolates and crackers up in the loft as well. If you did this, your default option would become to snack on healthy items and avoid unhealthy ones. Once behavioural norms change, attitudes and cognitions follow. In other words, one way to change social representations is through behavioural change. The elephant in the room remains – in whose interest has the nudge been devised (Sunstein, 2016). The answer is incontrovertibly 'in the nudgers' interests', but we have already seen how this reality cannot be overcome through communicative action (there's nudgers and counter-nudgers on every side) and we have thus settled on a license of social influence for all.

A second modality of social influence that has received a lot of attention is persuasion. This involves framing communication in line with tactics that the human mind is predisposed to concede. Cialdini (2007) has pioneered this line of research by studying successful persuaders and their tactics. He found, for instance, that we are likely to yield to persuasion attempts if we like the persuading agent more than if we do not, regardless of the features of the product itself. Which is why we have celebrities doing commercials rather than myself, for example. We know that many people already like celebrities (they wouldn't be celebrities if people did not like them), so we know that they have more persuading potential than I do. The principles of persuasion do not rely on coercion, they simply frame communication in ways that are likely to appeal.

There are other social influence modalities. Sammut and Bauer (2021) identify at least another six, namely (i) collective action, (ii) leadership, (iii) peer pressure (or conformity), (iv) authority, (v) the media, and (vi) objects and artefacts. All of these, alongside behavioural norms and persuasion, stand to influence others to do our bidding without recourse to violence. In whatever modality, social influence stands to recruit others to our cause such that we can institute our projects in a collective manner. What this means is that, through social influence, we are able to formally legitimate projects in institutional terms. As we have seen, institutions are required to preserve the common good in the face of the Tragedy of the Commons. One good way of influencing each other is by enacting laws that permit desirable behaviour but that also outlaw undesirable ones. Of course, we recognise that even organised crime has its own project, but this is not one that we want to legitimate. That might mean that our interests take precedence over the Mafia's, but this is not something that can be reasonably objected to.

In the social representations research tradition, Castro et al. (2018) have shown how the legal sphere, alongside the scientific sphere and the public sphere, is implicated in the enactment and exercise of social representations. It is interesting to note that all three spheres incorporate strategies for correcting wrong choices, unlike oppressive or totalitarian regimes that offer no remedy against dictatorial mistakes. In this way, law courts incorporate the possibility of appeal; academic institutions incorporate the principle of peer-review; and the public sphere in democratic countries incorporates elections through voting. In all cases, mistakes can be rectified through provisions that are built into the system. Should a project impinge unjustifiably over the interests of others, these systemic institutional mechanisms are capable of providing redress. Dictatorships do not offer such remedies. The only possibility of ousting a dictator to pursue an alternative project is through revolution (Moghaddam, 2013).

Conclusion

The issue with migration is that migrants are in pursuit of their own projects that might not match those of hosts. They might be fleeing war, so their aspiration is to find security. Or they might be searching for a better quality of life, or a better income, so they migrate to enjoy the proceeds of projects implemented by others. The project trajectories that migrants pursue differ from those of hosts even if they might intersect at some point. In this way, differences between migrants and hosts may pave the way to misunderstandings and misrepresentations of the other's interests and aspirations. At times, migrants are represented in thwarted ways, suggesting sinister aspirations that host societies would do well to clamp down on. Think of the claim that Jews hoard resources and skew the national economy. Or that Muslims are breeding to take over Europe (who says their offspring will be devout and will not internalise the host culture?).

When dealing with issues concerning migration, the social representations of hosts and migrants need to be unpacked with a view to deconstructing the projects these social representations have been designed to fulfil. These might be longstanding projects that have evolved for a certain people over a long period of time (Sammut et al., 2012; Obradović, 2019). Without a complete understanding of the intricate social psychological dynamics involved, our reactions serve merely to sustain our interests. As do those of others. This puts us on a collision course with other groups pursuing different projects. It is this possibility that the present volume aspires to avert. If we find ourselves in stark conflict, this means that our strategies to achieve wellbeing (even if only for ourselves) have not worked as well as intended and we now need to sustain them through non-peaceful means that are mutually destructive. Code: we need a better way.

CHAPTER 6

Multiculturalism and Competing Policies

A sad truth about the human condition is that cheating is adaptive, that is, cheats who do not get caught actually gain a clear advantage over others who do not cheat. Successful cheats end up doing better for themselves than they would otherwise have done. From an evolutionary standpoint, cheating is such an ingrained component of human nature that we are also capable of distrusting others on the basis of *imagining* the possibility that in a certain situation we could potentially be untrustworthy ourselves. This is a finding my colleagues and I unexpectedly made during an inquiry that was looking into the public's perceptions of community policing. Our team was tasked to study whether the public perceived any benefits to community policing over traditional station-based policing. Most respondents were in favour of community policing but some expressed scepticism, which we wanted to understand further.

Following an extensive set of interviews with sceptical respondents, we found that, in some instances, scepticism was rooted in suspicious reasoning that went along the lines: 'If I were a Community Police Officer, I would imagine that in these circumstances I could be tempted to break the rules [e.g. favouritism with acquaintances; overlook infringements, etc.]. Given that Community Police Officers are only human, like me, they are therefore corruptible in the same way that I could potentially be. Consequently, Community Police Officers cannot be trusted.' We called this finding 'introspective projection' (Sammut, Mifsud & Brockdorff, 2021a).

What seems to be happening here is that individuals engage in introspective processes that lead them to examine themselves and imagine what they would do if they found themselves in certain circumstances given their own thoughts and past experiences. They then project their imagined outcomes onto others and judge them accordingly. It seems thus that some of the stuff we do is not based on the reality we experience outside, but on the reality we conjure inside. So, if we know we might become cheats in certain circumstances we suspect others might become so too. In other words, we judge others on the basis of who we (not they) might become (not are) in similar (not current) circumstances – If I could be tempted to cheat, there's no reason to believe you couldn't be tempted too; therefore, I do not trust you. This is a social extension to Theory of Mind. In essence, we distrust others by projecting knowledge about ourselves onto them.

So where does this leave us in our quest to find ways for different groups to coexist? Clearly, if trust in institutions breaks down, we could not work through our differences well enough to collaborate on anything. Social life as we know it would break down. However much we distrust those around us, we still need medical care when we fall ill; we still need transport to commute to work; we still need to be rescued when our kitchen goes up in flames; and so on. Chapter 2 shows how societal laws and regulations provide a rudimentary social contract that constitutes the common ground for discordant interests. In this way, you do not need to trust that some person will behave morally on the basis of sound character. We force people to behave morally regardless of personal dispositions under fear of law. We know personal dispositions to be fallible from knowledge we have about our own selves. So, whilst we might not be able to trust individuals to act morally in all circumstances, we can build institutional systems that deter self-serving cheats and that promote harmony and collective well-being. We might not be able to trust others will not cheat. We might only be able to trust that some amongst us will execute the task to catch and punish cheats if it is their institutional duty to do so and if exercising their duty advances their own personal interests (e.g. getting a salary or promotion for doing so).

Institutions, therefore, are the mitigating measure against the human potential for cheating. They do not eliminate cheating tendencies. Nor do they eliminate discord. They serve rather to hack into social discord by pitching some personal interests against some others (police versus criminal), making sure that those personal interests that serve the common good prevail over those that serve only personal profit. Institutions do not eliminate cheating; human nature is well outside the remit of institutional jurisdictions. Institutions can only help detect cheating when it happens and punish it in ways that get perpetrators out of contention so that other interests, hopefully collective ones, prevail. Just institutions do no more than throw a proverbial spanner in the works of cheats, so that those who do not cheat gain ground in the long run. In this chapter, we will look at what this means in practical policy terms with regards to migration.

The Problem of Migration

There are certain kinds of migration that are largely unproblematic and that raise no eyebrows. For instance, short-term migration for tourism purposes is typically welcomed the world over, although many municipalities today, such as Barcelona, Venice, Valletta, and others are constraining tourist activities to avoid excessive disruption to locals. But, by and large, short-term tourism is welcome almost anywhere in the world. Or, take short-term migration for study purposes. Again, many universities worldwide strive to attract foreign students who typically also pay higher fees than locals. There is always the debate as to whether local spots at university are being sold to foreigners over locals for higher profits, meaning some locals end up not getting a spot at all because their 'seat' is sold to a wealthy foreigner. But, by and large, student tourism is an attractive proposition most anywhere as the profits made by selling seats to foreigners also translate into better quality tuition for locals. However, there are also other forms of migration that do raise eyebrows and that are heavily disputed. And the solutions to these disputes are in no way straightforward.

Imagine you are living a normal life in a relatively normal part of the world. You do your business as you do every day: you get up in the morning; you go to work or school where you spend your entire day; you get back home and sort out your meals; you have some time left at the end of the day for leisure, which you spend doing pleasurable activities with friends and family; you go to bed, sleep, repeat. And in all of this, you try to save some money for fun and travels, for getting onto the property ladder, for getting a bigger house, for putting together a pension pot and so on. This is a normal and regular day plan for billions of human beings worldwide. Now, let's imagine that things take a turn for the worse. An ugly way of doing politics rears its head and starts to take root. Initially it is limited to some extremist comments doing the rounds. These are so wild that they are almost laughable. But many think they nevertheless have a point to make.

Extremism on one side breeds extremism on the other side. Suddenly the political landscape starts looking very polarised. Things start to heat up and some brawls and skirmishes take place that attract local and international scrutiny. One day, the military steps in and takes over. International forces, armed militias, terrorists and extremists of every kind swoop in like a tide, seemingly coming out of nowhere. Fighting is taking place every day and the battle lines are drawing closer. At some point, you will need to decide whether to stay and face the slim chances that a raging war will leave you unscathed or pack up and take all you can with you to survive and tell the tale. Civil war and armed conflict are one of the biggest causes of human displacement worldwide, as we have seen in Chapter 1. One could also think of other calamities that might precipitate a similar move to another country or state. Think of disease outbreaks like Ebola or natural disasters like Hurricane Katrina. There are many good reasons to justify why some individuals decide that it's time to pack up and go. When they do, people typically migrate from places that are deemed too dangerous to other places that are deemed less dangerous. That is, there is an obvious migration flow from deprived countries to plentiful ones; from underdeveloped areas to developed suburbs; from war-torn environments to peaceful ones. Rarely does migration flow from a bad place to somewhere worse.

Imagine now that you have successfully migrated to another location, away from the dangers you were facing only some weeks ago. You now try to set up a new life. You try to resume your ordinary activities, but everything is much more difficult – you do not know how things work, you have little support, you left most of what you had behind. You try to learn, you try to adapt, but you look different and you behave different than everyone else around you. And what's worse, everyone can see that. Because what is normal to you is not quite normal to everyone else, and what is normal to everyone else is not quite normal to you. You realise that there are clear cultural differences that you somehow need to navigate.

Again, some of these differences might be mundane. The coffee might not be strong enough, the curry not spicy enough, the buses too busy, and so on. Other differences might be harder to swallow. Locals might binge drink, overeat, brawl. Minor contraventions might be completely overlooked, like car accidents or petty theft. Other behaviours are blown out of proportion, like yelling at pets. By your standards, the boys might be too macho, or too feminine; the girls might be too tomboyish, or too dollish. And then there's other things. No one dances the way you do, the music you like isn't played here, your favourite sport isn't popular, your religion is a minority religion and people like you are stereotyped as uncultured foreigners, possibly dangerous. Some refugees flee from terrorists only to be branded such themselves.

It doesn't stop there. You do not have the same rights as everyone else. You do not have access to good education and good health care, and you make nowhere near the money you need to afford these privately like the locals do because your qualifications are not deemed equivalent or you do not have local experience. So, you have to settle for underpaid, exploitative menial jobs. You pay taxes but your children do not enjoy residence rights, so you are effectively contributing towards somebody else's future. You turn to your religion. Spirituality is one way that human beings form congregations that support one another. Well, this is bound to get you into further trouble. If you practice your faith in private, at home, you might just get away with it. If you congregate, for the sake of community and social support, you are deemed to be claiming minority rights, that you are not integrating. Let us consider this point in a bit more depth.

Many argue that, at their core, religions are all the same, that they all share a basic set of common values that have to do with respect and care towards fellow human beings and the environment. Yet, religions also differ from each other and prescribe very different behaviours. Let us take a neutral example. The day of rest for Jews is the Sabbath. For Christians, that would be Sunday. For Muslims, that would be Friday. In *Life of Pi* (Martel, 2014), Piscine is a devout follower and believer of all religions. In most countries around the world, this is not a realistic possibility, however plausible a three-day weekend might sound. Now imagine you are a boss at work and you need to set your weekly roster. How does one manage that in a context of plurality where some workers need to be off on Friday, some others on Saturday, and some others yet on Sunday? Which couple of days will society recognise as its week-end?

Let's say we find ways to accommodate these different preferences. Some will take a day off one day, others take a day off another day, so that business keeps going every day. Places of worship proliferate as more people congregate, now that this practice is allowed and catered for. Now we need a bigger mosque, or another synagogue or a bigger church. The local community might not be big enough to afford a new mosque, but worshippers solicit the help of a donor whence they came from. They seek planning permission to build the biggest and most splendid mosque/synagogue/church in the area, that will dwarf every other religious establishment that has been built here for the past 500 years. Now the flavour is changing. New mosques, stronger coffee, spicier curry. You barely recognise the place! The tussle at the heart of migration issues is clear – change to accommodate migrant-induced changes or resist to preserve the ways of life that attracted migrants there in the first place.

The Question of Policy

In matters of migration, host–migrant relations can become very complicated. How are we to manage these? Some situations can be left to private individuals to sort out. Private worship is nobody's burden. Workplace arrangements that cater for inclusive practices keep the economy going. Other practices, however, need regulation through policy – the social contract. How high can minarets be? What ingredients and preparation methods (e.g. Kosher, Halal) are used for free meals in schools, hospitals, or care homes? What is the age of sexual consent? And so on. Different people coming from different cultures observe different habits, engage in different practices and pursue different collective aspirations. In other words, they pursue different interests originating from different locales that, due to migration, are imported from without and coalesce with competing interests within the host locale. As Solomon Asch (1952) pointed out many years ago, society cannot have different definitions of what constitutes crime. Somehow, if coexistence is to succeed, differences must be managed if not reconciled outright. As we have recounted, we cannot trust natural dispositions alone as these are prone to cheating. Many power asymmetries in many societies around the world are the direct result of self-serving natural tendencies that dominant groups institute to control non-dominant others. Migration plays right into this political power game.

Traditional politics is commonly divided between left- and right-wing ideologies. Those on the left typically pursue a socialist, welfare-based, collectivist agenda that puts a focus on those left behind, even if some argue that this makes welfare recipients lazy and attracts freeriding. Those on the right typically pursue conservative aspirations that preserve the social order whilst offering opportunities for mobility, even if some argue that this ensures the preservation of established hierarchies. Consequently, the rich remain rich and the poor remain poor. Neither left nor right-wing inclinations cater well to migration issues. Left-wing policies typically blunder in distinguishing between those deserving of welfare (disadvantaged ingroup members) and those who do not (outgroup members). Right-wing policies blunder in offering adequate incentives for effective social mobility that can institute cultural change. Either way, migrants are individually considered as an expendable and exploitable resource, regardless of the socio-economic benefits migration itself confers to society as a whole. In practical terms, resolving this challenge is a daunting task anywhere it manifests.

To Integrate or Not to Integrate

Integration can take many forms. First of all, there are different domains of integration, such as integration in the labour force, integration in schools, integration in welfare systems, integration in culture and society and so on. To go through the list, integration in labour means migrants are able to secure gainful employment; in school means they are able to follow lessons, learn and acquire suitable qualifications for the careers they wish to pursue; in welfare means migrants are able to access social benefits they are entitled to and to receive good quality care when needed; in culture and society means migrants are able to practice their own cultural ways without fear of persecution. An effort to integrate migrants, therefore, is an effort directed at migrants themselves that starts by seeking what realities migrants face when they come here, what difficulties they encounter in satisfying whatever needs they experience, and what changes we can undertake to lessen those difficulties and meet their needs. To integrate, therefore, implies also a willingness to change the system to accommodate needs that arise out of the condition of diversity as a result of migration.

To *not* try to integrate migrants does not necessarily mean that migration itself is not valued. It may still be valued in terms of securing resources that the economy needs to remain or become a developed economy. But this value is not extended to the consideration of migrants' *individual* needs. The burden of meeting individual needs is left to migrants themselves. For instance, a society might acknowledge that it needs more cardiac surgeons than it currently has, or more machine operators, and so on. There are cardiac surgeons, or machine operators, or any other required skill, knocking at the immigration door. A national jurisdiction can opt to let only those migrants in who already speak the language, or who have clearly matching qualifications already, or who have accumulated enough savings to not require any benefits and so on. This means cherry-picking migrants who do not need any tweaking of the system to function. That is, the host country does not take upon itself the burden of integrating migrants. It leaves that burden to migrants themselves and those who are not able to achieve this unassisted are naturally weeded out for failing to meet immigration requirements. Those migrants who are able to blend in seamlessly, and who through their own characteristics and abilities are able to find a way to contribute to society as is, without making any claims for special assistance, are allowed to stay. In other words, migrants are cherry-picked in terms of their underlying potential to *assimilate*.

The policy challenge underlying migration, as Moghaddam (2008) has clearly noted, is between integrating migrants into society through accommodation or assimilating them into the mainstream. The challenge gives rise to two focal concerns, that is, (a) the onus of the burden of facilitating a match between migrant and society characteristics and (b) determining what society we are currently working towards – the grand national project citizens pursue collectively. With regards to the former, some will place the burden on migrants themselves and refuse to fund upskilling opportunities at taxpayers' cost that provide migrants with the ability to integrate. They find little to no justification in devoting any taxes paid for by locals towards programmes that benefit outsiders who worked and paid taxes in another national jurisdiction. They argue that our taxes should be spent on programmes that benefit our quality of life, not that of unsolicited others who liberally chose to come here. Others argue that if we fund integration and enable migrants to become productive, we will reap the benefits of migration and become a stronger society as a whole. Integration is not an expense; it is an investment. With regards to the latter, some will argue that they want to live in a pluralistic society that reflects a diversified history. For that reason, they would be willing to make sure that different others have and acquire a visible presence. Others will argue that who we are needs to be defended against the onslaught of multiculturalism stemming from the outside. This only serves other people's needs, which might very well be justified but which will, if heeded, erode our ways of living at the expense of promoting another culture's ways, that elsewhere has already demonstrably failed.

In our studies regarding the integration of Arab Muslims in Europe (Buhagiar et al., 2018; Sammut et al., 2018), many Maltese respondents underlined the fact that Arab immigrants are well capable of integrating in Malta due to the fact that they are able to pick up the language, they share family values with the Maltese and they are entrepreneurial in the way they work and do business. However, we also documented anti-integrationist views that saw Arab Muslims as a threat in terms of their needs to congregate around their religious identity (just like the Maltese do!). According to some, Islam is problematic and its cultural prescriptions are not commensurate with liberal, secularist, European values. Consequently, allowing Muslims to gain a foothold only means importing the religious and cultural strife we witness in North Africa and bringing it home. They questioned why we would want to do that. The preferable alternative, they argued, was for migrants to shed their native identity at the border and assume a local identity by assimilating into our culture, that is clearly better than the one they left behind as they would not be knocking at our door if it were not.

Framed in this way, the case for assimilation should be very clear and it should not be too hard for anyone to comprehend the populist drive that has swept many Western countries over the past couple of decades on the ticket of rejecting proposal after proposal of inter-cultural or multi-cultural integration. The success enjoyed by populist movements is largely attributable to their anti-immigrant sentiments (Obradović, Power & Sheehy-Skeffington, 2020). The reasoning behind these is not much more complex than what has already been argued: we work and pay taxes here; we have a beautiful enough society but we are not without our problems; we vote for politicians who (a) intend to spend our collective resources on programmes that advance our own interests and (b) make sure that our hard-earned resources are not pillaged by others.

In other words, we are guarding against pillaging from outside. It is not that there is no acknowledgement that investing in migrant integration programmes does not benefit migrants and help them integrate. It is rather a question of whether and to what extent do locals want migrants to integrate and retain their foreign ways in mingling with locals. And, on another level, how high is the priority to integrate immigrants (who are foreigners incapable of assimilation in the first place) relative to better schooling, better health care, better transport, better policing and so on for ourselves – the ones paying contributions.

Even if immigrants are not freeriding, there is an obvious case for spending our savings on ourselves. Throw in the possibility of opening up your national savings to free-riders (or terrorists) and the case for assimilation should be self-evident. Even if any local changes undertaken by migrants are funded by donors from overseas, such that locals are not assuming a contributory burden, do locals care for more Mexico in the United States, more Saudi in Malta, more Syria in Hungary and so on? For most people the answer is most certainly not and this is reflected in their votes. The question, therefore, is whether there is any case for pursuing a strategy for integration at all.

The Case for Integration

Immigrants who reach their target destination face the prospect of habituating themselves to a new environment, about which they already have some pre-conceived beliefs and ideas. The process of learning the rules of another culture for the purpose of becoming capable of navigating it in everyday life is called acculturation (Berry, 1997). Not every migrant who acculturates, however, ends up internalising the hosts' cultural habits out of liking them. Migrants could very well develop a relative dislike of their new environment along with a nostalgic longing for home.

Similarly, immigrants also hold attitudes relative to their home country after they leave. Some remain affectionate with regards to their homeland and retain positive attitudes in its regard. Others might blame it for their ills and seek to disassociate themselves from it at every opportunity. What this means to say is that migrants demonstrate two inclinations during the course of executing their journey, that is (a) attitudes towards their country of origin and (b) attitudes toward their host country. Either or both could be positive or negative. One can conceive of migrants who leave their homeland out of frustration at how things have become. This negative attitude leads migrants to search for somewhere better. Once they settle, migrants might develop an attachment to their new home and regard it positively, or they might fail to develop a liking for it and remain unattached.

On the other hand, migrants might also leave their homeland due to certain circumstances but might nevertheless retain an affinity for their country of origin. They might be fond of it and look back on it with pride. They might have good reasons for leaving but they might nevertheless hope to return one day. Out of those that do, some will also be positively inclined to their new country. They might like the new culture, for different reasons and they might appreciate the benefits it has come to offer them. Others, however, might not very well like the new setting and the cultural ways that dominate there and they might spend their time waiting out their sojourn to be able to return to happier and more familiar sights and surroundings.

In similar fashion, host citizens express two distinct attitudes that bear on the acculturation potential demonstrated by their societies. Firstly, host citizens can like or dislike their native country. Not every citizen is a patriotic nationalist. Some citizens in immigrant-receiving countries might actually be looking to emigrate themselves. They might believe that calamities are merely around the corner. Or they might disagree with immigrants that the receiving country offers worthwhile prospects. In other words, host attitudes towards their own native land are likely to vary from favourable attitudes to unfavourable ones. Finally, host citizens also hold attitudes relative to migrants' country of origin. They might consider it favourably and be inclined to welcome immigrants from that land for the flavour they bring into their country, which they appreciate. On the other hand, they might regard it unfavourably, consider it as deprived in certain ways, and resist any efforts to integrate any of its cultural features. Berry et al.'s (2023) critical contribution in this domain, stemming directly from acculturation theory, is that acculturation preferences are mutual across inter-group divides.

What this means to say is that one could articulate distinct acculturation preferences on the part of migrants and hosts that might or might not correspond with one another (Mahendran, 2013). To what extent they do over different populations determines very directly the outcomes associated with inter-group relations (Berry, 2011; Sammut, 2011). To the extent that migrants demonstrate a high liking for their native country coupled with a high liking of their destination country, they can be deemed as favouring *integration* acculturation preferences. The corollary strategy for hosts is termed *multiculturalism*. We can think of a completely contrasting strategy, where individuals develop a dislike for their native country, which they blame for all their ails, but they do not demonstrate a liking for the country that is hosting them. They might wish to move on to someplace else, or they might have migrated with false expectations. The acculturation preference associated with this tendency is termed *marginalisation* for migrants and *exclusion* for hosts. One could also think of cases where migrants leave their homeland behind and settle in a new place which they come to like much better than their country of origin (Sammut, 2010). Migrants who demonstrate this preference are held to favour *assimilation*. Host citizens who dislike the ways of their immigrants and favour only preservation of the host culture are held to pursue *melting pot* acculturation preferences. Finally, immigrants and host residents could have positive attitudes relative to the migrants' country of origin but negative attitudes towards the host country. In this case, migrants are argued to demonstrate a *separation* strategy whilst for hosts this translates into a preference for *segregation*.

To sum up, both migrants and hosts vary along two dimensions, that is, their relative liking for (a) the immigrants' own native culture and (b) the hosts' culture. Migration issues typically arise in the contrast between locals pursuing assimilation and migrants pursuing integration. Migrants pursuing marginalisation strategies are unlikely to cause any issues due to the fact that they do not seek to change the host culture in a way to accommodate their own needs, for the simple reason that they do not like it and as a result do not identify with it. Even if hosts do not demonstrate a preference for exclusion, marginalised migrants are likely to roam under the radar anyway.

Similarly, migrants pursuing an assimilation strategy are also likely to experience few issues as they shed their native culture and assume the practices and habits of their hosts. Even if their native ways are valued by their hosts, failure to demonstrate these explicitly is unlikely to give rise to inter-cultural issues as the hosts' ways, which are adopted by assimilating immigrants, are routine in the host country anyway (Sammut, 2010; Sammut & Bauer, 2021). Tensions result in the mismatch between immigrants and hosts when the former retain a sense of attachment with their own native ways that they are prevented from importing into the host culture when hosts favour melting pot over integration. Issues may also arise when immigrants seek no association with locals and opt for a ghettoising strategy of separation, which is rarely endorsed by hosts in light of its segregated outcomes.

The case for integration stems from the fact that acculturation expectations determine relational outcomes. When individuals bind themselves together in groups, they generate *social capital*. This refers to membership ties that bind individual group members together and provide them with access to resources that accrue out of membership. Bourdieu (1986) argues that capital can assume different forms and that having access to one form of capital might pave the way for accessing other forms. For instance, an individual might use social capital to spread the word amongst kin and acquaintances that she is looking for a job. Through contacts, she might learn that there is a job opening in an organisation run by people who happen to be friends of friends. Their references, submitted with the application, carry a lot of weight and that individual might get the job because things were stacked up in her favour. Having a job – secured through social capital – provides the individual with a salary, that is, economic capital. The individual might then go on to use that salary to pay for further education, transforming economic capital into cultural capital, and so on. The crucial thing to note here is that the ties that bind group members together constitute social capital for members.

Immigrants who do not marginalise, therefore, are able to secure some form of social capital, either with other immigrants like them when pursuing separation, with hosts when pursuing assimilation or with both when pursuing integration. Similarly, locals too generate and maintain social capital. They do so with their own kind when pursuing a melting pot preference, with immigrants when pursuing segregation and with immigrants and other hosts like them when pursuing multiculturalism. And there we have it, the integration option stands to generate more social capital than any other. Let us break this down a little further.

Social capital, according to Gittell and Vidal (1998), can be of two types: (a) *bonding social capital* refers to intra-community ties that bind people together in some group and (b) *bridging social capital* refers to extra-community ties that bind people from different groups together in an overarching inter-group relationship. As Figure 6.1 shows, assimilation and separation offer relatively good prospects, as each is capable of generating social capital. Assimilation generates bonding social capital amongst the host citizenry. Conversely, separation affords migrants with bonding social

The Case for Integration

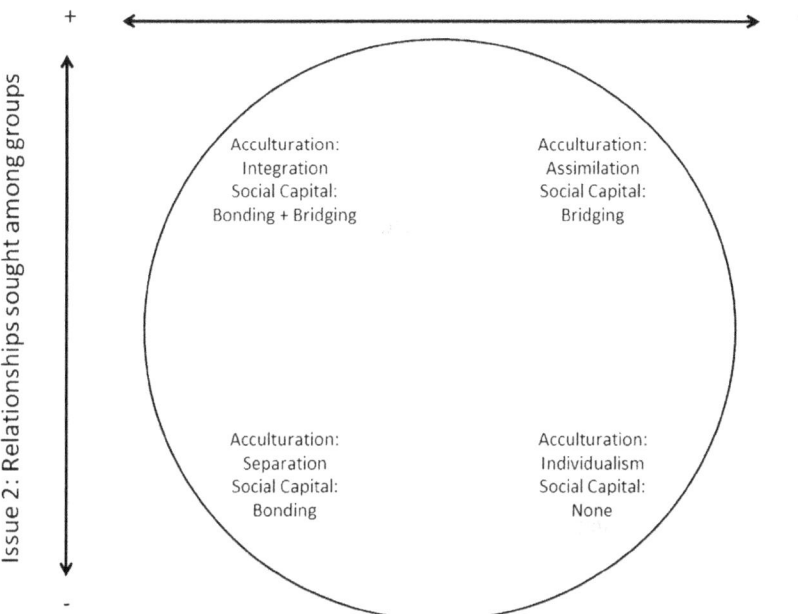

Figure 6.1 Acculturation expectations and social capital

capital in migrant communities within the host country but fails to establish links with the host's ways. Integration affords both bonding and bridging social capital. Migrants are able to inhabit native migrant communities within their host country (bonding), which are also valued by locals (bridging). This offers immigrants the possibility of branching out and building bridges with anyone in the host country who is in some ways favourably inclined to the immigrants' native culture. Consequently, immigrants who are able to retain a positive sense of their native cultural-self fare better than those for whom this prospect is denied (Berry et al., 2023). Such integrated individuals can go on to become assets in helping hosts develop better trade and security ties with the immigrants' native country. They provide the host country with bridging social capital it previously lacked. In a nutshell, the integration option offers a win/win solution regardless of whether immigrants or hosts favour one culture or the other, because neither is condemned or denigrated.

Conclusion

In this chapter we have considered the political implication of managing migrant–host relations through policy. We have seen that the characteristic policy debate rages over whether a nation should extend ingroup resources to outgroup members towards enabling their integration, or whether it should leave the burden on migrants themselves towards promoting their assimilation. We have seen that there are two variables underlying these policy strains that involve mutual acculturation preferences between interacting groups, that is, attitudes towards the host culture and attitudes towards the native culture.

We have also seen that policy outcomes are determined by the interrelations between groups, that is, migrants and hosts. We have seen how, in different locales, issues may arise out of discrepant acculturation preferences. As Sammut (2010) points out, non-discrepant preferences do not lead to any issues even if they do not promote integration. In Sammut's study, Maltese migrants to the United Kingdom expressed a preference for melting pot strategies that would enable them to shed their Maltese identity and adopt a British one instead, despite opportunities for integration provided by the British government. However, in this chapter we have also seen how integration offers the best inter-relational outcomes through its inherent potential for social capital. We have seen that integration is the only policy that aspires for the cultivation of both bonding and bridging social capital. By contrast, assimilation offers only bonding social capital within national identity groups. In Chapter 7, we delve further into social psychological processes marking reactions by hosts. We will seek an understanding for why integration is resisted despite its underlying potential as we take a closer look at the consequences of this resistance on migrants themselves.

CHAPTER 7

The Populist Backlash

Acculturation preferences and expectations vary across individuals and groups. Clearly, within any group, some will be more inclined towards getting along with foreigners and integrating them, perceiving their presence as adding some cultural flair to an otherwise monotonic culture. Others will adopt a different stance and strive to protect their native society's cultural ways against the incorporation of cultural ingredients from without, favouring assimilation. The latter are not necessarily xenophobic. They may simply wish to preserve their ways of life in the face of other alternatives which they do not personally value. They expect foreigners who migrate to their lands to shed their native culture and assume theirs, reasoning that immigrants are the ones who opted to move here in the first place. In other words, within any given society, some will express a preference for integration whilst others will be more inclined towards assimilation.

This policy dichotomy describes individual differences in preferences and expectations about migrant–host relations, as we have seen in Chapter 6. Group tendencies, in turn, are understood in the way the group, as a collective, leans towards one or the other preference. Typically, this insight is gleaned through some measure of central tendency, such as whether average opinion leans one way or the other given the diversity in individual preferences. Such exercises enable comparisons across demographically distinct groups, for example those with a high level of educational attainment versus those with a lower level and so on.

Consequently, we are able to observe that most immigrant groups worldwide lean towards integration whilst most migrant-receiving groups worldwide lean towards assimilation (Berry, 2017). There are also comparative differences regarding whether and to what extent particular groups are welcomed and integrated. For example, in our studies on the Maltese population we documented how Maltese attitudes towards Arab immigrants were consistently negative over a 10-year period whilst attitudes towards Western Europeans were consistently positive. Other ethnic groups, on the other hand, saw fluctuating preferences as the Maltese population either warmed up or cooled down in their regard over the same time period (African versus East European).

We also observed that the Arab group was subject to widespread antipathy across all other ethnic groups in Malta; not just the dominant Maltese majority but also other non-dominant immigrant groups rated Arabs negatively at both time intervals (Sammut & Lauri, 2017; Buhagiar et al., 2018; Sammut, Buhagiar, Mifsud, DeGiovanni & Brockdorff, 2022). This means to say that not all immigrant groups are received and treated in the same way; some groups will welcome certain immigrants but these same might not be well received elsewhere. In this chapter, we focus on how locals process the reality of immigration and its effects, as we seek to understand what drives locals' general resistance to integration despite the potential for bonding and bridging social capital that inheres in integrationist policies. Chapter 8 will then turn our attention to procedures that might help us get along in the face of this diversity.

The Personality Approach

Community

One of the earliest attempts to understand migrant communities and their relational outcomes with locals over time is Thomas and Znaniecki's (1918–20) study of the Polish immigrant community in the United States in the early twentieth century. Thomas and Znaniecki's study was based on the analysis of personal documents, media articles, institutional documents and other references to Polish peasants in the United States. It sought an understanding of intra- and extra-community relations that the Polish community demonstrated. The authors argued that the Polish immigrant community was shaped more strongly by its own internal dynamics than by official US government policy, which included circumstances pertaining to prospects for farmers in rural Poland pertaining to where migrants originated from.

Accordingly, over time, the conglomeration of Polish immigrants transformed into a Polish-American community that was distinctive in its own right and not reducible to either category on its own. The authors note that the community had adapted their cultural ways to fit the American context, but that it retained unique characteristics that were not present at all in American culture. This adaptation also meant that the community had diverged, to some extent, from its original native habits in Poland. The end result of immigration, therefore, was the beginning of something new that bridged community boundaries. Thomas and Znaniecki's study has become a classic across the social sciences for good reason. Whilst voluminous, its findings are relatively simple and point decisively towards the cultivation potential of social capital in migrant communities abroad, which we discussed in Chapter 6.

Authoritarianism

Other scholars, however, have noted that, whilst some people tend towards rigid, hierarchy-based social relations, yet others from the same cultural background demonstrate completely different inclinations. For these scholars, societal or cultural explanations like Thomas and Znaniecki's fail to distinguish immigrants who integrate or assimilate from those who do not. Migration outcomes, in their view, necessarily involve root causes of a personal, psychological nature.

In *The Authoritarian Personality*, Adorno, Frenkel-Brunswick, Levinson and Sanford (1950) argue that authoritarian personality types can be identified through a constellation of nine traits that cluster together and that are based in childhood experiences. These lead some individuals to develop fascistic tendencies that include a liking for authoritarian submission, stereotypy of outgroups and justification for institutional aggression against those perceived to subvert the social order through the violation of prevalent cultural norms. Adorno and his colleagues proposed the F-Scale (for *Fascism* scale) to measure these tendencies in individuals. The authoritarian personality is held to demonstrate conservative tendencies and stands in contrast to democratic or revolutionary inclinations demonstrated by other personalities that are comparatively more liberal and progressive. The Authoritarian Personality, therefore, maps onto the traditional demarcation between left- and right-wing politics.

The inter-mingling of psychology with politics carried through in subsequent developments of the F-Scale. Altemeyer's (1981) conception of right-wing authoritarianism retained the core features of the authoritarian personality but proposed an RWA-Scale (Right-Wing Authoritarianism Scale) to replace the F-Scale, that included a number of psychometric improvements which helped quantify authoritarian tendencies more reliably. Whilst the current version demonstrates high reliability coefficients (Fodor, Wick, Hartsen & Preve, 2007), the RWA-Scale nevertheless suffers from a biased conception that authoritarianism exists only in the right-wing of the political spectrum.

The Social Cognition Approach

Social Dominance Orientation

According to Jost, Glaser, Kruglanski and Sulloway (2003), right-wing authoritarianism is the manifest result of a socio-cognitive tendency that drives individuals to categorise the world into friends or foes. This is the root process in the development of social identity, as we have seen in Chapter 4. Authoritarians are those who demonstrate concurrent tendencies to (a) categorise the social world into different groups, whose relationships with one another involve an element of power and (b) preserve their own ways when relating with different others. Authoritarians, therefore, demonstrate political conservatism through a striving for dominance. It is for this reason that authoritarianism has been more strongly evident amongst right-wing political groups, although the striving for social dominance traverses both ends of the political spectrum.

The latter conception is prevalent in Sidanius and Pratto's (1999) social dominance orientation, which posits an individual disposition that leads to a striving for dominance in social hierarchies. Social dominance orientation (SDO) retains the core concerns of authoritarianism, without associating them with specific political leanings. Individuals high in SDO consider their groups to be superior to other groups, not merely different. Like Social Identity Theory, groups are held to be socially established on the basis of variable demographic criteria like age, gender, class, religion, race, ethnicity and so on. In this way, individuals are socialised into representations of particular categories that become meaningful and relevant to the self. High SDO individuals are motivated to secure power in an effort to preserve and advance the relative interests of their own group.

This means to say that those who are socialised into a world where their group stands at the top of the social hierarchy are more likely to be motivated to preserve it by developing high SDO, whilst those who find themselves at the bottom of the social hierarchy are more likely to be motivated to change it by developing low SDO. Pratto, Sidanius, Stallworth and Malle (1994) report that high SDO is strongly correlated with conservative political groups and opposition to equality promoting programmes (e.g. affirmative action and equal rights). Conversely, Besta, Akbas, Renström, Kosakowska-Berezecka and Vazquez (2019) report that low levels of SDO are associated with positive biases towards outgroup members. We have reproduced these findings in our studies in Malta, which are presented in Chapter 11. It is worth noting that SDO is not a fixed personality trait and one's social dominance orientation can shift due to changing circumstances. Rios and Ybarra (2009), for instance, claim that, in response to party identity threat, conservatives increase their SDO whilst liberals decrease it.

With regards to immigration, the prospect of integration appears as harmful to high SDO individuals given that integration requires institutional accommodation to cater to immigrants' alien cultural ways. High SDO individuals thus perceive integration as eroding their orderly ways of life. Even if others contribute to the collective in some way, integration inevitably precipitates a re-ordering of social relations that stands to benefit immigrants relatively more than it stands to benefit locals. Even if the new arrangement is stronger as a whole, the relative restructuring of social relations also means a diminished status for dominant (or dominating and domineering) groups. In this way, SDO helps explain the assimilationist leanings of dominant groups and the integrationist leanings of immigrant (i.e. non-dominant) groups worldwide, as the Mutual Intercultural Relations in Pluralistic Societies [MIRIPS] project has concluded (Berry, 2017; Berry et al., 2023).

Narrow-mindedness

Another socio-cognitive process that bears an influence on collective intergroup relations is social judgement. In the psychological sciences, the study of social judgement traces its origins to Rokeach (1951a, 1951b), who observed that liberals as well as left-wing individuals can be equally militant and dogmatic in their ideological outlooks. This insight contrasts with the psychological study of fascism that has confounded authoritarian tendencies with right-wing political ideologies specifically, as we have seen earlier in this chapter.

According to Rokeach, liberals (or communists for that matter) are capable of holding views in as intransigent a manner as conservatives. There is no reason to assume that it is easier to change the attitudes of one than it is to change the attitudes of the other. Rokeach (1951a) argued that the intensity and resistance of attitude change is a function of the underlying cognitive structure, which he describes as variable along a dimension of narrow-mindedness. He draws on Krech's (1949) dynamic systems model, which considers how systems differ from each other in the degree and type of interaction they demonstrate when interacting with other dynamic systems.

More specifically, Rokeach argued that individuals demonstrate three kinds of cognitive organisation when interacting with alternative views, namely (a) comprehensive, (b) isolated and (c) narrow. A subject's organisation was comprehensive if it was broad and integrated when relating a series of diverse concepts; isolated when the inter-relations were broken down into substructures; and narrow when individuals were unable to relate the entire series. Rokeach's studies provided the early impetus for research into narrow-mindedness, suggesting that some perspectives are narrower than others and that this evinces when considering alternative views. More open perspectives, by contrast, are considered to be better predisposed to engage differences and to identify ways to reconcile these in fabricating coherence. Narrow-minded outlooks fail at this task and transpire as incapable of incorporating a heterogeneous structure.

Need for Cognitive Closure

According to Rokeach, the three types of cognitive organisation seem to order themselves along a single quantitative continuum from more to less organised. Rokeach noted, however, that differences between the three types of cognitive organisation were qualitative in nature, which makes it methodologically impossible to collapse the tripartite typology onto a unidimensional measurement scale. This methodological shortcoming was arguably overcome by Kruglanski (1989, 2004) in a more recent development.

Kruglanski's approach is based on a lay epistemic framework of knowledge, where different cultures are held to subscribe to different belief systems that validate different perspectives. Cultural plurality also means that what different persons 'know for a fact' can be widely diverse, given the different interpretations and connotations that can be associated with subjective experience. Consequently, according to Kruglanski (1989), knowledge is derived from the association of beliefs with 'relevant' evidence. In scientific terms, evidence is standardised through the use of statistics and other methodological protocols. But, in lay terms, what counts as evidence is subjective logical inference. Consequently, what is deemed relevant for a particular social milieu is variable and a matter of social validation.

Knowledge plurality also means that the capacity for biased cognitive processing resulting in cognitive inconsistency is high and at times potentially overwhelming. Individuals facing such diversity are required to process an infinite amount of alternative perspectives where what they hold to be true or false might not be so when examined under a different cultural lens. Kruglanski (2004) argues that this is where the issue of open and closed mindedness becomes relevant – a slight development over Rokeach's term (i.e. narrow-mindedness).

According to Kruglanski, individuals are motivated by a need for cognitive closure (NFCC) that enables them to truncate information processing and fix their perspectives onto some derived conclusion. This process, which is held to be at the interface between cognitive and social processes, prompts individuals to seize on some notion that provides closure and to then regard that conclusion as logically true. The process is reminiscent of Herbert Simon's (1956) notion of satisficing, which refers to a cognitive heuristic by which individuals search for alternatives during decision-making and settle prematurely on an acceptable option that might not be the best option out of the entire sequence – just good enough. Similarly, individuals who obtain cognitive closure seize and freeze beliefs to then move on to other cognitive tasks. This strategy, according to Kruglanski, provides an operational understanding of closed-mindedness in terms of the closure obtained once beliefs are frozen, although Kruglanski himself goes on to admit that 'the road leading from need for closure to close mindedness isn't a straightforward one' (2004, p. 17). However, as Rokeach proposed before him, the crux of the matter in Kruglanski's conception 'is the failure to consider rival alternatives to one's initial conception' (2004, p. 164).

Points of View

In the various cognitive theories outlined in the Social Cognition approach to inter-group relations (i.e. SDO, Narrow-mindedness and NFCC), cognition is not an exclusively individual operation or inclination in the same way that attitudes are. Attitudes relate an individual to an attitude object, but other attitude-bearing individuals play no role in this conception. Other constructs have been advanced that include a reference to other people's attitudes when individuals engage in social relations and attune their attitudes to one another. This is the case, for instance, in Heider and Simmel's notion of equilibration, Festinger's notion of cognitive dissonance and Sammut's notion of social representations (see Sammut, 2015, 2016). The inclusion of others in social situations creates a minimal inter-relating triad of attitudes, that is (i) attitudes by Subject 1 towards the object, (ii) attitudes by Subject 2 towards the object and (iii) mutual attitudes by Subjects 1 and 2 relative to each other. In this model, the object could be anything that subjects hold attitudes towards, for example, recreational cannabis, Muslims or integration. Socio-cognitive orientations determine how these inter-related attitudes play out and attune during the course of social interaction, as portrayed in the Attunement Triangle model hereunder (Figure 7.1).

88 The Populist Backlash

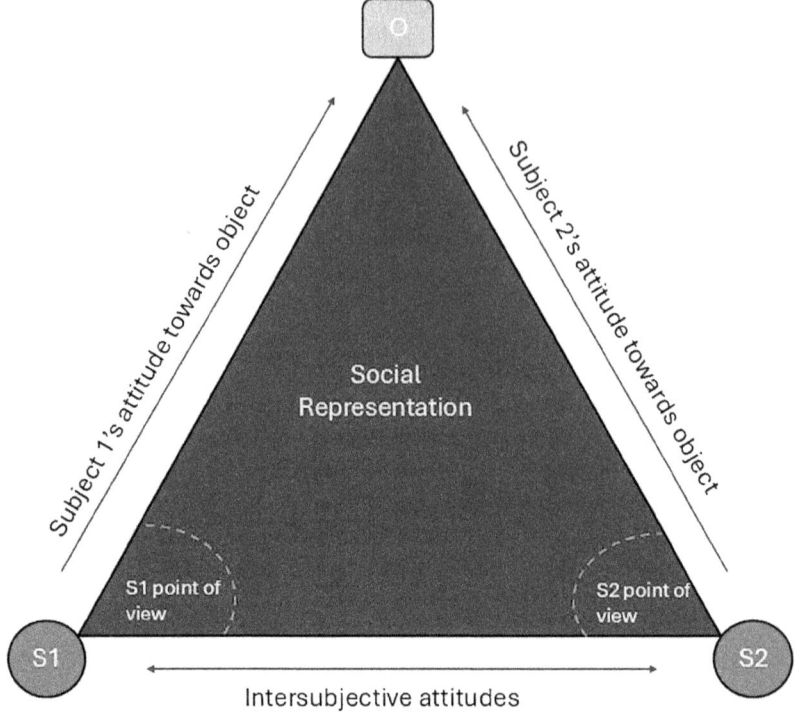

Figure 7.1 Attunement triangle

Our study of points of view provides an illustrative example (Sammut & Gaskell, 2010). We adopt the term *points of view* to denote relative plurality. A point of view is at once *relational*, linking some view to a particular point of perception, and *relative*, to other points that illuminate the view from elsewhere. Our original study of atheist and believer points of view in Britain revealed three distinct types as per Rokeach's (1951a, 1951b) original formulation. We found that monological points of view treated truth in exclusive ways, that is, they held their own views as right and correct whilst other's different views were considered as categorically and evidently wrong and in need of correction. Dialogical views understood that different people may have different beliefs and whilst they also retained their own beliefs to be true, like monological views, they conceded that others had a right to hold and practice their own beliefs even if these were incorrect. In other words, dialogical points of view extended alternative perspectives the right to be wrong. By contrast, metalogical views understood that different people have different beliefs, just like dialogical views, but that, whilst they believed their own perspectives to be right, they conceded that, from some other perspective, they could be wrong. In other words, metalogical perspectives doubted their own beliefs in the face of diversity and entertained the possibility of being wrong. They extended to alternative perspectives not only the right to be wrong but also the possibility to be right.

In this way, we agree with Rokeach that the differences between the three types of perspectives are qualitative in nature, due to the fact that monological views treat diversity on a single dichotomous polarity between right and wrong whilst dialogical and metalogical views are able to entertain relative veracity and the possibility that others can be right or wrong in their own right. This differentiation, however, provides obvious methodological limitations when operationalising different perspectives in terms of single measures, dimensions or indices (such as a single measure for cognitive closure), as these are not faithful to qualitative differences between types.

In our integration studies, alongside acculturation preferences and expectations we also asked respondents to indicate which of five perspectives came closest to their own views (Table 7.1). One perspective was metalogical, comprising a transcendental sceptical outlook. We then presented a dialogical and a monological point of view that were both in favour of integration. We also presented another dialogical and another monological point of view arguing against integration. In this way, we were able to examine whether closed-mindedness was indeed present across the polar divide for–against migrant integration.

We hypothesised that, if closed-mindedness was an exclusively conservative trait, we would identify it only amongst those declaring themselves against migrant integration. Conversely, we hypothesised that if, as Rokeach proposed, closed-mindedness evinces on both sides of the political divide, we would identify liberals whose views were as monological as those which they vehemently oppose.

Our hypotheses were confirmed (Sammut & Lauri, 2017; Sammut, Buhagiar, Mifsud, DeGiovanni & Brockdorff, 2022). In our first sample, in 2010, we found that 27.5 per cent of respondents expressed closed-minded views against integrating minorities whilst 5.2 per cent expressed closed-minded views in favour of integrating them. Almost a decade later, we measured the distribution of these views again. This time we found that 22.8 per cent endorsed closed-minded anti-integrationist views, whilst the proportion endorsing closed-minded pro-integrationist views rose steeply

Table 7.1 *Vignettes used to identify closed-minded, open-minded and dialogical views on integration*

Mindedness / View on Multiculturalism	Vignette
Closed-minded anti-integration	The Maltese must stand up for Maltese culture. We must never allow foreigners to change our way of life because they will soon take over our country.
Dialogical anti-integration	Immigrants have a right to their own way of life, but they do not have the right to impinge on the rights of others. Extreme tolerance should not be accepted.
Open-minded	Our way is not the only way, and to be free is to allow others to be free too. Everyone has a right to their own way of life. Similarly, everyone is free to take a view on the practices of another culture and has the liberty to express those thoughts. These rights are fundamental whether we agree with others or not.
Dialogical pro-integration	Immigration may be a challenge for people who are not accustomed to different ways of life. But the real problem of immigration is the intolerance of certain Maltese individuals towards other cultures, and not the immigrants themselves. Immigrants in Malta need our support not our hate.
Closed-minded pro-integration	Whatever people say, multiculturalism is necessary in today's world and there's no reason why different people shouldn't learn to co-exist in one way or another.

to 21.5 per cent of the population (Table 7.2) (Sammut, Buhagiar, Mifsud, DeGiovanni & Brockdorff, 2022). These findings provide evidence that individuals on both sides of the political debate are able to hold closed-minded views, both when they tend towards inclusion of different others and favour social change to accommodate cultural differences, as well as when they are exclusive and favour conservative policies that secure the dominant social framework. In other words, as Rokeach noted, closed-mindedness evinces amongst both left- and right-wing tendencies.

Our findings further show that, over time, closed-mindedness views on one side of the political spectrum were followed by a polarising shift that swelled the ranks of those expressing closed-minded views on the opposite side. We term this the spiral of conflict (Sammut et al., 2015). This is perhaps the clearest and simplest method to document polarisation over time. Politicisation of the immigration issue in Malta led to a higher incidence of extremist, monological thinking overall as the proportion of

Table 7.2 *Distribution of views on integration in 2010 and 2019*

Year		Monological anti-integration	Dialogical anti-integration	Metalogical	Dialogical pro-integration	Monological pro-integration
	Views on integration					
2010	Frequency	53	65	37	28	10
	%	27.5%	33.7%	19.2%	14.5%	5.2%
2019	Frequency	54	77	19	36	51
	%	22.8%	32.5%	8.0%	15.2%	21.5%

people holding closed-minded views rose from about a third in 2010 (32.7%) to almost half of the entire population less than a decade later (44.3%). During that time period, Malta experienced an economic boom that saw an increased number of immigrants move to the country. Malta's National Statistics Office (2023) reported that the country's foreign-born population stands at 22 per cent of the total number of residents, which is a 5-fold increase over a 10-year period. The hardening of attitudes amongst locals reported here has taken place in this shifting demographic context.

Contemporary Populism

The effect of demographic changes on attitudes towards immigration has been very well discussed by Kaufmann (2019), who notes that such shifts bear extensive political ramifications. Increased economic activity, as happened in Malta between 2010 and 2020, which also saw its GDP double from €6.4 billion to €12.8 billion over this time period (Sammut, Mifsud & Brockdorff, 2021b), leads to increased demand for labour in many industries that provides a powerful migratory pull. This contrasts with events elsewhere, such as protracted conflicts in neighbouring Libya and Syria, which generate a corresponding migratory push. In the face of evident demographic changes, some will react by incorporating cultural differences that they perceive to add flair to local culture. Others, by contrast, will perceive their ways becoming less routine in their own locale during their own lifespan.

The former, which Kaufmann identifies as left-modernists in political terms, pursue inter-cultural projects that require a bedrock of diversity which they perceive to contrast with narrow-minded, racist aspirations for homogeneity and stability. Right-wing populism, by contrast, promotes the interests of the dominant culture and seeks to prevent or limit its erosion in the face of ever-increasing diversity. It rests on a conservative coalition who are attached to their heritage and their own mainstream ways of life. Diversity is threatening not only because it changes the prevalent order and security of the dominant group, but primarily because it disrupts the sense of harmony and cohesion that is already in place. Consequently, the populist counter-reaction to cultural diversity involves both authoritarian efforts to maintain dominance and conservative tendencies to preserve local culture.

Ethno-traditional nationalists, as Kaufmann terms those inclined in this manner, favour slower immigration in the hope that immigrants assimilate into the majority culture without usurping or diluting local traditions. Whilst populist politicians typically portray the issue as a problem for the nation-state, Kaufmann observes that this is more pertinently framed as an issue for the ethnic majority. Nation-states are able to adapt to any ethnic configuration in a way that ethnic majorities are not, due to the fact that the dominant status of the ethnic majority is necessarily at stake should the proportion of ethnic minorities increase to 'majority–minority' status. Together with New Zealand, North America is projected to be majority–minority by 2050, with Western Europe and Australia following suit later in the century.

Put simply, according to Kaufmann, ethnic groups are communities that believe themselves to be descended from the same ancestors and who differentiate themselves from others through various cultural markers, such as language, racial appearance, religion, local customs and other cultural practices and ways of life. By contrast, nation-states are jurisdictions with clear territorial boundaries and political aspirations. National majorities in the West, Kaufmann goes on to argue, are every bit as ethnic as minorities are but, due to their dominant status, their sense of ethnicity and nationhood is conflated. Consequently, majority ethnicity within nation-states is typically backgrounded in everyday life, fuelling a spiral of conflict (Sammut et al., 2015) between those in whose interest it is to preserve it, for whatever reason, and others in whose interest it is that other cultural practices are accommodated within the mainstream. Ethnic majorities thus express their native identity in nationalistic terms, responding to the populist rallying cry to prevent their demise.

The polarisation we have identified in Table 7.2, therefore, is rooted in concerns over identity not realistic threat. Accordingly, Kaufmann argues, we need to understand identity not as a fabrication designed to maintain power but as a set of ethnic myths and symbols to which members are attached like any other ethnic group, including those striving for recognition. We are all, therefore, seeking legitimation of our own ways. It is worth noting the inherent paradox here that groups seeking conversion from other (majority) groups to accommodate national jurisdictions to their own ways can only do so by maintaining conformity amongst themselves. That is, they need to silence internal dissent in exactly the opposite manner they expect from others. Failing to do so would prevent them from mounting a coherent challenge (Sammut & Bauer, 2021).

The political polarisation over immigration involves those who identify with dominant cultural traditions versus those who, for whatever reason, do not. Both are valid identification processes in their own right. But, as Kaufmann posits, imposing either on an entire population is a recipe for discontent. Crucially, polarisation over immigration and how it should be managed fuels, in turn, political identity polarisation. Klein (2020) points out, in this manner, that disagreements over issues in democratic jurisdictions tend to be sorted through political party lines. Consequently, we observe that the kinds of people most attracted to liberal, progressive ideals are the kinds of people who are excited by change and by the prospect of cultural diversity. Their political preferences are merely an expression of their basic psychological temperament that also pushes them to live in cosmopolitan cities, try out new culinary experiences, travel and interrelate with curiosity when they meet different others. On the other hand, conservative people express political preferences aligned with the esteem with which they hold and value their place of origin and the family and friendship networks they built growing up, celebrating customs, traditions and practices they know and love.

Klein goes on to argue that open is not better than closed. As we have seen, closed and open mindsets are psychological characteristics, not compliments. They serve to incline populations towards ethno-traditional nationalist policies or liberal, progressive multicultural ones. The policy debate, as we have seen in Chapter 6, centres around what Berlin (1969) identifies as a distinction between negative and positive liberty. Negative liberty posits that people should allow other people to pursue their goals as long as these do not infringe on the rights of others. Tolerating difference is crucial for achieving this but loving it or celebrating it is not. Negative liberty contrasts with positive liberty, which consists in promoting overarching ideals such as diversity. Forcing this ideal onto conservatives is as coercive a political outcome as right-wing populism is in enforcing identity-based cultural assimilation. As minorities increase in size, therefore, through processes of immigration, the question of whether they will incline towards ethno-traditional nationalism or multicultural integration acquires political moment.

Conclusion

We have seen in previous chapters that human beings evolved to exist in groups. We have seen how social identity drives individuals to become members of groups that compete for scarce resources with other groups. Group membership, therefore, also means survival, whilst exclusion, or defeat in the competitive game, also means poverty, loss and, in a worst-case scenario, even death (Klein, 2020). It is little wonder, therefore, that political struggles over national group membership and the relative allocation of national resources to diverse ethnic groups that make up a national population is a highly charged affair. In this chapter, we have seen that economic prosperity, as in the case of Malta, materialises the struggle for resources that fuels closed-minded polarisation between those who strive to protect their interests and those who strive to institute their own.

We conclude by noting that political activity is intertwined with identity. As Klein points out, this is not because all politics is identity politics. Rather, this is because human cognition is influenced by identity, as we have seen in previous chapters, and political activity is part of human cognition. We cannot sever ourselves from our circumstances, Klein correctly notes. Consequently, we will never fully know how we've been shaped by our cultural contexts. Who we are, who we identify as and with, who we look up to, who we trust, who we love and respect, but also who we fear, who we hate and who we cannot stand, has a lot to do with where we grew up and who we socialised with in doing so. If identity-based politics is what drives us away from one another, then it must also hold the key to any conciliatory effort.

Our democratic systems are not designed to obtain consensus through suppression; they are intended to withstand the stress of dissent by outing deviance. But this, as we have seen, results in a monological hardening of attitudes that sets the stage for a spiralling of conflict. Conflict and conciliation, seemingly, contain within them the seeds of their own destruction. If we are not to charge down this gauntlet, we need to, as Klein advocates, become mindful of which identities matter to us and others in our midst so that we can become intentional about which ones we want to work to activate. In other words, we need for cultural conciliation to become the project that drives the social representations we collectively construct and the identities we enact in social relations (Sammut, 2018). If our politics is based on our psychology, as Klein correctly concludes, then the methods for improving our politics must involve a psychological component because systems can only work if the subjects making them up are able to acquiesce to systemic demands. It is to this critical insight that we turn next.

CHAPTER 8

Democracy
The Impossible Dream

In Chapter 7, we saw how attitude divergence towards migrant integration and assimilation in certain cases precipitates a polarisation of views that fuels a conflict spiral between opposing parties. When this opposition acquires political moment, through different party policies, the stage is set for intra-national conflict. This is presently proving to be a thorny issue in many Western democracies and has been so for quite a while. The issue of how to cope with immigration is an issue that will not go away. The downside to its persistent character is that it breeds discontent amongst a disaffected citizenry. In European Commissioner's Ylva Johannson's words (EU Observer, 2020), when it comes to migration pacts 'no one will be satisfied'. However, polarisation is not in itself altogether bad. As Klein (2020) argues, the alternative to polarisation is consensus, the achievement of which typically requires suppression of dissenting voices (Sammut & Bauer, 2021). Consensus, therefore, is a less preferable alternative than polarisation as it masks even more contentious practices. We commonly hold that democratic politics can handle the stress created by polarisation and that this is preferable to a unilateral view that requires blind conformity and nothing short of a revolution to overthrow (Moghaddam, 2013). Democracy, on the other hand, is not without its problems either.

One of the most famous claims ever made about democracy has to be that by Winston Churchill in the British House of Commons in 1947, when he proclaimed that democracy is the worst form of government except for all other forms that have been tried from time to time. Arguably, the prevalent view is that democracy is not only a good form of government, other forms (like communism, fascism, dictatorships, oligarchies, monarchies, or theocracies) are actually bad. The prevalent view also holds that any ails stemming from democracy can be redressed with even more democracy.

Whilst this might sound paradoxical, it is not the only governing procedure that can fix democratic shortcomings. For instance, in ancient

Rome, dictators holding executive authority were appointed from time to time to resolve particular issues in line with their specific mandate. The practice of overthrowing government through a military coup until a new government is appointed and handed the reins is also quite common through history. A recent example is Ukraine's contested overthrow of President Yanukovych's interim government in 2014 that led to the current Russo-Ukrainian war. That said, the conventional view about democracy also holds that, when democracy lets us down in some way, such as by appointing the wrong sort of people into government or when a majority appoints leaders that serve its interests over those of the entire nation, more democratic engagement and a strengthening of democratic practices serve to redress the ails. Democratic engagement brings more people into politics, airs subverted voices and in the process rights institutional and systemic wrongs. The same orientation is also common with regard to science, that is, the problems caused by science can be redressed through better science – scientific solutions solve scientific problems. And, whilst paradoxical, these views prevail for good reason.

Unlike other forms of government or learning, democracy and science both incorporate self-correcting mechanisms that have no parallel in other forms. In democracy, you get a chance to vote for someone else next time. In science, you get a chance to publish contrarian findings. Neither form is necessarily correct all the time. And, whilst the systems of democracy and science might be valued for their institutional implications, neither will satisfy those who stand dissatisfied with the outcomes. Under-valued immigrants will still shudder at bigoted practices permitted by democratically elected populist leaders. And disaffected nationalists will still quiver at the sight of multicultural celebrations. In this chapter we deal with the practice of democracy across two levels, that is, the institutional–collective level and the individual–personal level. We adopt a realistic view of democracy and analyse why it is commonly valued on the one hand (Harré & Sammut, 2013), but also why it commonly fails to deliver contentment on the other. Ultimately, we dispel the idea that democracy is a panacea for settling intergroup disputes. This paves the way for considering more pragmatic procedures, which we detail further in Chapter 9.

Politics

This might be evident to most, but it is still worth noting that the issue of immigration strikes right at the heart of politics. The word politics is etymologically derived from the Greek word *politikos*, which refers to activity of and by the *polis*, that is, the citizenry. Politics, therefore, refers to the activities of citizens that determine collective pursuits and the distribution of resources across different institutions. Insofar as social action is undertaken in a context that involves the regulated activity of citizens, then that activity can be deemed political within that context. For instance, if one goes to sleep in the comfort of their home in the knowledge that police are patrolling the area for criminals, that soldiers patrol the borders for defence, that nurses and doctors working the night shift in hospital are at the ready to provide medical care if needed, then even the individual act of sleeping acquires political overtones. Citizens can sleep with their minds at rest in the knowledge that their safety is catered for by the coordinated activity of similar others who have banded together to establish a community to care for one another, distinct from other communities established in other locales that cater to other citizens whose benefits one might not be able to claim or enjoy.

Contrast this with a solitary individual going to sleep in a dwelling they have fabricated 'off-grid'. In such circumstances, the activities pursued by that individual are not political – but they sure are highly vulnerable to plunder by neighbouring citizens seeking to expand their territory; more grazing land for their own, to use a metaphor along the lines of Social Contract Theory and the Tragedy of the Commons. The lone sleeper would do well to band with at least another to keep watch whilst they sleep. Should they do so, the decision-making process to determine who sleeps where, for how long and what resources are made available to whom to fulfil their duties becomes a political process.

The reason why immigration strikes at the heart of politics is because it involves a claim to practices and resources typically reserved for citizens. In the traditional Greek polis, citizenry was reserved for native Greek men. Foreigners held no vote in Greek democracy. Neither did slaves or women. And these restrictions were not characteristic of medieval Greek democracies alone. The entire emancipation movement represents a struggle for rights that permit political participation on an equal footing with recognised citizens. Immigrants enter the city (or, more pertinently, society in current times) with restricted rights (in the case of legal immigrants) or no rights at all (in the case of illegal/irregular ones). Naturalisation, that is, the process of acquiring citizenship, is typically a long-winded process in many countries that might take as much as a decade or more for legal immigrants to qualify for. In the case of illegal immigrants, the opportunity might never arise. The issue over immigration involves the extent to which political rights are extended to outsiders, who might then use the opportunity to pursue their interests over those of current citizens. The prevalent concern about immigration thus involves a citizenry's political control over its own habitat and membership, with all the resources it presently enjoys.

In practice, political activity involves different features. As Runciman (2018) notes, there is politics that produces stable institutions, such as parliamentary votes that enact laws assigning institutional authority to regulate the conduct of citizens. There is also politics produced by stable institutions, such as citizen or parliamentary debates about what should be done to make things better. In any case, as Runciman further notes, politics is about collective choices that enable people to live in a certain way and the choice they have in doing so. Ultimately, politics translates into the choices politicians and voters make about what laws to have and who must obey them. The exercise involves a trade-off between choice and constraint – who is free to do what and who isn't.

Runciman further argues, in line with Social Contract Theory, that the control of violence lies at the heart of politics due to the necessity to enforce enacted laws and regulations that emerge out of the collective establishment of a citizenry. They key to politics is therefore not violence, but control over violence. This represents the power involved in politics. There are two ways of thinking about this. The first involves control *through* violence. In its most basic form, this is what the armed forces are tasked to execute within society. Regular citizens, even gun-wielding ones, do not enjoy the authority to use violence to enforce their will (or anybody's for that matter) over others. But politics also involves control *of* violence, that is, who has access to it, whether citizens have a right to bear arms, when is it legitimate to use (e.g. defence of self or property) and against whom might it be warranted (e.g. waging war). In essence, politics involves the sort of actions that grant the right to use coercive force to some as a solution to conflict.

The virtues of politics involve giving humans the possibility of a stable existence without the necessity of violence. Politics enables human beings to escape the brutish condition of having to watch their backs from traitors, though the possibility of cheating can never be ruled out. In Chapter 6 we saw how introspective projection (Sammut, Mifsud & Brockdorff, 2021a) leads individuals to imagine possibilities of cheating based on their own subjective experiences and to use these to guard themselves from the potential negative actions of others. Even if we all know that we are better off living in peace, as Runciman (2018) notes, and even if we know that everyone else knows this, we cannot be sure that others will not see us as a threat, which means we cannot rule out the threat posed by others who perceive us as a threat to their own interests.

In such circumstances, we strive to neutralise the threat, one way or another. Which way we do ultimately determines what kind of politics we engage in. In a democracy, we rely on the armed forces to neutralise violence. To protect our other interests, we rely on the rule of law. We go to court to claim our rights from the state or fellow citizens. To change laws that do not grant us enough rights or the right kind of rights, we use parliamentary procedures. Politics does not make the difference on its own. It serves to create the spaces that, in conjunction with other institutional spaces, produce the social and material benefits we enjoy.

Doing Politics

The kind of politics we do serves to bring about the kind of life we want to enjoy. This enables us to go from our natural paranoid state of forever watching our back, to a convivial, civilised state where we can enjoy life in fellowship with others (Runciman, 2018). Imagine how long our life expectancy would realistically be if we could not rely on medical care provided to us by others in whom we lay our trust. Not even the best medical practitioner can cure themselves – you cannot perform heart surgery on yourself. Together we all go further and further, so it is vitally important that we do our politics right if we are to reap its benefits.

If we go back to ancient Greece, the cradle of democracy, we find that for much of history politics rested on the idea of virtue. Being a good citizen meant leading a virtuous life and becoming the best person you could be through politics (Runciman, 2018). In medieval times, this manner of living took on a religious dimension – the good man was one who observed God's precepts and acted in brotherhood (or sisterhood) with fellow citizens. In our modern era, the requirement for religious piety has abated – perhaps we have come to realise that we all are all too human – but we still battle each other to elect representatives worthy of political office. Think back to Bill Clinton's infamous affair during his US presidency, or Boris Johnson's COVID-19 parties during lockdown. Political careers can make or break on the back of personal scandals. A good party whip knows how to use politicians' sins to their party's advantage (Mitchell, 2021). And the media is replete with news about politicians' doings. Who in the world does not have an opinion about Donald Trump?

Doing politics in a democratic manner involves exercising political choice over who represents us in matters of politics. We want the right kind of people to represent us in the right kind of way. We use elections to do this and if we do not like how our choices turn out, we use elections to replace our representatives with ones who persuade us they can do it better. They are not necessarily able to, they just need to convince us they are worth a try over who is doing the job (badly) right now. We know they are fraught with human deficiencies like the rest of us, both the ones we elected and the ones we will elect to replace them in future. But we hope every time that they will at least do better than the outgoing ones.

We concede that politics comes with the risk of making mistakes, but we cherish the opportunity to correct them. We do so because we observe the collective rules of the game – when one side loses, it concedes power to the other side. This is not a given in every society. Even in self-proclaimed functioning democracies like the United States, some individuals find it hard to swallow and will rally in violence against the other party, like Trump supporters who stormed the Capitol in protest at John Biden's electoral win in 2021. In other places, like Assad's Syria and many of the countries involved in the Arab Spring, handing over the reins of political power to another person or party requires nothing short of civil war.

In essence, therefore, modern representative democracy is nothing other than a proxy for civil war. Instead of battling things out with guns on the streets, we battle each other over the number of votes our party counts in favour in an election and, by virtue of that, whose voice is the loudest and most numerous in parliament. Stable politics requires for people with access to guns to not use them. Done in this way, politics can rescue us from bad politics without recourse to violence (Runciman, 2018). Democracy is not held to be a good form of government because of all the good it does but rather, as Churchill posited, because of all the bad it helps us avoid.

Democracy does not mean that the best politicians are elected to power. Nor does it mean that those elected to power will live up to our expectations of virtue in their regard. It only means that, if we realise they are not serving us well enough, we can protect ourselves by electing others in their stead. In this way, modern democracy is adaptable and self-correcting in a way that other forms of government are not, as we have argued. Runciman (2018) points out that democracies are good at avoiding the worst because democratic citizens are prone to irritability and impatience in the face of neglected interests. They always push for more, no matter how good things already are. This keeps politicians on their toes. But democracy remains at its root a politics of restraint – it is a good way to stop bad things from happening (Runciman, 2018).

Democracy

Once we understand that democracy in its ideal form is different from how it is practiced, we can try to study the latter to examine where and how far we're falling short of achieving the former. Realistically, we cannot expect politicians to set a good example. They are people, like us, and every bit as biased in their cognition as the rest of us. What politicians are better at is politicking – the profession of politics if you like. But we also have that to say about the citizens who vote for them and what effectively sways them, including ourselves. How good are we at choosing the best people to represent us? In practice, we are all more or less aware of our and others' shortcomings. But what we tend to do is not bother much until we hit a tipping point (Gladwell, 2000) that spurs us into action. We do this individually; we've all got our personal thresholds. When enough people do it together, we observe a collective electoral swing. The latest ones have ushered a populist anti-immigration push in most Western democracies resting on a wave of renewed nationalism. Runciman (2018) cites Benjamin Constant with foreseeing the potential for reactionary voting where the public would wake up from a state of passivity and lash out at who is governing them. Constant argued that people who are disaffected by politics do not simply drop out and give up on it. Rather they become resentful and spring at the possibility of revenge.

Given the perennial difference between human cognition as we would like it and human cognition as it is when it comes to political affairs and the enterprise of achieving democracy, a deep understanding of the conventional view of democracy driving our political ideals is warranted. Achen and Bartels (2016) provide an insightful analysis of the folk theory of democracy. In this view, democracy begins with voters who choose leaders to act on their behalf or who act themselves by expressing their preferences in referendums. What the majority wants then becomes government policy so that effectively people rule themselves. Achen and Bartels (2016) quote Abraham Lincoln's expression for government 'of the people, by the people and for the people' for capturing this conventional folk view of democratically elected governments. The idea is that, when elected in this way, people make sure that they are represented by others who have their interests at heart and who act on the collective interest. Our ideals for democracy include effective participation by interested voters who ensure institutions respect principles of equality and inclusion by voting in virtuous politicians who see to that. In actual practice, what voters do is control elected officials through retrospective voting, that is, giving some people a shot at performing with the possibility of punishing them by withholding their support if they do not.

This is why the underlying economic bedrock made famous by Marx (1977) is critical in politics. When voters are doing well economically, they might complain but let things slide. When they are not doing well, they react and give someone else a try. Or, at the very least, they simply withdraw their support so that their party fails to put together the numbers. Given that politics is based on the social identities we choose to cultivate for ourselves, we are more likely to not vote for a party that has not lived up to our expectations than cast for the opposite side, though we might if we are willing to re-negotiate our identity on some policy line. In any case, we help sustain a push for our party but, when we feel let down, we ease the effort and let nature take its course. That doesn't mean democracy works. That might also mean democracy does not work if who seizes the opportunity of abated interest pulls things in a different direction, unsettling the whole institutional setup in the process.

So how do we get from a state of dysfunctional democracy to a functional one? As Achen and Bartels (2016) observe, there is a paradoxical folk view of democracy where people at once believe they are a free people controlling their own government and at the same time believe they are being badly governed by incompetent and untrustworthy politicians pursuing their own interests. We recognise both views as more or less true contemporarily. The everyday voter celebrates the wisdom of popular judgement and gets busy with their life whilst complaining about what the people did when they exercised that choice. However unfortunate things turn out, we still consider democracy to be a panacea for anything messed up by public opinion.

Actualised Democracy

The same distinction between ideal democracy and democracy in practice is found in Moghaddam's (2016) notion of actualised democracy. Moghaddam (2016) starts with a defence of democracy as the best sort of government for a number of reasons beyond simply voting out incumbents. He argues that democracy should be any society's goal for the fact that (a) it promotes freedom of choice and expression including that to criticise leaders; (b) it promotes government transparency, which brings about efficiency; (c) it provides the opportunity to hand over the reins to those who demonstrate themselves better at the task; (d) it promotes rule of law and an independent judiciary; (e) it upholds human rights and freedoms and (f) democratic nations are less likely to wage war against each other.

Moghaddam argues that, whilst we know the reasons that make democracy the most valid ideal, achieving it in practice remains a challenge everywhere. Effective *actualised* democracy requires the full, informed and equal participation of citizens in wide aspects of political, economic and cultural government. Many countries, including Western democracies, are still undergoing progress towards achieving this state. The fight for equal rights is nowhere more heated than in the migration debate, although gender rights also remain an ideal for the most part. In the EU, the migration crisis following the Syrian civil war has led to a resurgence of support for far-right movements battling multiculturalism in their effort to maintain the European way of life, including its fundamental values. This nationalist spirit has propelled many a populist leader to positions of government. In the United States, Trump's anti-immigrant stance set the stage for curbing the immigrant inflow. The United Kingdom has doubled up its efforts to prevent illegal boat crossings from France and to deport asylum seekers out of the United Kingdom before their claims are processed. These fiercely nationalist groups have polarised in response to other extremist movements, such as radicalised fundamentalist religious movements that pull in an opposite direction on the basis of what is held sacred to them.

Both of these extremes limit democratic progress as citizens in independent nation-states everywhere do battle over the rules of the game they choose to play within their national jurisdictions. In the process, they settle matters over whether and how many groups should be represented, how representatives should be elected and whether their terms should be time limited, whether and how much they can spend during elections to boost their support, how they should treat minorities who differ from them once they are elected, and so on. Put in this way, it is easy to realise how everywhere we are more or less close to achieving the ideal, but that nowhere has it been successfully realised as yet. It is still the case most anywhere that powerful elites are still more capable than others to influence public opinion and to protect their interests through mediated political communication – dictatorships and democracies alike.

The Sociology of Democracy

On the other side of leaders in the democratic equation stand voters themselves. We have just seen that the process of assuring good leaders are elected to lead, not just aspiring ones, is prone to the reality that elected politicians are merely human, therefore fallible in many ways. Democratic voters often consider themselves to be very capable of telling the wheat from the chaff. But this too may be no more than an illusion. Even the most informed voters, as Achel and Bartels (2016) argue, typically make choices on the basis of their own identity projects. That is to say, what party someone votes for says something about who that somebody is, regardless of the merits of specific policies or underlying ideologies driving the party. Voters tend to be more concerned about the former than the latter. This means that a leader might be propelled to power for being more cool than competent.

Achel and Bartels (2016) further note that disenchantment with democracy is widespread, even in seemingly unlikely places. They note that the Chinese and Americans are in fact indistinguishable in their support for democracy in its ideal version as well as their disaffection with how this is being implemented in their country's government. Most anywhere people find democracy to be a laudable ideal that their government is failing at.

Actualising democracy, as Moghaddam (2016) suggests, requires institutional structures that support its implementation. Moghaddam argues that the starting point for achieving actualised democracy is an educational system that develops critical thinking skills in the general population and which pursues the full and informed participation of all citizens as a virtue in every important aspect of decision-making. It is crucial for policymaking to reflect the true interests of every segment of society.

For this to materialise, educated citizens will need to pursue their interests in a democratic manner, which involves nine criteria: (1) leaders will need to be responsive to the wishes of the citizens who elected them; (2) systems and institutions need to follow rule of law over any other procedure, however routine or common-sensical this might be to those executing it; (3) leaders need to be removable through popular will; (4) citizens require freedom of expression; (5) minorities need to enjoy comparable human rights and freedoms like everybody else; (6) society requires an independent judiciary and adequate distribution of powers; (7) all adults should be free to vote; (8) positions of authority should be achievable on the basis of merit, not political patronage; and (9) institutions need to pursue distributive justice to enable the disadvantaged to get ahead and reduce social inequalities that breed resentment.

Moghaddam argues that leadership is at the centre of these democratic virtues because it influences each of these principles directly. It is crucial, therefore, for leaders to embody these democratic ideals. Voters identify with the leaders they would wish to be themselves (Sammut & Bauer, 2021). The leader is therefore an extension of the self. Leaders who embody democratic ideals offer their followers the possibility to incorporate democratic ideals into their very own identities. In this way, democracy becomes the province of the self.

The Psychology of Democracy

The psychological dimension of democracy, as opposed to procedural or institutional democracy, concerns the conglomeration of subjective thoughts, feelings and actions pertaining to democracy experienced in actual life. As with everything else, the subjective dimension of democracy means that not everything concerning the implementation of democracy is rooted in objective criteria. Indeed, many can be deemed inter-objective (Sammut, Daanen & Moghaddam, 2013) in the sense that they involve inter-subjective arrangements that are then objectified through the outcomes of democratic engagement, that is, official policy or black letter law. For instance, how large should traffic fines be? What sort of a prison term should particular crimes attract, relative to other crimes? For how long must a prisoner remain incarcerated before qualifying for parole? How are parole boards to be comprised? And so on.

There are also democratic procedures that in themselves require inter-subjective negotiation. How frequently should elections be held? How long is the term of the leader? Should leaders be allowed to run again once their term expires? Should deputy leaders also be voted in? Are there any thresholds in place to ensure fair representation? The inter-subjective outcomes of these topics often result in policies that can then be followed in an objective manner. Democratic engagement, therefore, involves more than voting for a leader every few years. It involves participation in inter-subjective experiences that result in the objective conditions we end up inhabiting.

As Moghaddam (2016) points out, we are all born into worlds and societies which pre-exist our arrival and which determine who we go on to become to some extent. If we, therefore, wish to be able to speak our minds and be respected for it, we need to implement free speech for everyone in society as a basic inalienable human right. This is the institutional dimension. Doing so might require voting in politicians who are ready to recognise free speech as a human right of law. This is the procedural dimension. We also need for other citizens to respect our right to free speech. This refers to the psychological dimension of democracy.

To achieve this, citizens might need to be trained, or educated, to develop a democratic skill set that permits democracy to bear its fruits. If, after granting a citizenry freedom of expression, the public's response is to mock and humiliate that expression or otherwise treat it with contempt and bullying, the result can only be self-censorship and resentment on the part of the victimised party. These are not the conditions that make democracy work. These are the conditions that make democracy not work, at least not for everyone. It works only for those who use their democratic liberties to bully others out of the running. Instead of leading us to a collaborative path across our differences, it leads down a sullen path of individuality where any difference from our own standards is grounds for desolation. The increasing polarisation in many democratic countries spells the latter more than it does the former.

Moghaddam (2016) further notes that the successful implementation of free speech requires psychological skills such as turn-taking, reciprocity, and empathic listening. Becoming democratic, therefore, also requires a sensitivity to democratisation processes that can help us travel further down the path of actualising democracy. We require political socialisation that targets cognitive styles, relational skills, social values and inter-personal skills to function in a political system that allows us to become the sort of person we are capable of becoming. If we suppress, impede or shut down others' dissenting opinions for what they do to us, we effectively throw a spanner in the works of giving disadvantaged others their voice, just because we can. And just because we can does not mean we should. In fact, we should not, however objectionable we find the contrasting opinion to be.

Achieving psychological outcomes of this kind involves implementing changes in thinking, in social skills and in individual actions that democratise the human mind. This is easier said than done, given the human mind in its current configuration. We have seen in previous chapters how evolution has shaped us in ways that aid our survival through enmity. The stakes of conflict at this point in time, however, offer more of a prospect for humankind to obliterate itself than the prospect of winning a war. It seems very clear, on the international level at least, that conflict is no longer necessarily adaptive and faithful to the 'survival of the fittest' maxim. No one alive is fit enough to survive a nuclear holocaust. The stakes of finding a way out of conflict that stretches from negative intra-personal experiences to inter-personal alliances that address discord involving an international dimension have never been higher, and it is my contention in this volume that they are now too high to pursue or entertain any further. As Moghaddam notes, Milgram's obedience studies demonstrate how poor we all are at resisting unruly authorities (Sammut & Bauer, 2021). That should be a wakeup call to educate more fully democratic citizens that can bring about more fully democratic societies – the kind who would be more likely to disobey than to obey orders to harm others, however benevolent you might perceive authority to be.

The Democratic Creed

Moghaddam (2016) rightly notes that the functioning of a democracy depends on the extent to which democratic values and democratic activities are embraced and enacted by its citizens and the extent to which these become integral to their own identities. A psychologically democratic citizen, for instance, would rather lose an argument to a brash opinion that is included in the debate than win the argument by excluding or ostracising opinions with which they disagreed. As Moghaddam (2016) further notes, democracy functions best when core democratic activities such as tolerance, support for human rights, respect for rule of law and so on become integral to individual citizens. In this way, democratic citizens are guided in their actions by a critical, open mind, an inquisitive disposition and a set of core values that promote engagement and reciprocity.

Moghaddam (2016) goes on to list a set of 10 convictions that democratic citizens need to internalise. Taken together, these constitute what he calls the Democratic Creed, that is:

(1) I could be wrong;
(2) I must critically question everything, including the sacred beliefs of my society;
(3) I must revise my opinions as the evidence requires;
(4) I must seek to understand those who are different from me;
(5) I can learn from those who are different from me;
(6) I must seek information and opinions from different sources;
(7) I should be actively open to new experiences;
(8) I should be open to create new experiences for others;
(9) There are principles of right and wrong;
(10) I should seek experiences of higher value.

Put in this way, Moghaddam's (2016) proposal sounds very compelling. At this point in our volume, we know that we cannot rely on human nature alone to inculcate citizens with these aspirations. We have seen in previous chapters how individuals are inclined to establish social identities that put them in communion with others, with whom they compete for access to resources against other self-interested coalitions. Human nature has seen to it that the human mind is inculcated with the right set of cognitive biases and heuristics that achieve the opposite of what Moghaddam prescribes. For instance, we have seen how our reasoning is motivated towards achieving group goals we have signed up to and that our reasoning process is biased in such a determined direction – we believe whatever evidence supports our views and we dismiss contradictory evidence even on irrelevant grounds.

Moreover, we are equipped with a mind that is easily plugged in to prevalent cultural norms and practices, regardless of their true nature. Human children growing up in China learn to speak Mandarin, those growing up in Kuwait speak Farsi, in Malta children speak Maltese and in the United States they speak English. As human beings we are born capable of learning any language, but we grow up speaking the one we have been exposed to. Similarly, most children growing up in the West tend to believe in Christianity, in the Middle East and North Africa they tend to believe in Islam and in China they tend to believe in Confucianism. Like learning a foreign language, we are capable of comprehending and mastering a different skill set than the one we have acquired through socialisation. The human mind permits this through our lifelong potential for learning. But what we believe and what we question is more easily aligned with the cultural norms we have been socialised in than any other set of principles which also speak to the same issue.

In essence, the potential for democratic citizenry is part of our evolved cognitive package. We are capable of open-mindedness as much as we are capable of closed-mindedness. This is because the ability to open or close our mind was essential to the survival strategies our ancestors might have pursued. Sometimes they needed to move on, which required an open mind as to what might be better elsewhere. Immigrants tend to think like this. At other times they might have come across a patch that was good enough for purpose, so they closed their mind to other options and settled. This is the local mindset. The potential for both is inherent to the human mind.

What Moghaddam (2016) proposes in his psychology of democracy is that the time has come to precipitate a shift from closure to openness by focusing more strongly on what enables us to act democratically relative to one another, due to the fact that the potential for conflict that inheres in any other strategy is, at this point in time, too big a risk for all of us. In a sense, Moghaddam's proposal is like teaching resilience to schoolchildren.

We start by acknowledging that some are naturally more resilient than others, but we do not leave it at that. We also teach schoolchildren that bullying is wrong and that it should not happen. And we do not leave it at that either. Rather, we go on to teach resilience techniques to everyone because we recognise that no matter how good our children already are, it would not hurt to boost their capabilities a little bit further. So, we teach them how to cope with bullying. Similarly, no matter how many formal elections we will participate in over our lifetime, it would not hurt for us to learn further that democracy works best when the guns are left at the door and that our staunch defence of nationalist ways and values might light a spark that ends up engulfing us all.

Conclusion

In a sense, all world religions and philosophies have already attempted universal reconciliation between different kinds of human beings. Let's put it like this, if everyone converted to Catholicism then we would not fight each other when we disagreed, we would simply request papal oversight. Likewise, for the Chinese communist party or the Russian oligarchy. We would not fight each other if one of us had the final word, be it Xi, Putin or the Pope. All forms of social organisation pursue dominance to some extent in pursuit of a cause that can unite us all – if we all converted.

Assimilating foreigners to local cultural ways and practices does the same, as does integrating them with enough freedom to maintain and celebrate different habits and cultured practices. So, in a sense, all creeds fail for the same reason, that is, human variability. Some are inclined one way, some another. This does not bring peace, but it has brought about survival of the fittest over our species' evolutionary time. Those better able to withstand whatever challenges they faced survived, whilst those less able perished. One way of going about the issues we have discussed so far is to observe from a distance to see which collective organisation will survive in future. All religions and ideologies in circulation have made it this far, but will they make it 100 years hence? How about 1,000, or a million years hence?

Ultimately, nature takes its course. But, as Moghaddam (2013) pointed out, the stakes of conflict in the nuclear era are simply too high to overlook because they come with a catastrophic end for us and our progeny. We are also naturally equipped to be alarmed about this prospect and to try to do something about it. As Runciman (2018) notes, the truth is that we do not know how to fight wars for peace. Nor do we know how to turn democratic negatives into positives so that the benefits of politics spread to those who need them. We know that we want things done better, but we do not even know when what we are doing is actually not good enough. With regards to politics, we can see how pursuing peace promotes easy options but that easy options encourage bad politics, which can be disastrous (Runciman, 2018). And as far as democracy goes, we all agree that it is a good thing but we also agree that we do not have a good system yet. In the meantime, we go about our everyday business enjoying what we do and despising other systems that do things differently.

The real problem is that the incommensurability of worldviews means that some culture clash is inevitable in democratic systems that do not oppress (Benhabib, 2002). This leads to disillusionment and dissatisfaction within our societies, frustration with our political representatives, distrust of institutions and toxic ingroup–outgroup relations. In the end, we might tolerate but despise one another – a situation where literally no one is satisfied, to echo EU Commissioner Johansson once again. So, is there an alternative? I want to be honest about this – I am not entirely sure there is, but I believe there might be. What if we turned our focus from what we disagree about to what we effectively agree upon, and started to patch up those incommensurable worldviews? What if, instead of a canvas depicting an ordered and manicured landscape, we fashioned a slightly messy collage out of our cultural practices? What would the ultimate inclusive omnicultural portrait look like? (Mahendran, 2017; Moghaddam, 2020). I believe my proposal is justified if we start by acknowledging that fighting one another further will not lead to the superior race amongst us winning and flourishing, as many have proclaimed. It will more likely lead, in my view, to a dismembered Vitruvian who has lost a limb or two in the course of war. And, along that line of thought, isn't a whole Frankenstein better than part Vitruvian? Allow me to explain further in Chapter 9.

CHAPTER 9

Building a Bridge over Babylon
Patching up Discord

Let the words of my mouth, and the meditation of my heart, be acceptable in thy sight . . . here tonight – Boney M.

Chapter 8 showed us that, whilst democracy makes for a utopic aspiration everywhere, it remains most anywhere unfulfilled. And, through the various chapters of this volume thus far, we have seen that what stands in the way of democracy's effective actualisation is nothing less than human nature. Our evolved human tendencies incline us to consort with others in an effort to pursue our own interests, which necessarily puts us in competition with differently interested parties. Fulfilling some interests also means we fail to fulfil competing others. The Beatles sang how 'all you need is love' but the truth is that resolving human discord takes much more than that. We all understand that unbridled love provides an opportunity to cheats to advance their own interests at our expense. We need to be careful whom to love if we want to do so in our own interest.

Whilst this is clear, we also understand that we cannot sustain social relations in either a paranoid or a predatory manner. We cannot distrust everyone and everything. To do so would put us in utter isolation, which for us is a disadvantage relative to other species. On the other hand, we cannot become total cheats ourselves either. This would see us ostracised and potentially locked up behind bars. Human survival involves an intricate balance in our behaviour regarding whom to collaborate with in an effort to compete with others over scarce resources. The other side of conciliation is competition; peace with one, conflict with another.

The problem we face now given the scale of technological development that marks our ecological habitats everywhere is the very realistic threat of a man-made nuclear holocaust. Sure, there are other threats in nature that risk obliterating the human species. We opened this volume with reference to the COVID-19 pandemic. We all learned a very hard lesson over that period; that a miniscule superbug or super-virus risks gaining the upper hand and wiping out humankind. This is perhaps not as likely as we might imagine, as in wiping out our species such parasitic organisms would also be wiping out themselves. Perhaps it is more likely that we will end up messing up the climate so badly as to make the world uninhabitable. For this we turn to science and technology in an effort to identify the main polluting agents and alternative sources that can stop or reverse some of the damage done. We could still get hit by a hypersonic meteorite, but hopefully we would have enough warning of that kind of danger to nuke that threat into smithereens. And right there lurks the ultimate danger. The biggest threat to the human species at this point in time might well be the human species itself.

The issue we face at this point in time in our evolutionary lineage is that we know that no one can win World War III. That conflict stands to end us all. The atomic bombs over Hiroshima and Nagasaki brought World War II to an end. That might have been the last time peace was achieved through warfare. In an era of nuclear proliferation with MAD (mutually assured destruction) capabilities (Futter, 2015), we need to find other ways of bridging our differences than imposing order that is right in our view but wrong in others'. We can no longer afford to pursue a single truth. Not Islam, not Christianity, not Marxism, not Communism, not Capitalism, not any other. Every single holy truth is worth fighting for, for some, and worth fighting against, for others. Welcome to Babylon.

We need to bridge our differences whilst conceding that we are every bit as self-interested as others are, and that others are every bit as good as us. Vilifying others to uphold a self-assumed virtuous standpoint takes us down a warpath we can no longer afford to thread. We can no longer divide the world into virtuous and infidels – this makes us all virtuous and all infidels at the same time, relatively speaking. Our starting point needs to be a twofold recognition that (a) our cognition is as motivated, as self-interested, as subjective and as biased as that of others with whom we disagree and that (b) others are pursuing collective projects that are as honourable, as virtuous, as aspirational and as utopic as ours. We are no better than them and they are no worse than us. The counter-argument is that we should then block migration so that we can leave them to mind their affairs whilst we mind ours. Again, human nature stands in the way of that. They have things we want; we have things they want. And if we were to build impenetrable borders, where would we draw the lines? Who do we want in and who would we want to chuck out? Would erecting national boundaries resolve political enmity within? It certainly would not. So, we must start with recognising our human nature in its variable complexity and we must proceed then to build a bridge over it.

Deconstructing Conflict

Projects

Let us start with a simple observation – that we are all busy, doing something or other. We are busy working to make a living; studying to make a career; investing for our future; saving for our children; worshipping to save our souls; protesting for a better world. I am busy writing this book. You are busy reading it. For whatever reason. I might be writing this book for teaching purposes, or for research purposes, or even recreational purposes. You might be busy reading it for learning purposes, or for research purposes, or recreational purposes. For all I know, you might be taking pleasure in finding fault with whatever I've been arguing, convincing yourself even further how wrong I am and how right you are!

The fact remains, the lives of human beings are imbued with purpose. Even in doing nothing, we are busy. In my country, sunbathing is a national pastime. Many Maltese will leap at the opportunity of lazing in the Mediterranean sun for hours on end, doing little more than splashing sunscreen to protect their skin, turning around for an even tan and wading into blue waters to cool down their body temperature. What are they doing? – they are relaxing, unwinding, washing the stress away. We pursue collective values of what we consider to be the good life and all it entails (Sammut, Tsirogianni & Moghaddam, 2013; Tsirogianni, Kostas & Sammut, 2021). Finding time to chill (i.e. busy doing nothing) with friends in the Mediterranean sun is a key marker of quality of life for many Maltese.

In essence, human action is purpose-driven and, by extension, purposeful activity fulfils our interests. Chapter 5 showed us how interests are something we pursue with others (Sammut, 2011). They are a way for us to connect with others and be together. To do this, we create conceptions of objects and activities that enable us to fulfil these interests. We call these conceptions social representations (Sammut & Howarth, 2014). We conceive of life as a transient spiritual journey and of God as the ultimate spiritual being who will grant us eternal serenity for engaging in the right kinds of acts and refraining from the wrong ones. We conceive of the planet as a finite resource that we need to manage for the benefit of future generations, including our progeny. We conceive of climate change as a threat to this purpose and we proceed to make the effort to recycle our refuse, avoid the use of plastics, cook with an air fryer and so on, to fulfil that purpose.

Crucially, we are not dispassionate or disinterested about what social representations we construe – social representations are conceived in the service of the purposeful projects we pursue (Buhagiar & Sammut, 2020). This goes back to Moscovici's (1961) original insight. Catholics, communists and liberals in twentieth century France construed the psychological practice of psychoanalysis in very different ways according to their own established convictions. More recently, we showed how the use of cannabis can be conceived of variably as drug abuse, recreational activity or medication (Sammut, Mifsud & Brockdorff, 2022). That is three social representations of the same object, each of which prescribes very different practices, some of which some would argue should be outlawed. Our study showed how Catholic NGOs in Malta drove the anti-decriminalisation agenda. Catholic morality prescribes worship to deal with whatever cross we bear, not getting stoned. Every organised religion, philosophy or political movement will have its own prescriptions for achieving some ultimate ends.

These are the projects that surround us, that we are born into, that we grow up to understand and that we end up identifying with (Buhagiar & Sammut, 2020). Some of them predate us, most will outlive us. Think about your own pursuit of happiness and whether and how family features in that. Now ask yourself, what do you understand by family? What makes for a good family? What kind of family will you rest happy with for yourself? What do you think of an extended family, where you share your living space with uncles, aunties, cousins and other relatives? Would you marry into one? What do you think of polyamorous families – would you marry a polyamorous partner? What do you think of monogamous families? Do you think these are realistic over an entire lifetime? Do you think people should be allowed to divorce as they please, dissolving monogamous marriages rather than bearing the burden until death do them part? Homosexual marriages? Homosexual families? Asexual marriages and families? The use of one word – family – is enough to unravel plural conceptions of its meaning, all of which are associated with deep-seated political agendas that strive to legitimise some practices at the expense of others. And, in this state, some will identify with one project and others with different projects, you and I included. As Giddens (1991) has noted, no one today can assume any conviction without also knowing that others around us subscribe to completely different and potentially incommensurable convictions.

Our ecological habitat thus includes competing projects that transcend us, that determine the social representations we construe, the political leanings we assume and, ultimately, the interests we pursue, the activities we engage in and the kind of identities we negotiate for ourselves that communicate to others what kind of person we are and who we choose to be. This purpose serves as a thread that runs through everything we do and across all levels of human activity, from the thoughts and attitudes we harbour as individuals to the battles and wars we wage as collectives. Whatever we do, we do for reasons that define us.

Argumentation

I want to extend this point further: whatever we do, we do for *good* reason. Here is another fundamental insight. We commonly attribute ignorance or faulty thinking to those with whom we disagree (Sammut & Sartawi, 2012; Sammut et al., 2015). We claim that if others were as objective and as well informed as us in their thinking, they would conclude that we are right. We discount the fact that they might be reasoning differently from us, that we also have blind-spots in our reasoning stemming from our beliefs and our subjective experiences, and that they might have access to some truth which we lack. We simply assume that their reasoning does not add up. Well, it does. Just like human action is motivated by purposeful projects, human thinking is reasonably justified. That is, reasons can be articulated for claims we make that justify the actions we engage in and the projects we pursue. What we do, we do for a reason. And the same goes for those who disagree with us. They also have good reasons for doing what they do even if we hold their reasoning to not be good enough for us.

This insight goes back to Harré and Secord's (1972) suggestion for studying accounts to understand human behaviour. Harré & Secord claim that, to understand behaviour, we should ask individuals to justify their actions by providing accounts for why they do what they do. If human behaviour is agentic and motivated, that is, intended to bring about some desirable ends, then human reasoning can account for manifest behaviour whether we agree with it or not. Think of the narco-trafficker in the Peruvian jungle. We might not condone their trade, we might not endorse consumption of their product, we might justifiably oppose their activities and support law enforcement in their fight to eradicate their industry. But that does not mean that narco-traffickers themselves do not have their own reasons for doing what they do. They might argue that their product is a natural crop for which there is a viable market, that their industry provides jobs to locals who would otherwise starve, and that their product is unfairly targeted to give an edge to big pharma. Obviously, none of these reasons might be good enough to quell our concerns. But that does not mean that they do not have good reason for doing what they do in their own eyes. Marinaci, Venuleo, Infurna and Di Maria's (2025) study as well as Gambetta's (1996) study of the Sicilian Mafia show how native Sicilians resort to the mafia for dealing with everyday issues that are left unaddressed by the state – there are not enough legitimate jobs going around, the police do not provide adequate security, insurance companies are a rip-off, the judiciary is politically biased and so on. In such a state of affairs, organised crime becomes legitimate industry and people join for what they consider to be good reason.

Think about it, imagine your home was burgled and you had some sentimental possessions stolen off you, like an heirloom that did not really cost much but that meant a lot to you. You then found out that the police were not going to do anything about catching the thief and retrieving this for you because, they claim, they had other more urgent business to attend to and you are getting an insurance pay-out anyway. You might see their point, but you would not be consoled. Imagine you had an inkling who the burglar might be. You saw the local junkie in your backyard two days ago and you warded him off. You told this to the police, but they did not bother. They said what's the point, he would have traded it off by now and if we were to prosecute, he will simply be released with another warning. Been there done that, they tell you, pinning it on the judiciary. You think: who knows, they might be right. But how do I get the heirloom back?

Now imagine you went to school with the local 'Don' – the local Mafia guru. You know he's a rotten character, he always has been. He comes from a crime family and you know better than to do business with him. But you also know he oversees the illegal drugs trade in your area. Imagine if you bumped into him on the corner, and you asked him whether he can help, and he told you in typical Mafia style: 'I'll see what I can do'. And then imagine a couple of days later the heirloom is dropped into your letterbox, and you have no idea who brought it back. And then you bump into Don again, somewhere you did not really expect him, and he comes over to check on you and asks if you're good and whether you needed anything? You do not know anything for a fact, but you suspect it was him behind the letterbox. What would you say to him? Would you thank him? Would you use his services again in future? Would you cover for him if you saw him do anything untoward? What Marinaci and colleagues' (2025) study as well as Gambetta's (1996) study illuminate is that mafiosi do mafia for their own interests. That much we know. But the thing is, they do it for their own good reason.

This insight shifts our focus from trying to correct erroneous views to trying to comprehend misunderstood ones. In essence, we move away from trying to educate or persuade those we disagree with, acknowledging they have their own good reason for doing what they do. Rather, we try to understand how their actions are justified in light of their circumstances. In this manner, we can find what it is that does not add up about what we think, in their view. And we can then go on and do something about that.

In our Minimal Model of Argumentation (MMA) (Buhagiar & Sammut, 2023a), we develop a qualitative analysis protocol for understanding accounts in terms of their justificatory reasoning. We propose that accounts can be deconstructed in terms of the argumentation structure they evince, which is made up of four types of qualitative data. First, arguments present a *claim*. The claim is the derived conclusion that justifies a course of action. The claim follows from a set of *warrants*. These are statements that constitute reasons for linking *evidence* with a derived conclusion, or claim. Evidence is thus the third component of MMA. Crucially, this involves statements pertaining to facts, statistics, or other objective criteria. But it could also involve subjective evidence like personal experiences, beliefs or deeply held convictions. Warrants provide an interpretative link between evidence as cause and claim as effect: If X [evidence], then Y [claim], by virtue of Z [warrant]. This is the chain of human reasoning that reasonably justifies motivated action. The final component of MMA is *qualifiers*, which might specify particular circumstances or conditions under which the reasoning chain might not hold. A formulaic depiction of MMA would be:

> Unless A [qualifier], if X [evidence] then Y [claim] by virtue of Z [warrant]

The identities we negotiate, the social representations we fabricate, the projects we fashion, are not trivial. In a context of plurality, we subscribe to some activity and not another because we perceive it as something that helps bring about desirable ends. We are able to argue our position to justify our actions with good reason, whether others agree with us or not. Sometimes, we do not see eye to eye with those who disagree with us. We think their reasoning is faulty and they need to be educated so they can link the dots. In their turn, they think our reasoning is faulty and we need to be educated to be able to link the dots. Mutual attribution of ignorance across both sides sets the stage for a spiral of conflict and polarisation of views masking a failure to understand how they cannot see what is obvious to us, and vice-versa.

We used MMA to understand the polarisation of views presented in Chapter 7 (Sammut, Buhagiar, Mifsud, DeGiovanni & Brockdorff, 2022). There are obviously two sides to the debate concerning the integration of Muslims in Malta, that is, (a) for and (b) against (Sammut et al., 2018). We asked Maltese respondents what they thought about the integration of Arab-Muslims in Malta and why. Respondents articulated various arguments supporting their position in terms of cultural, socio-political, psychological, religious, stigmatising and economic criteria. Crucially, both sides of the debate were justifiably argued. Sometimes views were diametrically opposed. For instance, a socio-political argument supporting integration efforts claimed that 'The Maltese never had problems with Arabs, they integrate and we get along'. The conclusion was derived from evidence that 'I have Arab friends and we get along' and 'Race does not bother me', warranted by statements including that 'In Malta we never had Arab segregation', that 'Arabs have been coming to Malta for a long time and this has led to more acceptance' and that 'problems arise between individuals, not because they're Arab'. Across the set of respondents, the favourable integration position was qualified in terms of 'certain people from certain cultures integrate less well with us, but not Arabs', that 'it's high-end Arabs that are coming over', that 'Arabs with strong Muslim views integrate less'.

As stated, however, we identified diametrically opposed views amongst respondents that reject Arab integration. These claimed that 'Arabs expect special treatment due to racism', that 'Arabs impose their culture on others' and that 'Large proportions of foreigners give rise to political problems'. Respondents used as evidence the fact that 'People cannot wear masks or helmets in certain places due to security issues but Arabs wear burkas' (PS: these are extremely rare in Malta), that 'Malta is already densely populated' and that 'in some countries crucifixes had to be removed from classrooms'. They warranted their conclusions with statements such as 'Arabs do not take on our local ways', that 'the Maltese are welcoming but Arabs take advantage of that', that 'Arabs are more dogmatic about their culture than the Maltese are about theirs', that 'Maltese culture is inspired by Christianity', that 'they are not used to democratic laws and practices'. They also qualified their views by stating that 'Not all Arabs are bad', that 'other socio-ethnic groups impose their cultures too', that 'if we become more like them, we become worse off' and so on.

What this simple exercise reveals is that, amongst the same population, views for and against integration are both justified in terms of good reasoning. It is not the case that some are knowledgeable and others ignorant about the situation. The integration project is a complex project that involves exceptions of all kinds. It largely depends on what it is that one chooses to focus on. If one argues that integration brings positives, another is able to point out tragic instances of conflict. Conversely, if one argues that integration is negative overall, another can point out instances of economic, inter-personal and cultural benefits. The polarisation of views may boil down to black and white political thinking, but personal views involve all 50 shades of grey that stand in between.

The same holds true for the other group in question, that is, Arab-Muslims in Malta. As part of the same study, we proceeded to interview them about what they thought of their integration in Malta. We found a similar diversity of views (Buhagiar & Sammut, 2023b). Some claimed that 'there are good relations between the Maltese and Arabs', that 'integration is the only option' and that 'integration is improving with time'. They supported these claims by recourse to personal experiences and friendships at work that warranted Arab contributions to local communities, qualifying their arguments by criticising authorities handling their documentation. However, other immigrants claimed that 'institutionalised discrimination hinders integration', that 'integration is not taking place at all', that 'Arabs are disengaged and stick to their own communities', that 'racism should not be tolerated' and that 'the Maltese fear Islam and do not want to integrate Arab-Muslims due to this'. They cited delays in processing work and residence permits by the relevant authorities, differential working conditions for migrants and everyday racism on the part of the Maltese as evidence for their claims. These were warranted by statements such as that 'integration was not well marketed', that 'non-Arab Europeans are treated differently', that 'many migrants dream of going back home someday', that 'some do not behave well', that 'some practices are better kept private' and that 'some lose faith in the system'. Interestingly, respondents also qualified their arguments by noting that 'cultures reason differently'.

Bridging the Inter-group Divide

From what we've seen here, we clearly note a diversity of opinions concerning migrant integration, both amongst the native Maltese as well as amongst the Arab-Muslim immigrant group. In both groups, we find some who are in favour and some who oppose the integration ideal. In practical terms, some are happy to pursue integrationist projects, others are happy to settle or advance assimilationist or segregationist ones. Within both, the possibility of a hardening of attitudes and polarisation is very real. The potential for a spiral of conflict between staunchly assimilationist Maltese and staunchly segregationist Arab-Muslims is evident. The political implications of migration in this case contain the seeds of discord both within and between the two distinct socio-ethnic groups. Reconciling this divide and building inter- as well as intra-community bridges that foster bonding and bridging social capital represents the new challenge of migration in our current era. We do not purport to have a silver bullet to resolve these ails. There is no magical solution that we can propose to satisfy all views. However, armed with the findings of our argumentation studies amongst the two communities, we are able to suggest an empirical procedure that stands to bridge discrepant views.

We start by collating the list of claims identified in the course of our argumentation inquiry on both sides of the inter-group divide. Some claims will be unique to one of the groups and will have no corollary amongst claims advanced by the other group. Some other claims, however, will recur and will articulate somewhat similar conclusions. For example, in our study, the claim that 'Arabic Islamic culture and Maltese Christian culture are too contrasting for integration to succeed' was articulated by both Maltese and Arab participants. The argumentation structure varied between the groups. The Maltese argued that 'Arabs do not relate with Maltese Christian traditions' and that 'Integration difficulties boil down to Islam'. On their part, Arabs argued that 'Islam makes Arabs stick out' and that 'certain religious restrictions (such as alcohol) are hard for the Maltese to understand'. Both arguments, however, supported the same conclusion. Similarly, the claim that 'Similarities between Arab and Maltese culture, heritage, language and mentality can help us get along' also transpired across both groups. The Maltese argued that 'We share similar practices regarding hospitality', 'We have similar food' and 'culturally, we are close'. The Arab group argued that 'We have a similar language', 'We're both laid back' and 'Shared cultural elements help integration'. The list of claims that recur across the inter-group divide provides a point of convergence whether the claims stand for or against integration.

The second step in this conciliatory exercise is to subject the list of claims to a ranking procedure to identify which arguments articulate positions for and against the project of integration more strongly than others. We used expert ranking for this, to sort out claims in a sequence that runs from those that support integration the most to those that oppose it the most. The result of this exercise was an ecological scale that sorted claims concerning the project from the most extreme positions on either side of the debate to those that were relatively more neutral. Out of the total list, we then chose six claims for and six claims against that were the most clearly ranked in the sorting exercise across our participants. We thus ended up with the following list of twelve claims supported across both groups, scaled from the most pro-integration item to the most anti-integration item:

1. Maltese and Arabs can definitely get along whilst fully keeping their cultural and religious differences; living together is mutually beneficial.
2. It would be better for society if the Maltese and Arabs engage with each other (e.g. at school, work) instead of isolating themselves.
3. Having Christian and Muslim places of worship side by side makes for a strong and diverse society, both here in Malta and elsewhere.
4. The similarities between Maltese and Arab culture, heritage, language and mentality can help us get along.
5. As a minimum, there should be no discrimination between the Maltese and Arabs.
6. As with other cultures, cultural contact between Maltese and Arabs can be good in some respects (e.g. food, music).
7. The religious and cultural differences between Maltese and Arabs can be problematic when it comes to living together.
8. Migrants would do well to keep certain cultural practices private in order to get along with locals.
9. Maltese Christian culture and Arabic Islamic culture are too contrasting for us to get along well.
10. At the end of the day, Arabs or Maltese will want to impose their way of life on the other.
11. It would definitely be better if the Maltese and Arabs avoid dealing with each other altogether.
12. Racism between Maltese and Arabs makes sense; we simply should not mix.

Once this ecological scale was compiled, we proceeded to administer it in a survey including samples from both groups (Maltese: $n = 217$; Arab: $n = 105$). Respondents in the survey were asked to rate their level of agreement or disagreement with each item. Crucially, the items were weighted in data analysis so that an integration score could be compiled for each respondent. The pro-integration items were weighted from +1 to +6 whilst the anti-integration items were weighted from −1 to −6, depending on their order in the scaled sequence.

We presented the ecological scale to respondents twice. In the first instance, we asked them to express their own level of agreement with each of the items, as described. In the second instance, we asked respondents to estimate to what extent they thought the other group would endorse the respective items. This allowed us to investigate not only personal preferences, but also attributions to the other group. We could then analyse, for each item, the mean level of endorsement by each group as well as the mean attributed endorsement for the other group. The results revealed what the Maltese thought about the integration project, what the Arabs thought about the integration project, as well as what the Maltese thought the Arabs thought about integration and what the Arabs thought the Maltese thought about integration.

The findings of this study revealed that, broadly speaking, both Maltese and Arabs expressed pro-integrationist views but the Arab group reported favouring integration significantly more than the Maltese. This finding was in line with previous studies reporting stronger acculturation preferences for integration amongst immigrant groups (Berry et al., 2023). Crucially, however, we found that both groups attributed lower integration scores to each other than actually reported. The Maltese attributed a higher pro-integration score to Arabs than they did themselves, meaning their attributions were correct albeit much lower than that actually reported by the Arab group. On the other hand, the Arab group also correctly attributed a lower integration score to the Maltese than they did themselves but, as with the Maltese, the attributed score was significantly lower than the one actually reported. In other words, both groups under-estimated the extent to which the other group endorsed integration.

We then conducted pairwise comparisons for each of the scaled items. The Arab group endorsed all pro-integration items more strongly than the Maltese group. The opposite was true for the anti-integration items, which received higher endorsement by the Maltese group except for item number 8, for which mean differences between the two groups were not statistically significant. The crucial finding, however, was that item 7 presented a point of convergence between the groups. Items that were more pro-integrationist than item 7 received higher endorsement by the Arab group, whilst items that were less integrationist than item 7 received higher endorsement by the Maltese (Figure 9.1).

When juxtaposing actual scores with attributed scores, further insightful findings emerged. When comparing Maltese views with what Arabs attributed to the Maltese, we found a clear pattern that showed that Arabs correctly perceive the Maltese trend across the items, although at every

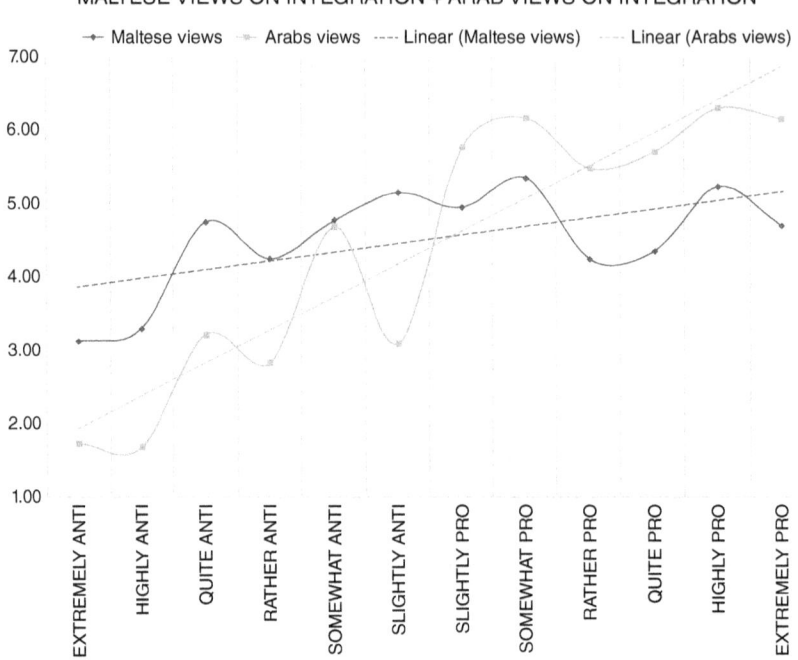

Figure 9.1 Maltese and Arabs views towards Integration

point they under-estimate the extent of Maltese support for the item. The discrepancy is more pronounced for the pro-integration items (Figure 9.2).

When juxtaposing actual Arab views with Maltese attributions to Arabs, however, we found that the Maltese misperceive integrationist intent on the part of Arabs by attributing significantly higher anti-integration sentiment and significantly lower pro-integration sentiment to the Arab group (Figure 9.3). In other words, the Maltese think that the Arabs amongst them do not wish to integrate – when they actually do. This is a critical insight regarding a locus for intervention. There is no point in trying to sell the integration project to the Maltese; they already support it. There is also no point in trying to sell the integration project to the Arab minority, as the Maltese are inclined to do; the Arab group also already support it. The inter-group difficulties stem from the fact that the Maltese misunderstand the Arab groups' intent, incorrectly assuming that Arabs affirming their own identities do so because they wish to stand apart from the Maltese.

There is yet another implication from these findings regarding an intervention to reconcile inter-group divergences. Any intervention that

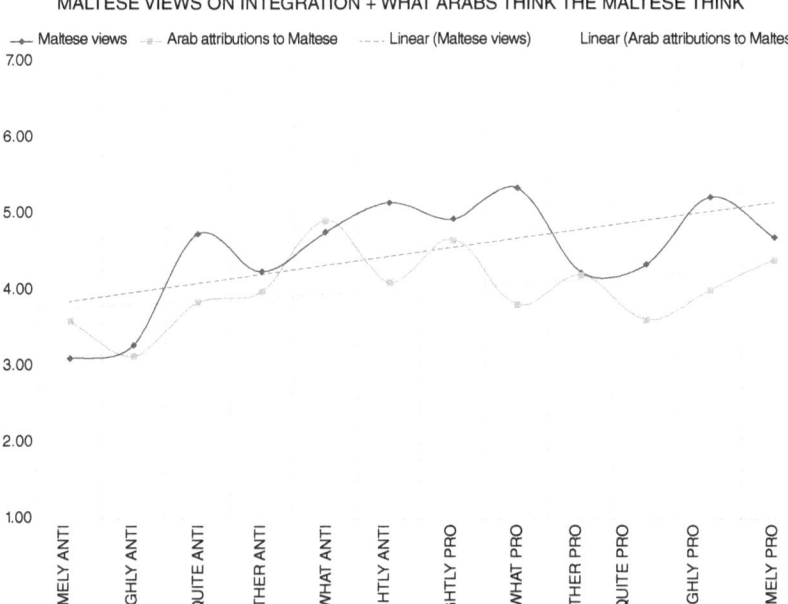

Figure 9.2   Maltese views towards integration and Arab views of Maltese views

aims to reconcile inter-group relations between the Maltese and Arabs should start by promoting Item 6 for the reason that this item is already endorsed by both groups and divergences on this item across both groups are at a minimum relative to divergences for other items. In this way, it represents a convergent point in divergent trends (Figure 9.1). In other words, one would be preaching to the converted as, when presenting this item, both groups stand to agree that this would be a right way forward. Moreover, promoting this item as a strategy for inter-group conciliation should be done in a manner that is faithful to the argumentation differences between the two groups on this respective item. This stands to convert intra-community sceptics. That is, the claim that 'Cultural contact between Maltese and Arabs is good in various respects' is one that stands to be endorsed by both groups, but it should be sold to the Maltese using the Maltese argumentation structure whilst any promotion with the Arab group should rely on argumentation support provided by the Arab community. In this way, intra-community agreement can be garnered for

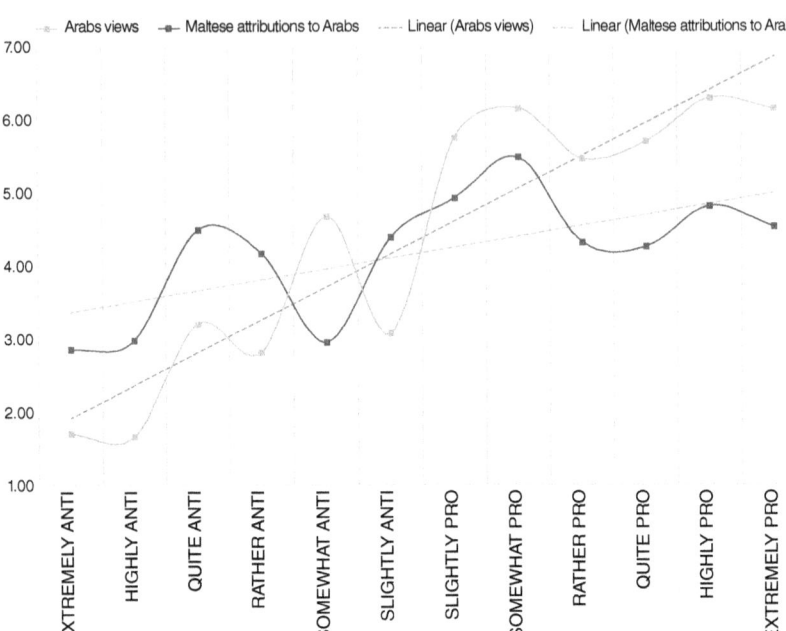

Figure 9.3 Arab views towards integration and Maltese views of Arab views

extra-community reconciliation. Item 6, thus, stands to bring most people on board both within and across community differences of opinion.

If one then wished to promote a more integrated position, one would staircase up the ecological scale to the next item (no. 5) to promote the claim that 'As a minimum, there should be no discrimination between Maltese and Arabs'. Once again, one would need to rely on arguments advanced by the different groups to promote the item within its rightful justificatory context. In this manner, the ecological scale described in claims 1–12 stands to serve as an instrument to patch up differences between groups concerning particular projects in a manner that is differentially reasonable across the group divide. How far can this patchwork across community divides go? There is no telling in advance. Once agreement has been forged concerning some item, other issues might arise necessitating the investigation of some new inter-community project. The exercise is one that necessitates a degree of structured imagination (Nicholson & Howarth, 2018; Nicholson, 2019). The end result is not to live happily ever after. We realise this is no more than a myth. The end result is to get a grip on reconciliation and work from there in a manner that is respectful of opinions on both sides (Obradović & Howarth, 2016; Nicholson, 2019). International conflict often distinguishes between the heroes on one side (us) and the villains on the other side (them). The truth is that there are heroes and villains on both sides. The procedure we have outlined in this chapter is intended to serve as a handle to peace-makers, whichever side they might be working from.

Conclusion

The opening quote of this chapter originates from Psalm 19 verse 14. Boney M, a disco group from the 1970s, revised the words of the psalm in their hit song 'Rivers of Babylon', which was itself a cover of a former Rastafari song by The Melodians. In both versions, Babylon refers to modern day Iraq and the rivers Tigris and Euphrates, where Jewish people were exiled following defeat in the Jewish–Babylonian war. Curiously, the term Babylon shares the same etymological roots with Babel, another reference in the biblical narrative where a single people conspired to build a tower that would withstand a second great flood in case this ever occurred. God presumably took offence at the challenge and intervened by confusing their language, dividing the collective into different linguistic groups which could not understand one another. Consequently, the tower of Babel was never built and humankind thereafter stood divided. Metaphorically, this seems to be very much where we are now – one's person's good reason is another person's ignorance, and so on.

Boney M's revision of the psalm, however, introduces a new focus with which this chapter and the proposed reconciliatory effort is aligned. Their lyrics replaced the reference to the Lord in the original psalm with a focus on the here and now. In my interpretation, 'thy' does not refer to an omnipotent supernatural entity but the 'Other', whom we misunderstand. If the words of our mouths and the meditation of our heart are acceptable to others with whom we stand in conflict here and now, and vice-versa, then we have established good grounds for bridging the differences that divide us. The methodological procedure we have outlined here relies on empirically derived argumentation building blocks that make sense to conflicting parties *in their own respective right*. Its point of departure is establishing a consensus that is already agreeable. It moves from there to the next agreeable target to climb the stairs of solidarity and reconciliation. We call this the PASS method of reconciliation (Buhagiar & Sammut, 2025), which involves the following four steps:

1. PROJECT: Identify the project that is contested across the intergroup divide.
2. ARGUMENTATION: Analyse the range of claims and their justificatory grounds for and against the project to understand the reasoning that sustains the various positions. The claims must be empirically derived for utilisation in an ecologically valid scale, that is, reasonable in the here and now.
3. SCALE: Formulate an ecological scale by ranking the list of claims that recur in both groups from those that support the project the least to those that support the project the most,
4. SURVEY: Measure the extent of agreement with the various claims in both groups as well as their meta-perceptions of the extent of agreement attributed to the other group(s). This reveals comparative preferences as well as convergences and disparities and misperceptions regarding the other group's intent. Use convergences as a starting point to communicate a stair-cased reconciliatory strategy that is reasonable to the respective groups in their own right.

CHAPTER 10

Ethics–Politics Morality
What's Good for the Goose Is Not Good for the Gander

Chapter 9 advanced the contention that, in inter-cultural and inter-group disputes, we should try to understand one another in terms of each other's underlying reasoning, over trying to persuade the other that our views are right and their views are wrong (Sammut & Bauer, 2021). We have seen that, unless we grant the other party the benefit of the doubt and explore their reasoning regarding their own practices, we risk misunderstanding their intent, such as when Arabs' self-affirming identity claims (e.g. veiling) are understood as a cultural affront to integration. This line of thinking would suggest that inter-cultural communication is a panacea for inter-group conflict resolution, based on the naïve premise that if only we communicated with each other well enough we would discover that we are all well-meaning individuals and that we can all live in peace and harmony if only we bothered to talk to one another. All you need is love, right? Well, no doubt misunderstandings and miscommunication do not help. But there are also dilemmatic situations where good intentions alone do not suffice either. Consider the following example, adapted from Kohlberg (1981):

> Heinz's wife has been diagnosed with terminal cancer and she has only a few months left to live. Heinz discovers that a pharmacy down the road has recently stocked a ground-breaking new drug that in medical trials has been proven to cure the cancer his wife is suffering from. The pharmacy, however, is aware that stocks are in very low supply as the drug is very new and has only just come onto the market. Consequently, it is selling the drug at a premium, as much as ten times what it cost to produce. Heinz desperately tries to put the money together anyway by borrowing and crowdfunding, but he only manages to raise about half the money he needs. As his wife's condition deteriorates, Heinz grows progressively desperate. One night, he takes matters into his own hands and breaks into the pharmacy to steal the drug that will save his wife.

According to Kohlberg (1981), human beings go through three stages of moral reasoning, that is, from pre-conventional to conventional and post-conventional thinking. As in the Muslim integration example we reviewed in Chapter 9, one could argue both for and against stealing the drug. It is not whether one thinks Heinz should or should not have burgled the pharmacy that reveals one's stage of moral development but one's justificatory reasoning for doing so. In the pre-conventional stage, reasoning is based on obedience and self-interest; in the conventional stage it is based on conformity concerns and law and order issues; and in the post-conventional stage it is based on concerns related to the social contract and universal human ethics. That is, in Kohlberg's theory, moral development follows a normative and linear trajectory. However, we wonder whether it is really the case that a concern with universal human ethics constitutes a higher moral state than self-interest – at all times and in all circumstances? Some readers might remember quite vividly the protectionist horse-trading by nation-states all over the world in securing supplies for Moderna's, Pfizer-BioNTech's and Oxford-AstraZeneca's COVID-19 vaccines some years ago at the height of the COVID-19 pandemic. This saw some countries introduce vaccines only after other nations had double-vaccinated their entire populations! Again, is it really a concern with universal human ethics that stands to guide our choices, when it's our lives and those of our loved ones at risk?

Let's problematise Heinz's situation a little further; after all, moral reasoning is consequential in practical terms, as the COVID-19 pandemic has bitterly taught us. Imagine Heinz's wife makes a full recovery one week after the pharmacy reported the burglary. The police suspect Heinz had something to do with it, but they also suspect that Heinz's brother-in-law might have had something to do with the crime too. Heinz and his brother-in-law are picked up for questioning. Heinz now finds himself in a prisoner's dilemma:

> The police tell Heinz they understand his and his brother-in-law's motive for the robbery but they are duty-bound to prosecute them formally according to criminal law as otherwise it would look like the police are not doing their job. The police detective lets Heinz know that if both Heinz and his brother-in-law admit to the burglary, they both stand to get one year each behind bars. The police further advise Heinz that they lack forensic evidence. No DNA samples were retrieved from the scene and CCTV cameras were not operational. Consequently, if both Heinz and his brother-in-law deny the charges, they will be handed a suspended sentence because whilst the motive is clear there is still reasonable doubt that it was actually them who committed the crime. However, if Heinz admits his involvement but his brother-in-law denies his, Heinz will get a three-year jail term whilst his brother-in-law gets to walk free. The same trade-off

applies to his brother-in-law, who is being kept in a separate cell, and Heinz has no way to communicate with him at this point to coordinate a strategy. And neither of them is a hardened criminal, they never discussed what plea they would give the police. What will Heinz do now?

What this example makes clear is that moral reasoning is not only a function of what we think is right or wrong. It is complicated by what we perceive others are doing and what we think about that. It is all well and good to claim that we ultimately should be concerned with everybody's welfare, the good of the planet and future generations. The real question in social relations arises when we see that others are not sticking to their end of the bargain and that they are not abiding with the same moral standards as we are. That is, what moral grounds will we occupy when we see that some others in our midst are free-riding or cheating? How do we deal with that?

Normative Rationality

Heinz will admit his responsibility in the crime he committed with his brother-in-law, or he will not. Whatever he does, the next time he is reunited with his brother-in-law over a thanksgiving dinner, he will have some explaining to do. And he will do that by appeal to grand theories of what people do or what they ought to do, in similar circumstances or aside from such circumstances. And he will use those grand theories to justify his personal moral judgement in the present circumstances and the situation he now finds himself in. And, likewise, his brother-in-law. And they might agree or disagree.

Recent advances in cognitive science point in the direction of intuitive folk theories that serve as meta-judgement frameworks for understanding diverse reasoning patterns in individuals embedded in cultural contexts. These frameworks call for greater attention to ecologically sensitive studies of judgmental variability (Grossman & Eibach, 2024). A key feature of folk theories of judgement, according to these authors, is whether judgements are made in a principled manner or whether they prioritise a focus on consequences. In philosophy, the difference between the two is known as deontological versus utilitarian ethics (Alexander & Moore, 2021). We will have more to say about this later in this chapter.

According to Crockett, Kim and Soon Shin (2024), moral cognition is a uniquely human attribute that enables us to reason about what is morally appropriate, permissible, required or forbidden. In this way, different folk theories afford different kinds of action in what they prescribe as morally blameworthy or praiseworthy, as well as different inferences about the moral character of those individuals who execute these actions. What is good or bad, therefore, hinges on what moral folk theory an individual uses to justify their actions.

Why do we even have intuitive folk theories in the first place? Gabriel and Schneider (2024), in the same issue, claim that evidence suggests that folk theories fulfil a basic need for social embeddedness that has arisen in our evolutionary past. They claim that human beings survived by banding together to share resources and help out with securing provisions in a hostile environment teeming with predators. Our evolved need for social embeddedness made sure we did not wander off on our own to face dangers we were ill equipped to overcome naturally. Or rather, those who did so did not fare well in evolutionary terms as they fell prey to predators rather prematurely. Those who were prone to a stronger need for social embeddedness would have stuck together, faced challenges together, and lived to tell the tale. They are our ancestors, through whom we have inherited our evolved predispositions. Folk theories of the world and how it works, including what is good and what is bad for us, fulfil this basic need.

Tomasello (2022) provides a compelling and elaborate explanation of how intuitive folk theories have proven adaptive in evolutionary terms. He argues that, in our evolutionary history, humans inhabited an experiential niche that relied on worldviews shared among respectful and responsible cooperative agents. In his work, Tomasello examines the psychological notion of agency, which denotes an element of freedom with regards to decision-making and consequent action. He argues that shared worldviews arose when central-place foraging became a successful survival strategy. This would have involved small parties that obtained more resources than they themselves needed, who carried these resources back to a central location to share their bounty with the rest of the group who could now afford to devote themselves to other tasks in the meantime.

In other words, division of labour, as we argued in Chapter 2. This would have marked the rise of extended families. Again, those who successfully collaborated with neighbouring extended families fared even better than those who did not, who would have fared relatively worse. In times of hardship and scarce resources, such as droughts or attacks from predators, the larger groups were better able to hunt for even larger prey, defend their territory from intruders and so on. Ergo, tribes – entire networks of extended families, who bonded together through rituals, ceremonies, arranged marriages, communal childcare, collective defence and so on. Ergo, villages, cities and so on. At some point in this evolutionary lineage, a challenge arose that emanated not from other predatory species but due to competition with one's own kind; city versus city, tribe versus tribe. As humans became apex predators, the survival challenges they faced arose from within by way of inter-group competition – with which we still struggle today!

In this environment, the primary challenge for modern humans was none other than coordination with *ingroup strangers*. Social identity, which we reviewed in Chapter 4, resolves precisely this challenge. It serves to create affiliation beyond blood relations. As groups became too large for individuals to have personal common ground with all other members, culture arose to cater for this requirement. In other words, those groups who evolved culture were able to capitalise on affiliation ties between ingroup strangers and these groups fared better than those who did not and who relied solely on family ties. In Chapter 6 we called this social capital. Social capital is the derived benefit of cultural common ground and it can be fostered both within and across different groups (bonding and bridging). As Tomasello makes clear, this is based not on individuals' personal experiences but on a *commonality of experience*. In other words, some cultural features are better able than others to foster it. This is the grounds on which we made our case for integration in Chapter 6.

According to Tomasello, establishing a cultural common ground requires a capacity for a cultural-type theory of mind where the individual expects ingroup strangers to conform to conventional practices and where they in their turn expect the individual to conform to the same and so on. This is precisely what Heinz and his brother-in-law will argue over during their next thanksgiving dinner. Coordination with ingroup strangers, Tomasello claims, requires group-minded cognition that emanates from the collective agency of the group, which relies on mutual expectations established in the cultural common ground. This is how we judge whether what another person chooses to do is right or wrong, that is, by appeal to the group's overarching perspective of what is right or wrong. The individuals' point of view is thus immersed and participates in an overarching collective worldview.

In Tomasello's terms, collective self-regulation (what we choose to do when we live together) is achieved through the emergence of social norms, which require conformity to prescribed behaviours. For social groups to achieve this level of solidarity, individual members must be committed to following prescribed social norms and to punish transgressors. To reconcile variable expectations, cultural groups objectify these norms as institutions, policies, laws and so on. Their social obligations no longer appeal to each other's perspectives, they come to appeal to objective standards, or standards that have been objectified. The social contract is therefore no longer perspectival, it becomes objectified into law. It is not objective in the sense that it is physically tangible. Rather, it is a socially constructed objectivity. Elsewhere we have termed such class of phenomena as *inter-objective* (Sammut, Daanen & Moghaddam, 2013).

To extend Tomasello's argument, modern humans came to understand their obligations to one another not in personal inter-subjective terms but in collective inter-objective terms. Contraventions of the social contract are not resolved personally, but by appeal to civil or criminal law. In settling grievances, one reports matters to the police, hires a solicitor, makes recourse to the courts and so on. We are no longer allowed to take matters in our own hands, not even to resolve personal issues. You cannot choose to not recognise unlawful behaviour as criminal. If you do, you become criminally liable yourself. As Asch (1952) pointed out, society cannot have multiple definitions of what constitutes a crime.

We therefore recognise, as the sociologist Bruno Latour (1996) proposed, that modern humans live in inter-objective worlds in which agency is shared with objects and entities that act with us and upon us in normatively inscribed ways. In these worlds that we share experientially, moral values are no exception. Once human beings started operating on the basis of inter-objective moral standards and representations, they became normatively rational agents who thought about and did things in the right way for the right reasons. Naïve realism, which we reviewed in Chapter 3, marks this evolved adaptation. According to Tomasello, human thinking about moral dilemmas provides evidence for precisely this claim. Once an individual enters group-minded agency, other 'voices' tell her what she ought to think or do. Unlike the other great apes, we might well find ourselves in situations like Heinz's that do not admit a single correct answer. Unlike the great apes, who as Tomasello demonstrates are rational agents in their own right, human beings experience genuine moral dilemmas that involve internal conflicts among different agencies with different goals and values and no single best one.

This point is worth considering in some more depth. Tomasello shows that adaptations that have resulted in the branching out of vertebrate species along different times of the evolutionary tree have resulted in distinct types of cognition between that of reptiles, mammals, the great apes (also known as hominids) and finally humans, based primarily on how they relate with other creatures.

For reptiles, which evolved first, most of the uncertainties in their experiential environment arise from the erratic behaviour of insects, that is their prey. This requires flexible decision-making, which is necessary at times also to avoid predation. For mammals, which branched off at a later time in evolution, the primary survival challenge arises from the behaviour of conspecifics who compete with them for food. This requires added flexibility such that the right behaviour is not necessarily the only successful behaviour, it might be merely 'better' (i.e. relatively more efficient). For great apes, who are also mammals, uncertainties arise again from the behaviour of conspecifics, but due to social living conditions that include an added pressure of predicting the behaviour of competitors and correcting poor decisions before execution. This requires reasoning things out to select not only more efficient alternatives but also possibly waiting for the right time to execute them – delayed gratification (i.e. inhibitory control). Accordingly, hominids (i.e. bonobos, chimpanzees, orangutans and gorillas) also seem to be more or less *sapiens* after all, if the term is deemed to denote inferential thinking as per its etymological roots (i.e. knowing).

For humans, uncertainties arise due to the complexities of coordinated group life, which require new social-cognitive skills for decision-making and self-regulation that align one's behaviour with that of the social group. It is not that humans live together socially, like the great apes; it is that human beings *function* socially. They fulfil their goals, needs and requirements in coordination with others, whilst competing with others yet. In Tomasello's words: 'an organism's agentive behavioral organization depends on whether it is mainly solitary, mainly competitive with conspecific group mates (via either scramble or contest competition), or mainly collaborative with conspecific group mates' (2022, p. 124). What seemingly marks the human species from other vertebrate species' cognitive repertoires, therefore, is their ability for politicking – the art and practice of soliciting support for particular courses of action over other competing alternatives. Aristotle seems to have been right all along, *Homo* is not only *sapiens*, by virtue of its sociality it is also *politicus*.

To go back to our story, we can expect Heinz's reunification thanksgiving dinner to proceed along some very clear argumentative lines. As Tomasello (2022) points out, collaborative partners *respect* each other so they treat one another fairly. Have Heinz and his brother-in-law treated each other fairly in their claims to the police? To the extent they have, they will both rest satisfied even if they have both been punished. But if one of them thinks the other did not, things will turn out different. According to Tomasello, in the event partners do not respect each other, they are legitimately entitled to *rebuke* them by appeal to inter-objective institutions and procedures. Did Heinz or his brother-in-law rat each other out?

If they did, they will *resent* their treatment and protest it on normative grounds. They will argue that the other had a *responsibility* to act cooperatively in the way they *deserved* to be treated according to their joint commitment at the outset. Finally, if one of them is deemed to have acted selfishly, they will need to offer some *excuse* or *apologise*. Otherwise, they will be expected to suffer *guilt* and to be treated as traitors (pp. 103–104). So, all in all, was Heinz streetwise in the end? Or was he upright? Was his brother-in-law common sensical? Or was he naïve?

Worldviews

Crockett et al. (2024) note that, what intuitive folk theories have in common is that they provide explanatory structures for causality beliefs that guide people's choices and actions in everyday life. What varies between them, however, is what types of beliefs they generate and what actions and behaviours they advocate. Whilst all folk theories are somewhat accurate in describing particular elements of the world that they home in on, they are only ever approximately accurate as other elements remain unaccounted for. Think, for instance, of how the Christian faith treats some hard to resolve concepts in its theological doctrine by recourse to 'mysteries' (e.g. the Holy Trinity as a single God; the doctrine of transubstantiation, etc.). In like manner, all folk theories trade off precision for efficiency – you might not have the full details but you know that stealing is wrong. The positive side-effect of folk theories is that they serve to bring like-minded people together. In this way, they serve social adaptive functions. As we have argued in the previous section, folk theories serve to build solidarity amongst ingroup strangers. As Crockett et al. further note: 'Even if moral conduct does not perfectly generalize across domains, the efficiency offered by essentialized character theories might be worth the cost of occasional errors' (2024, p. 216).

Situated Cognition

The situated view of cognition posits that any description of human action is only meaningful if it rests on a foundation that caters to the role cognition serves in establishing communicative mutuality. This is due to the evolved human disposition for social embeddedness (Gabriel & Schneider, 2024). Elsewhere, I have argued that this foundational bedrock is a necessary premise for understanding any and all psychological activity, as cognition is essentially geared towards the establishment of social identities around collective interests (Sammut, 2012, 2019). This form of sociality, however, is only relatively enduring as individuals' interests fluctuate and the composition of social groups changes accordingly. This results in situational influences on group members which individuals are required to negotiate in pursuit of self-interested goals. The situated view of cognition stands in contrast to the idea that our inclinations flow invariably from invariant cognitive processes located within the minds of fully autonomous agents. It posits rather that motivated functions determine the nature of these processes (Sammut, 2019).

Psychologists, for instance, have long argued that our behaviour is largely a function of stable dispositional orientations in human personality. The Big Five model of human personality, which posits a five-factor personality structure, remains a cornerstone of the discipline (Costa & McCrae, 1992). More recently, research on the Dark Tetrad of human personality (Paulhus, 2014), comprised of the traits of narcissism, Machiavellianism and psychopathy, has gained prominence due to its concern with explaining the behaviour of malevolent agents like terrorists. What personality models fail to explain is how and why trait-based dispositions change in the same individual over time, or why behavioural responses shaped by the same dispositions are inconsistent across situations for the same individuals. We are all personally aware that some people, or some situations, are better able to bring out our good side (or bad side) more than others.

The same can be said of sociological models, such as Hofstede's (1991) Cultural Dimensions, which posit that human behaviour is a function of cultural values transmitted through socialisation. These claim that different cultures prioritise different values. Depending on which cultural dimensions are salient in a particular society, individuals socialised therein become more or less inclined to particular behavioural tendencies. What these models fall short in explaining in turn is how and why individuals demonstrate similar behavioural dispositions across different cultures, or how within a given culture individual differences may be highly marked.

What scholars have reliably observed over the years is that such psychological and sociological structures are inherently unstable across variable circumstances. Specifically, it seems that the factor concerned with 'Openness to Experience', both in psychological as well as in sociological research, has something to do with their *relative instability* (Connelly, Ones & Chernyshenko, 2014). Elsewhere, I have argued that such reconfigurations are adaptive and contingent on the individual's situated circumstances. I proposed that personality serves as a psychological camouflage, by which dispositional inclinations can be reconfigured to match situated ecological demands. This is observed in personality research as *relative* stability (Sammut, 2019).

For instance, we can understand how cultural differences might influence preferences for certain behavioural responses through social norms. We can also understand how within the same culture some individuals are more prone to exhibit certain behaviours than others. What the psychological and sociological sciences have failed to successfully address is how the same individual, within the same culture, behaves in one way in one situation and a different way in another situation. This is situated cognition. Moreover, whilst cognitive science has furthered the agenda regarding the role and function of folk theories and their basis in social psychology, it remains moot on their substantive nature. It is to this topic that we now turn.

Substantive Cognition

As we have seen, human beings have evolved a predisposition for social embeddedness that directs them to use social norms as a reference for judging their and others' behaviour. In Chapter 5, we saw how social representations serve the function of describing elements in our environment for the purpose of guiding action. Power et al. (2023) have extended this line of thinking to worldmaking notions, that is, intuitive beliefs that we use to describe ourselves and the world around us. These intuitive beliefs or theories, once expressed and once they gain social moment, take on a loosely structured form that includes specific content. In other words, different ways of worldmaking result in a range of worldviews. In this way, social norms are both descriptive and prescriptive – they describe not only what some people do, but also prescribe what people ought to do in certain circumstances. Their prescriptive nature enables their use as a behavioural referent for particular courses of action that, for like-minded individuals, serve the need for social embeddedness.

The literature on worldviews remains scant (Koltko-Rivera, 2004) but a number of theories have looked at the content of social beliefs to understand what and how people think. Remarkably, these have converged on a five-factor typology (Sammut, 2019). Sammut, Mifsud and Brockdorff (2022) review four literature strands supporting this typology, namely: (i) symbolic universes (Salvatore et al., 2018); (ii) social axioms (Leung & Bond, 2009); (iii) moral foundations (Haidt, 2012), and (iv) deep stories (Hochschild, 2016), noting various similar features. First, none of these theories focus exclusively on individual dispositions but they situate individual dispositions within cultural networks that are held to shape the way individuals interpret their social world. Moreover, they are all held to serve the practical purpose of enabling individuals to adapt suitably to different situational demands, as Tomasello (2022) argues with regards to human cognition and its evolved capacity to reference social norms.

For instance, Mifsud and Sammut (2023) note that the symbolic universe *Inter-personal Bond*, the moral foundation *Loyalty/Betrayal*, and the deep story profile *Team Player* all emphasise pro-social behaviour. Conversely, the symbolic universe *Others' World*, the social axiom *Social Cynicism*, the moral foundation, *Authority/Respect*, and the deep story profile *Cowboy*, emphasise selfish behaviour. The Thomas-Kilmann conflict mode instrument (Kilmann, 2023) identifies a similar five-factor typology of conflict resolution methods, namely: (i) Competing, (ii) Collaborating, (iii) Compromising, (iv) Avoiding and (v) Accommodating, based on the extent to which individuals choose to be assertive and cooperative.

In light of these commonalities, Sammut, Mifsud and Brockdorff (2022) propose a fivefold typology of worldviews aimed at unifying the above-mentioned concepts. These include the (i) *Localised*, (ii) *Orthodox*, (iii) *Pragmatist*, (iv) *Reward* and (v) *Survivor* worldviews, summarised in Table 10.1. Each worldview is associated with a respective symbolic universe, social axiom, moral foundation, deep story profile, to which we have now added conflict resolution styles.

In essence, the *Localised* worldview involves the desire to fix problems or address social issues. It is immanent and focused on fixing laws and institutions so that these can cater to everyone's needs. The *Orthodox* worldview seeks to preserve the status quo representing a dogmatic outlook on life that relies on rigid adherence to some overarching code. The *Reward* worldview contends that life challenges are overcome with effort that opens up new possibilities and centres around determination to work hard to obtain a desired goal. The *Pragmatist* worldview is protective and revolves around self-interest, promoting adaptation to circumvent potentially adverse circumstances. Lastly, the *Survivor* worldview involves fatalism, distrust in others and the need to overcome adversity, representing a cynical outlook that requires stoicism as good people get exploited whilst the selfish get ahead (Sammut, Mifsud & Brockdorff, 2022).

Sammut, Mifsud and Brockdorff (2021b, 2022) tested the hypothesis that the content of beliefs is not independent of how people think about them. They studied the relative influence of worldviews with regards to various issues that were salient in Malta at the time, including the use of

Table 10.1 *Intuitive belief theories*

Worldviews	Symbolic Universes	Social Axioms	Moral Frameworks	Deep Stories	Conflict Resolution Styles
Localised	Inter-personal Bond	Social Complexity	Loyalty/ Betrayal	Team Player	Collaboration
Orthodox	Ordered Universe	Religiosity	Sanctity/ Degradation	Worshipper	Competition
Reward	Caring Society	Reward for application	Care/Harm	Cosmopolitan	Accommodation
Pragmatist	Niche of Belonging	Fate Control	Fairness/ Cheating	Rebel with a Cause	Avoidance
Survivor	Others' World	Social Cynicism	Authority/ Subversion	Cowboy	Compromise

cannabis, prostitution and euthanasia. Worldview differences transpired in the endorsement of proposals for the legalisation of recreational cannabis. The debate at the time was based on the objectification of cannabis as a gateway drug to other illegal substances, a medicinal product to treat certain ails, or a recreational drug for private consumption. Their findings showed that the Orthodox worldview, based in the Catholic faith, stood in contrast to all others in opposing the proposals. It represented the only resistance group to legalisation even though in public this included numerous NGOs which, however, were all associated with the Catholic Church. This is sensible in light of the fact that the Church advocates religious observance to deal with difficult life circumstances, not getting high. Even in instances with no clear resolution, Catholics are expected to behave like Jesus and 'carry their cross'.

Conversely, no other worldview unilaterally supported the proposals and all other participants' responses expressed themselves in favour of the proposals. Interestingly, the statement that 'cannabis consumption is already very common, so it should be legalised' also received popular support. But the same statement applied to the practice of prostitution in the same study was popularly rejected. This means that the way participants were thinking about these issues varied across situations (situated cognition) and worldviews exercised a significant influence in one domain but not in another (substantive cognition). What's good for the goose is not good for the gander – both with regards to how the same issue is appraised by different respondents as well as with regards to how different issues are appraised by the same respondents. The study further revealed that the proportion of variance accounted for by worldviews was comparable to that demonstrated by demographic variables.

It is worth noting that the worldview influences reported by these authors rely on categorical distinctions between the five types using self-reported measures. These arguably provide a rich and holistic formulation that may otherwise not be captured through the sum of a sequence of Likert scales. Specifically, the measures offer a flexible approach by which respondents consider a range of generalised situational outlooks when interpreting them. Arguably, a *Survivor* worldview in rural China might be despairing about altogether different reasons than a similar worldview in downtown New York. Worldviews, however, capture the element of despair that transcends particular conditions. They serve as a phenomenological lens by which individuals interpret their own personal experiences. On the other hand, it is worth noting methodological limitations that might lead to deflated effects, primarily in terms of the use of a single self-categorical measure of worldviews over more robust multi-item instruments. Further research is required to flesh out a robust instrument that is also easy to administer and that is useful in typifying worldviews given their role in human cognition, as we detail herein.

In summary, it seems that human cognition has evolved a capacity for grand outlooks (i.e. worldviews) that confer meaning to human existence and enable action in pursuit of goals that are sensible enough to like-minded others to enable joint action, even in the face of adversity and competing alternatives. In this way, human beings are able to overcome setbacks by reconstructing meaning according to a revision of worldviews that are adopted as a normative referent. Sammut (2019) argues that worldviews operate in a manner that is akin to changing gears in a moving vehicle to enable adaption to a changing terrain, regardless of whether one is driving an off-road truck or a sports car. Sammut (2019) contends that this constitutes the essence of human adaptability to situational demands.

Human cognition thus demonstrates substantive phenotype switching, which enables individuals to camouflage their dispositions adaptively to meet situated ecological demands. Sometimes, it pays to be open, positive, or innovative. At other times, it pays to be otherwise. An open and positive mindset enables the individual to explore and reap opportunities for growth. At other times, it pays to adopt a more cautious demeanour and focus on worst-case scenarios. For the behavioural response to be adaptive, the behavioural strategy needs to match the situated ecological demand. A growth mindset when facing bankruptcy is as maladaptive as a fixed mindset when opportunity beckons (Dweck & Yeager, 2019).

Clearly, as Sammut (2019) points out, adaptation in the human species is psychologically, not biologically, based. Human beings do not demonstrate biological camouflage. Rather, their adaptation involves variable action tendencies that rely on the ability to change one's mental outlook to a more profitable one given the circumstances. The capacity to switch mindsets transpires as relative (in)stability in personality-based research and is key to understanding a host of dynamic behaviours such as creativity, decision-making, empathy, communication styles, resilience, morality and so on.

The Ethics–Politics Moral Compass

Let us return to the issue of measurement. Koltko-Rivera (2004) advocates a dimensional approach to the study of worldviews whereby individuals will demonstrate variable tendencies towards a range of concurrent ones. Some worldviews will be more strongly endorsed than others, but individuals are not held to operate within the confines of specific worldviews. This may or may not be right and the issue is easily resolved in operational terms by asking respondents to rate different worldviews over selecting any particular one. Whilst we agree with Koltko-Rivera (2004) that any worldview typology rests on a set of underlying dimensions, we think that it is also useful to study the direct influence of worldviews on particular behavioural tendencies.

In this light, we carried out a study to investigate the relationship between worldviews and higher order values (Mifsud & Sammut, 2023). We looked specifically at Schwartz's (1992) theory of social values. We found that worldviews map onto two value dimensions in particular, namely 'Self-Enhancement versus Self-Transcendence' and 'Conservation versus Openness to Change'. In our study, we found that the *Localised* and *Orthodox* worldviews both rate highly on self-transcendence but disagree on the value of conservation. An individual who endorses either of these two worldviews is thus someone who subscribes to a dogmatic outlook that either puts a moral code (e.g. religious dictates, black letter law, etc.) or local concerns (e.g. protectionism, climate change measures, austerity, etc.) above all else. What differentiates the two is the extent to which they are willing to abide by the prevalent social order. Those who endorse a *Localised* worldview are open to change whereas those who endorse an *Orthodox* worldview rate most highly on the measure of conservation amongst all worldviews.

Like the *Orthodox* worldview, the *Reward and Survivor* worldviews also value conservation. Unlike the *Orthodox* worldview, however, the *Reward* and *Survivor* worldviews do not value self-transcendence. The *Reward* worldview in particular rates highly on self-enhancement. This is also the same for the *Pragmatist* worldview. Both worldviews prioritise their own interests over any grand transcendental aspirations of what might be correct. This is characteristic utilitarian thinking – what is of benefit to me is what is right for me. Unlike the *Reward* worldview, however, the *Pragmatist* worldview perceives that getting ahead means having to change things around. It loads negatively on conservatism and positively on openness to change. Curiously, we found that the *Survivor* worldview does not lean towards self-enhancement either. This worldview seems to embody two fundamental dictates, that is, learned helplessness and better the devil you know.

Conceiving of worldviews in this manner is enlightening. We can see that, with regards to higher order transcendental aspirations, the *Orthodox* and *Localised* worldviews are mirror images of each other. In their pursuit of transcendental causes, however, *Localised* worldviews work to change things for the better, whilst *Orthodox* worldviews work to preserve the established order. Similarly, the *Reward* worldview and the *Pragmatist* worldviews mirror each other in pursuing their own personal interests. But, like the *Localised* worldview, the *Pragmatist* worldview is committed to exploit opportunities for change, whilst the *Reward* worldview focuses on exploiting whatever opportunities it is able to identify given the way things are. Where one claims 'this is how things work', the other responds 'this is how things *do not* work'. The impetus for change distinguishes the *Localised* from the *Orthodox* and the *Pragmatist* from the *Reward*. That said, it is also the case that the *Reward* and *Pragmatist* worldviews are working to get ahead personally, whilst both *Orthodox* and *Localised* worldviews prioritise the common good because if we all do well, I will do well – one for all and all for one (Figure 10.1).

Conceived of in this way, worldviews thus provide a starting point for understanding how human beings form coalitions for action. Specifically, the empirical relationship between worldviews and values facilitates our understanding of how individuals may come together and agree to support a cause or a course of action despite clear and widespread intra-group differences. In the pursuit of any cause, some stand to agree for some reason whilst others may disagree – either with the cause itself or with the means taken to pursue it. For instance, a worldview might ally with another worldview in the pursuit of conservative projects. This would be the case, for instance, in an alliance forged between those holding a *Reward* worldview and others holding an *Orthodox* worldview. That coalition, however, might crumble in the event that self-enhancing versus self-transcending projects

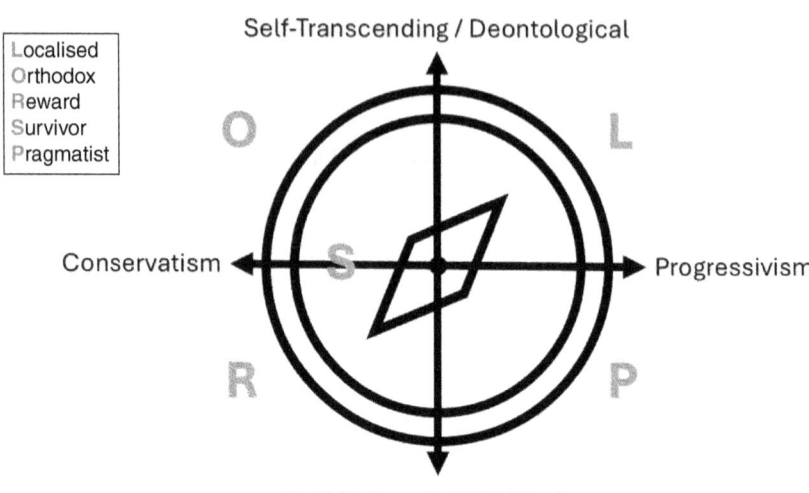

Figure 10.1 The ethics–politics moral compass

rise to the fore. The *Reward* worldview will resist personal sacrifice for the good of all. In this, it stands to find an ally in *Pragmatist* worldviews, whilst the *Orthodox* will emerge as a common opponent.

Worldviews, in terms of the values they embody, help explain shifting coalitional dynamics in contemporary political landscapes and reveal a moral compass that guides human action. On the one hand, the moral compass enables a bearing on political concerns that either seek to preserve the status quo or that pursue change to ameliorate conditions. The traditional distinction between conservatives and progressivists or liberals maps directly onto this value dimension and distinguishes some worldviews from others. Additionally, worldviews are also distinguishable with regards to an ethical dimension that maps onto deontological or utilitarian ethics. The latter are synonymous with self-enhancement strategies that justify *Pragmatists'* and *Rewards'* willingness to cut corners to get ahead. By contrast, *Localised* and *Orthodox* worldviews are guided by deontological principles where the ends do not justify the means.

Political Activity: Engagement and Mobilisation Effects

The moral compass we have just outlined has ramifications that should lead to differential orientations with regards to political phenomena. We have already seen how *Orthodox* respondents aligned themselves differently from other worldviews with regards to the introduction of recreational cannabis legislation in Malta. Unlike *Localised* and *Pragmatist* respondents, they place a value on conservation and maintaining the status quo. And, unlike *Reward* and *Survivor* respondents, they place a value on prescribed dogma. As we have seen, the other worldviews were non-committal with regards to the proposals; only the *Orthodox* respondents adopted an explicit alignment. In this light, we wanted to examine the role worldviews play in policymaking in further depth.

Policymaking serves to regulate the activities of citizens in a way that helps society chart a direction for the future. A common difficulty in policy-making concerns well-intentioned proposals that fail to solicit uptake due to misunderstanding on the part of citizens. Whilst policies can be well meaning, they do not always necessarily meet citizens' expectations. We looked at environmental policy and health policy in Kuwait as part of a broader investigation to understand cultures of science (Sammut, Sartawi, Bauer & Mifsud, 2024). Kuwait is currently undergoing transformation towards more renewable technologies on the one hand and in implementing health enhancing measures targeting the high prevalence of diabetes and coronary heart disease in its population on the other. In two parallel attitude surveys we conducted in 2022, we measured a number of science culture indicators to examine Kuwaiti attitudes to science and the way these resonate with particular worldviews.

Our findings showed that culture of science indicators did not directly vary by worldview type. What this means is that the Kuwaiti public's inclination to science is not directly a function of the worldviews they assume. This finding might seem surprising at first sight, but it simply means that it is not the case that some worldviews are pro-science and others are not. Upon further scrutiny, we found that only once individuals are *engaged* with science do differences in worldview types underlie discrepancies in culture of science indicators. That is, amongst those who are sometimes engaged, the Localised worldview scored significantly higher on Reservations to Science than the Orthodox worldview, whilst the Pragmatist worldview leaned significantly more towards Categorical thinking than the Survivor worldview, which leaned towards Relational thinking. Moreover, amongst those who are regularly engaged with science, the Localised worldview scored significantly higher on Knowledge than the Reward worldview. Conversely, the Localised worldview scored significantly higher on Technocracy Tolerance and Reservations to Science than the Reward worldview. We termed this the engagement effect.

We then looked at differences *within* worldviews with regards to Knowledge, Technocracy Tolerance, Reservations and Relational–Categorical thinking, focusing on the same engagement with science cohorts (i.e. 'sometimes' and 'regular' engagement). Here, we found that, amongst those who are sometimes engaged relative to the non-engaged, significant differences transpired in the Reserve indicator for the *Localised* and *Orthodox* worldviews, in Knowledge for the *Reward* and *Survivor* worldviews and in Relational–Categorical thinking for the *Pragmatist* worldview. With regards to those who are regularly engaged relative to everyone else, significant differences transpired in Technocracy Tolerance and Reserve for the *Localised* worldview, in Reserve for the *Orthodox* worldview, and in Knowledge for the *Reward* worldview. In summary, these findings indicate that, when comparing individuals endorsing the same worldview type, significant differences in culture of science indicators emerge between those who are engaged with science and those who are not. Crucially, as a function of engagement, some move to increase their support for science whilst others become more concerned with its effects. We termed this the mobilisation effect.

Now let's extend our thinking a little bit further to the political domain. Naturally, politicians come in different shapes and sizes. And they cannot all be classified according to a single characteristic type. But as we have observed in our Kuwaiti study, some people are moved in some ways and others in quite different ways. This begs the question as to who stands to move whom – if we consider the five worldview types. I believe that at this point we are able to propose a rudimentary classification of political types that engage different people in different ways. Let's start with politicians who acknowledge that there are some issues that need to be addressed because some members of the community are currently not being served very well. Things must change, but in a considered fashion. We do not want to do more harm than good, but we do not wish to leave things as they are either because the present system does not currently offer a remedy to some disadvantaged groups. So, they propose change guised in a caring demeanour. This was the key argument in my country for introducing recreational cannabis legislation, in an effort to decriminalise those individuals who were being sent to prison for personal use of the drug. I would equate these Localised concerns with Modernist politicians, to use Kaufmann's (2019) term.

As stated previously, this argument was vehemently opposed by others, who insisted that cannabis products remain entirely illegal. They argued against decriminalisation; sending users to prison sets the right example for everyone else. They demonstrated an Orthodox inclination to conserve the system, however disadvantageous this was to anyone who needed use of the drug for whatever reason, in the name of prioritising the common good. Introducing change in this domain also risks opening the doors to unforeseeable consequences, the effects of which we do not currently understand and cannot fully anticipate. During the debate, proponents of this kind of thinking chose to selectively focus on drug addicts, noting how many of them used cannabis in the process of getting themselves addicted to harder drugs. They never considered that proportion of the population who had used cannabis but never got themselves addicted to harder substances. They merely conjectured doom and gloom scenarios that Malta would now develop a national problem with hard drugs, that workplace productivity will fall as workers get stoned at their place of work and that traffic accidents will increase as users get stoned behind the wheel. I propose this represents Technocratic politicians who are experts of how the system currently works, even if some claim it doesn't work well for them. Any novelty lies outside the technocratic competence that such politicians rely on.

Another class of politicians seeks to preserve the established order to safeguard the interests of those who are currently doing rather well. These are typically politicians who represent lobby groups to preserve and promote their own interests. There are many such lobbies in any democratic country, from developers' associations to medical and pharmaceutical industries, tobacco and oil producers, as well as military products. These lobby groups fund Traditionalist politicians who propose that we need to safeguard jobs, protect local interests, maintain social order and so on. What they fail to note is that safeguarding jobs also safeguards profits, protecting local interests means killing competition from start-ups and other entrepreneurs and maintaining the social order means those who are on top stay on top.

The political counter-position is represented by Revolutionaries, who see Modernists as appeasing those who benefit from the system and who therefore argue that we need to tear up the social contract altogether because, unless we do, those in power have a way to maintain power. Never mind the trickle effect, let's open the floodgates to change and pull the rug from under their feet. Revolution is lauded as the solution because, in their eyes, progressive change is always too little too late. The long-term prospect overlooks the present structural imbalance. We need to do something and we need to do it now before things get even worse. We cannot make an omelette without breaking some eggs, let's figure out reparations once we are victorious. This political standpoint equates with a Pragmatist worldview that proposes to do what we can do now and worry about unintended consequences later. Things are not well, we know that much, so things need to change and we know that much too. Nothing further is needed for now, let's get the change underway then we can take it from there.

Finally, I propose that the Survivor worldview equates with Populist politicians. The focus here is on how bad things are and on how little hope there actually is to make them better. The political aim is to not make things much worse by making the same mistakes that landed us here in the first place. We might not have a well-budgeted and well-researched solution, but things are not right and we are honest and upfront enough about it to say it like it actually is, without any of the usual political glitz and glamour. Our numbers might not add up, but we are surely more honest than anyone else – just look at the experience.

Conclusion

Why do people vote for who they do? The answer this volume proposes is that they vote for those that move them the most, regardless of what others might think of that. You might not understand why anyone would have voted for Trump, Harris, Meloni, Berlusconi, Orban, Macron, Sarkozy or any other contested politician in the history of democracy. Those who voted for them, however, do. Our studies on worldviews show that this concept does not help in distinguishing individual inclinations amongst those who are not engaged. Some individuals are seemingly happy to live and let live and their generalised outlooks on life do not serve any purpose for them in such regard.

It is when they become engaged that worldviews reveal political alignment and whether they will move to join others in supporting or resisting a political proposal. As we have argued in Chapter 9, individuals are self-interested and they forge social identities to advance self-serving projects with like-minded others, fabricating social representations to suit their interests in this process. The bottom line of ethical and political activity is our ability to make recourse to social norms that help us get along in life. A bone of contention arises regarding which social norms to peruse – different worldviews prescribe different courses of action that implicate individuals both ethically and politically. Poor Heinz! Interesting though the thanksgiving conversation might be, we would not want to be seated at that table if he and his brother-in-law disagreed.

CHAPTER 11

The Dark Side of Politics
Who Dares Wins

> Power, real power, doesn't come to those who were born strongest, or fastest, or smartest. No. It comes to those who will do anything to achieve it
> - Silco, in Arcane (Season 1, Episode 2)

Chapter 10 revealed that we not only sometimes disagree, but that we do not seem to have a way to settle certain disagreements. We are all able to justify our decisions by recourse to overarching moral frameworks. But at times there is no telling which course of action is right or wrong. Even if we agree on some fundamental precepts, we might still end up on opposing sides. Some moral dilemmas have no answer and no clear way out. The issue becomes a matter of choice, or personal ethics – no more, no less. Moreover, all choices can be defended and justified on the basis of good reasons. But, similarly, all choices can be equally rebuked for other good reasons. The end justifies the mean, or does it? In such instances, we choose what we think is the right thing to do, for us personally or for everyone generally, but crucially always according to us and from our perspective. According to somebody else and from another person's perspective, we might very well be wrong. What's worse, due to our biased social cognition, which we reviewed in Chapter 3, we will assume that our choices are objectively right and others' choices are objectively wrong, even though we know them not to be so.

Faced with this prospect for human psychology, the only thing that seems to make any sense at all is to 'live and let live', as the common aphorism goes. But, as we will see in this chapter, the 'let live' bit of this equation transpires as a thorny issue. Think about it, in real terms, what would this mean? Turn a blind eye to what others are doing whilst claiming they have good reason to do so? In other words, turn a blind eye to corruption, to exploitation, to bullying, to abuse? We know that if we did, some amongst us will take advantage regardless of whether they hurt others in the process. They will do so, for the simple reason that they can, even though we all know that just because one can does not mean one should. So, some things we cannot simply let slide. We must acknowledge that some things are worth fighting for. This is the key point that we unpack in this final chapter. Once again, this is not just us, it's everyone. All of us have our limits. All of us will at some point stand up and do something about something that in our view is just not right. And we will hold that if we do nothing, we and others will suffer even more than we and they already have, and even more than what we must endure in doing something. In other words, we all have red lines that are based on a personal interest tipping point – the trade-off between the cost of doing something and the cost of doing nothing. So, all in all, what do we do in circumstances that prod us to take action?

To Do or Not to Do

Let's go back to Heinz to spell this one out. So, Heinz and his brother-in-law did meet over a family dinner – three years later (wink wink!). One of them had served time; only one of them had! At dinner, they were all very glad that Heinz's wife was still around to cook a delightful meal for them. Her cancer had gone into complete remission, and she thought thanksgiving would be the ideal opportunity for everyone to meet and bury the hatchet. But dinner that day did not go as planned. As Tomasello (2022) himself would have predicted, one thought the other irresponsible and it became clear that they both resented each other. One rebuked the other, demanding an apology. The other replied saying his conscience was clean, one should have known better. And so it went all evening. In the end, they fell out and things between them became rather frosty.

For good reason – they both told Heinz's wife separately when she tried to talk to them about reconciling. Heinz's wife was truly heartbroken. She loved her husband as she did her own brother, and she could not stand them falling out over something they both did out of love for her! So naturally she felt like she had to do something about it. Wouldn't anyone? And she could not expect anybody else to do something about this either, it had to be her as she was the linking pin in this family feud and the cause of all that happened. She thought long and hard about what she could do to smooth things over. And then she had an idea.

She thought that the best way to reconcile her husband and her brother would be to somehow create a set of enabling conditions such that they would then be required to work together for a common purpose.

A multilateral solution of sorts. She was reading a lot of psychology at the time and amongst other things she had come across Allport's contact hypothesis, which suggests that prejudice is lessened in conditions of positive contact. And she also read about Sherif's Robbers Cave experiments, where these two groups of boys who had been fighting through summer camp eventually made peace by working together to resolve a common problem when their water supply was sabotaged (Sammut & Bauer, 2021). And then there was this political psychology book she was reading about bridging cultural, social and political divides. The author was going on about projects and how people fabricate social representations that enable them to advance their own interests with similar others (Chapter 9). So, she thought this must be the key to reconciliation. She needed to get them to work together towards achieving a higher goal than whatever grudges they were immersed in, and in taking up the task they would both get something out of it. So, she put her plan in motion then convened them once everything was in place.

When they met, she informed them that she had gone ahead and registered a charity, 'Same Crime, Same Time', which she was going to personally chair, so that they all together could help spread the message and raise awareness about what had happened to them. Hopefully this would lead to a revision of policy for police to question and prosecute suspects together, so that in future others will not suffer the same nasty fate they had. Heinz and his brother-in-law agreed (wink) that this was a bad idea. They did not want to work together, and nothing they did now could take back time. On the other hand, it was a good cause and the dice had already been cast: Heinz's wife needed a secretary and a treasurer for her charity, and how could either of them say no if they both wanted the moral high ground. By the end of the evening, they were obviously all on board. The only thing that remained to be done was to put the plan in motion. In other words, doing what needed to be done to change things for the better, once and for all.

Doing Something about Something

So, what was the plan? Where to start? The obvious starting point for changing the world these days is to make yourself a nice gingerbread latte (my fav), take a sassy snap, head over to the couch and post your message on Insta. With an estimated 95 million posts every single day, you should also consider going the extra mile and tweet on X, post on Facebook, reel on TikTok and do the rounds on all other types of social media. Be warned though, you're unlikely to make much of an impact unless you are an influencer. So, the first task must be to become an influencer. Or perhaps to recruit one, if you do not wish to sacrifice your private life completely, online and offline. Maybe you could recruit a journalist, to help you get the message out there in a way that influencers might pick up. Or maybe you could organise a peaceful protest, that will bring you 'likes' and journalists. Or maybe cut through the chase and talk to a politician to push through legislation. But politicians have a habit of swinging things their way. So maybe become a politician yourself. But do you really want to run up against the likes of Trump, Putin and Xi?

In 2023, along with many other colleagues, we were tasked by the European Commission's Horizon Europe programme to study political extremism and find ways for limiting its spread. The project, which goes by the name of OppAttune (www.oppattune.eu), sought to understand the evolution of 'everyday extremism' and how this relates to political activity like citizen activism, social movements and other democratic activities that, whilst well-intended, potentially open up the door to civil unrest, disorder, disaffection and other anti-democratic effects. The overarching impetus was to find ways to stop discordance from degenerating into efforts aimed at destruction of the opposition. Because, even though we all seemingly value democracy, we do not seem to be very good at dealing with opposing views. We want debate, but we all seem to strive for consensus when it comes to our views and, when we do not get it, we tend to use our democratic freedoms to protest, because we can, so why shouldn't we! In the process, sometimes we make things worse by turning up the temperature and fuelling hate.

To do all this, OppAttune sought to establish a set of benchmarking metrics for tracking and measuring everyday extremism, and to us at the University of Malta fell the task of devising the Everyday Extremism Scale.[1] Our conception of everyday extremism relied on the combination of the two terms, that is, behaviours that are commonly regarded as relatively outlandish (i.e. extreme) but that might be rather commonplace in their occurrence due to permissive norms (i.e. everyday). In this way, we distinguish 'everyday extremism' from 'extremism in the everyday', such as when a bus is blown up in a terrorist attack, to give an example, where an everyday event such as boarding a bus becomes subject to extremist activity. By contrast, everyday extremism refers to those sorts of behaviours

---

[1] Deliverable 6.1; https://ordo.open.ac.uk/articles/dataset/Everyday_Extremism_Scale/26411599.

that most people will find squeamish but that are also warranted in certain, perhaps extraordinary, circumstances.

In our view, everyday extremism is a form of escalation that fuels the spiral of conflict between opposing parties (Chapter 7) and that precedes more drastic behaviours synonymous with extremism in the everyday. The rationale is that if you target everyday extremism and impede further escalation, things will not get out of hand by going too far. In essence, we studied what people do when they want to do something about something, amongst the possibilities for action that one could realistically do. To develop the everyday extremism scale, we relied on the scaling procedure detailed in developing the PASS method (Chapter 9) and revised it for use with publicly sourced data. This helped us develop a more efficient and equally effective procedure for incremental behavioural scaling, which we proceed to describe next.

Incremental Behavioural Scaling

We started by immersing ourselves in Reddit for the best part of two months over the summer of 2023. We reasoned that we would find on Reddit whatever we stand to find through other forms of qualitative data gathering, like interviews or focus groups, perhaps more in view of Reddit's anonymity feature. Moreover, on Reddit, opinions were expected to be unadulterated as they are not moderated along editorial lines, which would be the case for published media. Our data gathering proceeded along two lines, that is (a) general and (b) domain-specific content. For the former, we looked at posts and comments that described taking action or doing something that was not tied to any particular policy domain. We searched Reddit for 'activism', 'activist', 'raise awareness', 'advocacy' and 'how to'. We did not limit any of these searches to specific subreddits. In the domain-specific condition, we used the same search operators but focused our searches to target 'LGBTQI', 'anarchism', 'progun', 'abortion', 'Bernie Sanders', 'environment', 'climate' and 'vegan' subreddits. We then read through the posts and comments that described behaviour/action strategies and we extracted these for subsequent analysis. By the time we reached saturation, we extracted a total of 218 posts providing a list of over 350 different actions. The data file listing actions and sources is publicly available on the Open Science Framework repository.[2]

[2] https://osf.io/fv7rs/?view_only=569c83d475e34b7484a76bbe7a9edf88

We proceeded to validate our findings through online searches of mainstream media in four different countries, namely the United Kingdom (*The Guardian*, *The Telegraph*, *The Times*), Greece (*efsyn*, *Kathimerini*, *Ta Nea*), Kosovo (*Prishtina Insight*, *Koha*, *Nacionale*) and Malta (*Times of Malta*, *Malta Today*, *The Independent*). We searched for articles containing the following keywords: 'extremist', 'extremism', 'activist', 'migration', 'vaccination', 'protectionist' and 'protectionism'. We analysed over 540 articles in total, following a random selection of articles returned by the searches we carried out. No additional behavioural acts beyond the ones we originally found on Reddit were identified in this exercise.

We then returned to our Reddit data and conducted a two-step thematic analysis where similar behaviours were grouped to avoid duplication and thematised according to the type of activity entailed. In this way, we reduced the original list to 113 actions categorised into ten themes, namely, 'Activism', 'Engagement', 'Lifestyle', 'Lobbying', 'Opposing', 'Organisation', 'Politics', 'Social Media', 'Support' and 'Violence'. We removed the themes of 'Lifestyle' (e.g. change one's own personal habits) and 'Violence' (e.g. do something that lands you a prison sentence so that journalists cover the news) from subsequent analysis, the former for being too every-day and the latter for being too extreme (Table 11.1).

Inspired by the PASS method outlined, we proceeded to subject the list of items to two rounds of expert ranking in which experts were asked to

Table 11.1 *Everyday extremism themes and actions*

Theme	Example of Actions
Activism	Attend public demonstrations
	Block activities through sit-ins
Engagement	Associate with like-minded people
	Convert neighbours and friends
Lobbying	Enlist politicians to the cause
	Establish an NGO
Opposing	Blackmail
	Become a whistle-blower
Organisation	Associate your cause with successful projects
	Develop a members database/list
Politics	Become active in local politics
	Email/write to politicians
Social Media	Anger troll
	Block those you oppose
Support	Build credibility
	Buy merchandise and wear it

rank the items from the most extreme to the most every-day. The first round used actions presented in thematised lists. We then looked at the mean rating for each item and selected three or four actions per theme that demonstrated statistically significant mean differences between them in the ranked order. The thematically ranked lists typically included the highest ranked and lowest ranked items, then either the item at the 50th percentile or the items at the 25th and 75th percentiles for three or four item lists, respectively. We proceeded in this manner depending on whether statistically significant differences in means transpired between the uppermost ranked and lowermost ranked items and any in between at the noted percentiles. We thus made sure that the items we retained following the first round of ranking that went into the second round demonstrated statistically significant mean differences between them. We used paired samples t-tests to conduct this exercise, which reduced our list of actions to 25 items (Table 11.2).

We then undertook a second ranking exercise relying on a different group of experts to reduce the list further, this time bringing all items together and doing away with themes. Once again, we asked them to rank the items from the most extreme to the most every-day. We conducted a Wilcoxon-rank test on the items, where the results were not significant. This showed that the ranking of the items demonstrated a symmetrical distribution around the median. We then conducted a Principal Components Analysis to examine factor loadings. Out of the 12 actions that loaded most strongly, 6 loaded positively and 6 loaded negatively onto a single factor which explained almost 20 per cent of the variance. A final Wilcoxon-rank test with these 12 items once again returned non-significant results, demonstrating a symmetrical arrangement. Finally, we examined internal consistency, which returned a Cronbach's alpha of 0.822, suggesting very strong reliability. In this manner, we devised a final list of 12 items to measure everyday extremism quantitatively, as detailed in Table 11.3. The final list, in simple terms, involves a selection of incremental behavioural actions that people do when they decide to do something about something.

Fight Fire with Fire

Let's go back to Heinz and apply incremental behavioural scaling to his case. Heinz's wife asked everyone she knew for advice on what she could do to get her charity off the ground. Some said one thing, some said another. She also spent a lot of time on Reddit browsing for ideas. In the

Table 11.2 *Ranked everyday extremism items*

Theme	Action	Average of Rating	SD of Rating
Activism	Storm an event	3.96	2.25
Activism	Fake signatures on a petition	8.35	2.62
Activism	Attend public demonstrations	13.13	2.26
Engagement	Flood comments sections online	3.75	3.69
Engagement	Support allied politicians publicly	6.63	3.29
Engagement	Share upcoming events for others to attend	9.38	3.35
Lobbying	Lobby government officials	4.55	2.94
Lobbying	Team up with journalists	6.50	2.89
Lobbying	Develop affiliations with researchers/universities/industry	9.27	2.59
Opposing (undermining)	Gaslighting (question/deny the truth with an opposite version)	5.52	3.07
Opposing	Undermine the opposition personally	7.48	3.47
Opposing	Submit (false) allegations of misconduct	10.60	4.12
Opposing	Call out those responsible	12.68	4.13
Organisation (organising)	Organise campaigns	3.70	2.03
Organisation	Develop a members database/list	6.91	1.62
Politics	Become active in local politics	4.10	2.79
Politics	Vote for candidates that endorse particular reform and action	8.29	2.28
Social media	Anger troll	4.25	3.73
Social media	Public shaming/criticism (e.g. through social media)	7.17	3.74
Social media	Block those you oppose	9.92	3.75
Social media	Publicly endorse (e.g. through social media)	14.17	3.21
Social media	Like & Share content (Actively Promote/Publish Content)	16.67	4.05
Support	Organise a street party (public events)	4.00	2.65
Support	Post stickers/signs/posters in public places	8.05	4.19
Support	Donate money and time to the cause	11.41	3.81

end, she devised an action plan that she shared with Heinz and her brother. She would start with the least intrusive option then scale things up as she gathered momentum. Heinz and her brother agreed, there was no point in shooting for the stars if they hadn't laid the groundwork. So, the first thing they settled on was to start promoting their NGO in public. They wanted to put it out there, so they commissioned a website with information about the charity, they registered accounts on the various social media platforms, and they printed leaflets, brochures and business

Table 11.3 *Everyday extremism incremental behavioural scale*

Action	Average of Rating	Median	SD of Rating	Factor Loading
Submit (false) allegations of misconduct	4.81	2	5.74	0.673
Gaslighting (questions/deny the truth with an opposite version)	5.62	4	4.86	0.775
Storm an event	4.30	4	3.44	0.459
Anger troll	6.62	5	4.77	0.759
Public shaming/criticism (e.g. social media)	7.84	7	5.18	0.516
Undermine the opposition personally	8.46	7	6.14	0.595
Publicly endorse (e.g. social media)	16.24	16	6.58	−0.491
Actively promote/publish content	16.78	17	5.53	−0.448
Become active in local politics	17.24	17	5.04	−0.486
Post stickers/signs/posters in public places	16.19	17	5.81	−0.560
Share upcoming events for others to attend	18.76	21	5.72	−0.720
Vote for candidates that endorse particular reform and action	19.32	21	6.38	−0.448

cards to disseminate. They agreed to post something on social media at least once a week, to get things underway and to keep their audience interested. Soon enough, they had a few hundred followers and their posts attracted a few likes every time as well as a few encouraging comments now and again. But things then hit a plateau and, however enthusiastic their activity was, they quickly realised things would not achieve their mission by posting on social media alone. So, they reached out to politicians in their locality and they resolved to vote for those who supported their charity regardless of which party they came from.

Supporting the right politicians could really help, but Heinz's wife wondered whether at some point she needed to bite the bullet and run for town mayor herself. Sure, she would be unlikely to win, but there was the off-chance that she would secure enough votes to get a seat on the board of elected representatives and if that were to happen, she could try to put the charity's work on the town's agenda. It would involve doing a lot more other town work that had nothing to do with the charity's business, time which could be spent promoting the charity directly, Heinz argued, but there was no change to be expected without some form of political clout. Somebody had to try.

As the elections drew near, a frenzy of political activity took place all around them. They had all voted in the town's mayoral elections in the past and they obviously had come across political propaganda but being directly involved took things to a whole new level. For starters, even though Heinz's wife was running as an independent candidate, the charity was approached by other well-established politicians from the two big parties for endorsement. This was so tempting, as they would then spread their message with the big party voters on the big party channels. Even if Heinz's wife would not be elected, their message could now reach thousands instead of hundreds of people. In exchange, they would be granting the big party politicians a foothold amongst the charity's voter base. The flip side of this was that our trio were effectively in competition and the other guys seemed to have much more manpower and much deeper pockets, propped up as they were by big party funding.

In for a penny, in for a pound, argued Heinz's brother-in-law. They asked for donations from their followers and spent every penny, including some of their personal savings, on the campaign trail. Their evenings were now spent politicking around town, putting up signs and posters in public places to showcase their message to potential voters. Social media posting would have to be done on the road, long gone were the days of posting comfortably from the sofa whilst watching an episode from the latest series. This was exhausting work! And there were still two weeks to go to election day. But they had to give it one final push. They needed to do what they needed to do, not necessarily to win, but to get the message out there. They needed to organise a political rally – a mass meeting to round up and catalyse their troops for the big day.

So far, so good. Many of us would not be prepared to go anywhere this far to bring about whatever change we think is needed. It is one thing to complain with mates over a beer at the pub; it is quite another to personally run for office. But most of us were not cured from cancer by loved ones who went to prison for stealing drugs for us who then fell out. So, fair enough for Heinz and his company. How about you though, how far would you go?

Heinz himself would not have gone a step further than endorsing other politicians. He would not have directly contested. As far as he was concerned, he would have left the heat to them as that kind of stuff comes with the job description and any who find that kind of thing unpalatable should have known better. Heinz's brother-in-law agreed. As far as he was concerned, he would not have lifted a finger beyond posting on social media. The truth is that they were always unlikely to succeed in changing things, and if they did succeed, there was nothing saying they would change things for the better. With the way politicians run their business once in office, it was more than likely that things would actually turn out for the worse. Heinz and his brother-in-law were chatting over a barbeque that Heinz's wife had organised for their families to lift up everyone's spirits. With one week to go, their campaign had hit a snag.

They realised that something was amiss when they saw that the posters they had been putting up were being removed and painted over. Finally, they figured that the police were fighting back! The police were actually harassing them; stopping them on the streets to check their driving licenses every night they were out. This was a huge waste of time that was keeping them away from the campaign trail. At one point, the three of them were arrested only to be released without charges the following day, which was obviously very disruptive. The police permit for their political rally was inexplicably delayed and issued only on the eve of the day when the rally was due to be held. By then, the market stalls they had planned to host had pulled out and the event ended up being a mere shadow of what it was meant to be. And to make things worse, Heinz himself was back in the dock facing tax evasion and money laundering charges, after failing to pick up a receipt for an ice cream he bought at the rally to make the best out of a bad situation. Things got to a head, though, when deep-fake images of Heinz and his wife appeared on 'OnlyCans' (a private photo sharing website) the night of the rally. Heinz's wife was utterly devastated. She was doing her best at the barbeque, wearing a smile and keeping everyone's glasses full. But the mood had decidedly dampened and Heinz and his brother-in-law both felt they had to fight back. After all, they were seasoned criminals by now and one of them had actually served time. All knowledge they were ready to put to good use. So, over a couple of chargrilled steaks that evening, they hatched another plan.

They agreed on the same strategy they had when they decided to promote their charity – start slow then scale things up. To get the ball rolling, they would disrupt the upcoming police event where 20 constables where being promoted to a higher rank. They got wind that a parade was planned for the occasion. A couple of smoke flares thrown over the wall would be sure to cause a stir. Heinz would throw the flares whilst his brother-in-law would work the camera, armed with a cheap but fancy telephoto lens that would provide a plentiful stock to take jibes at the officers on social media that evening and make a laughing stock of the lot of them. Moreover, as it happened, Heinz knew someone who had been to school with the current Chief-of-Police, and he had more than a story to tell about their childhood days even though the source was known to like a drink or two. Still, maybe not enough to force a resignation, but more than enough to embarrass the man. And they resolved that the next time they would be picked up for questioning, they would head straight to hospital after their release and claim they had been beaten up in custody. That story was sure to go viral. The police would surely deny, so they would then proceed to name two particular officers they had identified through social media that were a little loose with their words and who could be trusted to lose their temper if provoked. They would allege these two officers were involved, and it would not take much to get them to embarrass themselves and the rest of the force with them. And come what may – this time they agreed in advance – whatever statement the police released the two would counter by gaslighting them, that is, claim the opposite had actually happened and that the police were making false allegations. In the end, it would take years to prove things one way or another in court. What was certain was that the public did not think much of the police already, and their victimisation could enlist enough voter sympathy to get Heinz's wife elected after all. In the end, it serves them right.

All Is Fair in Love and War

By and large, we all want the same things in life. We all want to have good healthcare for ourselves and our families. We want good education for our children. And, ideally, we want others to have that too. We want to be able to put food on the table and enjoy quality time with our loved ones. And we would all rid the world of poverty if we could. We do not all agree on how to deal with climate change, but we all want nature to thrive and we all want to leave the world a better place than we found it. We all want to be treated respectfully. We all try, in our way, to cope as best we can. And if there is an afterlife beyond our mortal existence, we are all trying to make it to that afterparty. But we obviously disagree on how these basic yet grand human ambitions are best served. The problem with achieving any of these ambitions, quite simply, is other people.

Moral reasoning, as the Heinz example makes clear, is not only a function of what we think is right or wrong. It is complicated by what we perceive others are doing, and what we think about that. The real dilemma in social relations arises when we see that others are not sticking to their end of the bargain, that they are not abiding by the same moral standards as we are. The Everyday Extremism incremental behavioural scale we presented in Table 11.3 spans two polarities. The positive polarity is made up of a list of actions that involve what we can do to promote our own views. Of course, there is a cost to everything and, in speaking one's mind, one runs the risk of being challenged, contradicted or stereotyped even.

In democratic societies, we like to celebrate freedom of expression that gives everyone the right to speak without fear of persecution. But then we also observe people speaking and saying all sorts of rubbish, with which we fundamentally disagree. Conspiracy theories abound, sometimes with highly adverse effects. And we observe that some people are very gullible as well. So, we find ourselves compelled to point out the errors in others' ways. And this pits us against each other. The negative polarity of the Everyday Extremism Scale is all about what we can do to impede what others are doing. And some of those actions are rather shady. Would you submit a false allegation of misconduct to prevent someone from speaking their minds and wreaking havoc amongst a gullible populace? Would you be prepared to gaslight the opposition if you could not stop them any other way? Bear in mind that, whilst these actions include some that are ethically shady, they are also all perfectly legal in democratic jurisdictions that uphold rule of law. Whatever issues might arise as a result are resolved not through obedience, but through litigation. The thing is, some abuse that and rely on democratic freedoms to pursue anti-democratic, subjectively justifiable ends.

And that is the fundamental question we face in politics, that is, what do we do about what other people are doing about the problem we all face. Think about it, what if you found yourself in Heinz's position? How far would you go? How far is too far? Bear in mind one thing, you might be up against an opposition that does not have a red line and who is prepared to go all the way. The BBC reported how some protest organisations, like Just Stop Oil for instance, require their members to be willing and ready for imprisonment if it came to it. That is how ready some people are to make their case. Substantively, we might actually agree with them. But is it worth taking things that far? Would you pat your child on the back if they took things that far and you're now having to visit them in prison – for the good of the planet? Where would you draw the line?

The Everyday Extremism incremental behaviour scale is useful in two ways: qualitative and quantitative. In qualitative research, it can be a useful tool to stimulate discussion regarding how far some individuals are ready to go. In OppAttune, we used the scale to stimulate focus group discussions in a variety of locations across the EU border. Similar scales can be produced with little effort to investigate other topical issues beyond extremism that have to do with escalating actions. Another way the scale is useful is in quantitative terms. This involves computing an index of everyday extremism by asking respondents to rate their agreement with each item on a scale from 1 to 7 (least to most agreement), then weighting their response by multiplying the answer by the rank order of the item from 1 (most everyday) to 12 (most extreme), and subsequently dividing the weighted score by the sum of weights to obtain a weighted mean. The higher the final score, the higher the propensity for extremism.

In this way, the scale combines Likert measurement with Thurstone scaling, enabling a comparative appraisal of attitudes that is sensitive to their intensity. Without such weighting, a vegan's attitude towards eliminating meat from their diet, eliminating all farmed produce from supermarkets and eliminating all animal farms from the face of the Earth are all weighted equally. If we are interested in escalating attitudes, this will not do (Roberts, Laughlin & Wedell, 1999; Drasgow, Chernyshenko & Stark, 2010). Weighting the items according to their rank in the sequence circumvents this problem. Moreover, aside from the composite score that is obtained from summing up the weighted scores, the Likert ratings themselves are useful inasmuch as they enable a comparison of the extent of endorsement for the various items. In other words, it tells you just how far a population is ready to go.

We administered the Everyday Extremism incremental behavioural scale to a panel of 410 respondents in Malta immediately following the European Parliament elections of 2024. There was no shortage of political controversy prior to the election. The debate was reminiscent of the 2002 French presidential election that saw French President Jacques Chirac reconfirmed after appealing voters to 'Vote for the crook, not the fascist'. The campaign leading to the European Parliament elections in Malta in 2024 was marked by corruption charges issued against serving members of government, which led to the suspension of the governor of the Central Bank of Malta and the resignation of the Minister of Health. The charges, however, were delayed for years and the date they were effectively issued had been predicted by the Prime Minister months in advance to coincide with the start of the electoral campaign, and so it came to be – alleged crooks on one side, alleged fascists on the other. In this charged political context, respondents rated the items as listed in Table 11.4.

There is one very interesting thing to note in the findings, that is, all responses bar item number 2 are rated below the neutral midpoint 4, on a scale ranging from 1 (Strongly Disagree) to 7 (Strongly Agree). In other words, Maltese respondents personally disagree with every action, including promoting their own views, which is recognised as a fundamental

Table 11.4 *Everyday extremism scale responses for Malta*

Action	Mean	SD
1. Actively promote your own views	3.72	1.897
2. Vote for candidates who support action in line with your views	5.49	1.717
3. Become active in local politics	3.36	2.013
4. Endorse politicians whose views align	3.77	1.939
5. Post stickers & signs in public	2.58	1.820
6. Promote events for others	3.32	2.036
7. Disrupt formal event	2.17	1.666
8. Publicly shame and criticise	2.53	1.809
9. Undermine opponents personally	2.40	1.805
10. False allegations of misconduct	2.33	1.789
11. Harass to provoke	2.48	1.768
12. Gaslighting	2.61	1.812

human right in Maltese legislation. The only action rated in positive territory is to vote for candidates whose views align with yours. In essence, send someone else to do your bidding.

The Art of Politicking

Politics is a dirty game. We think we have the moral high ground when we stand up and speak our mind about whatever we think is wrong, until we realise that they are playing dirty and, because they are playing dirty, they have the edge. And if we do not do something drastic about that, we stand to lose. So, we end up getting drawn into the issue, not so much the substantive concern but the actual rules of the political game. Our cherished democratic freedoms, are they all fair enough? Or do desperate times call for desperate measures? Many question how we ended up with the populist leaders we have. They struggle to understand how people like Trump, Bolsonaro, Orban and others have been able to sway their electorates despite their abrasive and largely non-charismatic political styles. The answer to this question should be pretty clear by now. They were voted in because they were perceived to have what it takes to do what voters thought needs doing. Voters did not necessarily agree with their policies, they did not necessarily think these were charismatic leaders and they did not necessarily fall for their charms. Neither did voters necessarily think they were more virtuous than the opposition. They simply thought these leaders were the ones who would do what was needed, what was right – for them and according to them: the voters. You and I might well disagree. But one reason populist leaders are elected is because they seemingly do not care and they do not play by the rules. They go the extra mile. If they did not, the charismatic, self-righteous, self-proclaimed non-populists would win. The only way to beat the charismatic, self-righteous, self-proclaimed non-populists is to take things further, regardless. And they are not the only ones ready to take things to the brink.

In Chapter 10, we examined the role of worldviews and the role these play in engaging and mobilising political support for certain policies. We noted five worldviews, which we articulated as political styles. The Technocrat adopts an orthodox style, placing emphasis on how things work and what happens in society when you tweak things one way or another. The Modernist wants to fix problems and change things for the good of all, not a select few. The Revolutionary wants out of a messed-up system, once and for all; tear it down and we will rebuild from there. The Traditionalist claims that some will always do better than others, tearing things down benefits no one. The Populist claims that things are bad enough already and there's little hope they can be better; we cannot keep hoping for the best whilst ignoring the rest.

We used the Everyday Extremism incremental behaviour scale to examine how these worldview/political styles leaned in their democratic engagement. We used the computed index as outlined in Table 11.3 to study this, relying on a computation of weighted scores for each item and a final summing up of all scores for each respondent. We then measured a list of other variables in the same sample as well as the extent of their agreement with the five worldviews. Crucially, we asked them about their levels of institutional trust (in parliament, the legal system, the police, the banks, the mass media, the scientific community, political parties, European institutions and NGOs) and the extent to which they felt they had a legitimate voice to express their political opinions (ability to say what I truly believe when talking to others; concerned that my political opinions will be censored on social media; political correctness is harming free speech).

We started by testing main effects for Anomie, Democratic Disaffection, Political Participation, Political Voice, Inequality, Institutional Trust, Life Satisfaction, Political Disaffection, System Justification and Social Dominance Orientation on Everyday Extremism.

We found that Political Participation ($B = 0.109$, $SE = 0.55$, $p < 0.05$), Political Voice ($B = 0.138$, $SE = 0.043$, $p < 0.01$), Institutional Trust ($B = 0.278$, $SE = 0.066$, $p < 0.01$) and SDO ($B = 0.135$, $SE = 0.053$, $p < 0.05$) exercised main effects on Everyday

Extremism. We then tested main effects on Everyday Extremism for the various worldview stances. We identified a negative main effect for the Modernist stance [Localised worldview] (B = −0.188, SE = 0.052, $p < 0.01$).

We then tested the main effects of worldviews on each of the influencing variables, in other words, indirect effects on Everyday Extremism. We found that the Technocratic stance [Orthodox worldview] (B = 0.094, SE = 0.044, $p < 0.05$) and the Traditionalist [Reward worldview] (B = 0.143, SE = 0.049, $p < 0.01$) both exert a positive effect on Political Participation, whilst the Modernist [Localised worldview] (B = −0.123, SE = 0.052, $p < 0.05$) exerts a negative effect. These findings are precisely in line with the Ethics–Politics moral compass we reviewed in Chapter 10 and demonstrate a higher propensity for Technocrats to push the temperature bar higher due to their attitudes concerning political participation, whilst the opposite is true for Modernists, for whom political participation serves as a disinclination for everyday extremism.

We found a positive direct effect for the Populist stance [Survivor worldview] on Political Voice (B = 0.124, SE = 0.048, $p < 0.01$). This too is as predicted by the ethics–politics moral compass, inasmuch as populists who feel they lack a political voice are more inclined to engage in everyday extremism. Presumably this is the only way they can make themselves heard, being mostly overlooked by the mainstream parties. Similarly, we found a positive direct effect for the Traditional stance [Reward worldview] on Institutional Trust (B = 0.16, SE = 0.043, $p < 0.01$), such that high levels of institutional trust for Traditionalists incline towards everyday extremism. Traditionalists are aware that this remains fair game in a democratic society.

Finally, we found that the Revolutionary stance [Pragmatist worldview] (B = 0.094, SE = 0.038, $p < 0.05$) and the Populist stance [Survivor worldview] (B = 0.095, SE = 0.035, $p < 0.01$) exert a positive effect on SDO, whilst the Modernist stance [Localised worldview] (B = −0.150, SE = 0.048, $p < 0.01$) exerts a negative effect on this variable. This replicates the findings we reviewed in Chapter 7 regarding conservative and liberal influences on SDO. It also means that not all left-leaning political views pull against everyday extremism, only Modernists do. Revolutionaries and Populists concerned with social dominance both push everyday extremism higher.

The political tug-of-war that shifts the standard for everyday extremism, therefore, looks like this: Modernists actively try to tone down the political extremism temperature directly as well as express opposite views to Technocrats regarding Political Participation, to Traditionalists on

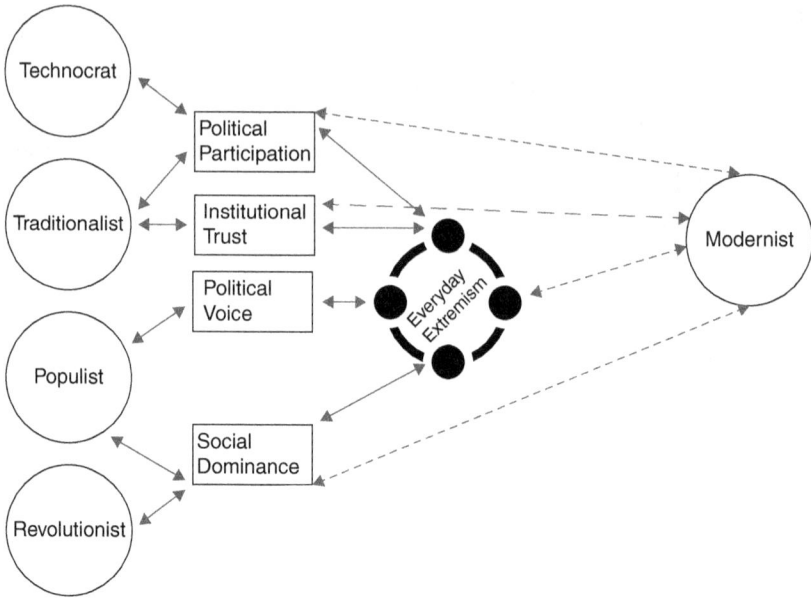

Figure 11.1 The political tug-of-war

Institutional Trust and to Revolutionists and Populists on Social Dominance. On the other hand, Technocrats concerned with Political Participation, Traditionalists concerned with Political Participation and Institutional Trust, Revolutionists concerned with Social Dominance and Populists concerned with Political Voice and Social Dominance all act to push the extremism temperature higher (see Figure 11.1).

Conclusion

The question regarding how far people go has been decisively answered by Milgram in his obedience experiments. The answer is simple – when individuals are commanded by an authority aligned with their worldview, most go all the way. Many of us believe we won't, but most of us actually do. This is in line with Tomasello's (2022) findings concerning agency in the human species. Once we buy into a normative framework, we simply proceed to implement it in presumed unison with others. Milgram's subjects bought into the scientific establishment and proceeded to administer potentially harmful or deadly shocks to fellow participants in the name of science. Others do likewise in real life in the name of the Church,

Islam, the Motherland, the Party, Democracy. Milgram was criticised that his experiments were unorthodox, that people do not go about everyday life being asked to harm others and give them electric shocks. Maybe his were artefactual findings. In other obedience experiments with higher ecological validity, where subjects were only asked to stress their participants enough to ruin their prospects for employment, obedience rates increased even further (Meeus & Raaijmakers, 1995; Sammut & Bauer, 2021).

On the other hand, people do demonstrate a capacity to disobey. Look at the various social movements that make the news from time to time. This suggests that as human beings we also have the potential for disobedience and that we might not be conditioned one way or another after all. As we have argued in this volume, however, the crucial variable that seems to make all the difference is self-interest. In Meeus and Raaijmakers' (1995) Utrecht studies, obedience rates fell sharply when participants were informed that they were legally liable themselves for any harm incurred by the participants and that the University's insurance policy would not provide legal cover to them. In this case, most disobeyed. In essence, we are all advancing our own interests according to what we think is right.

Faced with the enormity of his findings, Milgram ultimately sought solace in conscience. We make our own personal choices in the end and where things end up and how far they go is a collective consequence of our combined actions. Conscience is that personal individual space where others do not tread, a matter between us and God that many consider to be a spiritual voice within that provides ethical guidance. The grounds we have covered in this volume are not equally promising. What about naïve realism, stereotyping, ingroup identification, dehumanisation and utilitarian ethics? Perhaps these issues have no clear answer. Conscience is not directly amenable to experimental control and observation. The study of moral dilemmas in light of the extremism incremental behavioural scale presented in this chapter provides an opportunity to delve into these issues and constitutes a promising avenue for future empirical inquiry. But much is left unanswered.

Perhaps it could be that we cannot even help ourselves in matters of conflict. In the Netflix documentary *Chimp Empire*, Joya is an orphaned chimpanzee who finds her place amongst the Western Ngogo community. Upon reaching adulthood, she will need to leave this group and cross the community's boundary to a different tribe for her to start her own family. This basic patriarchal arrangement ensures variability in the genetic pool and limits the potential for inbreeding. In other words, social fragmentation amongst chimpanzees in the wild turns out to be adaptive for the species, however crude and misogynistic it looks to be in human eyes. Perhaps conflict is what we do as a species once our basic survival is assured, ironic as this might be. Survival of the fittest where intra-species conflict is the absolute measure.

On the other hand, we are nevertheless equipped with agency, which gives us the ability to make choices, including those that help us avoid conflict and pay the price for excessive self-righteousness. Regardless of where we come from, we are all able to make choices in the present which go on to shape our future. The basic human response in the face of danger is fight or flight, which, like the hunter-gatherer adaptation we have discussed in this volume, comprises of two equally adaptive alternatives. Sometimes it pays to curl one's palm in a fist, at other times it pays to open the palm and offer a handshake. How things pan out rarely goes according to anyone's plan. As we have seen in this chapter, the political tug-of-war involves many players and there is very little telling where it settles other than it is hardly ever entirely predictable. Some might push in one direction but others will step in to veer the ship off course. Where we end up, more often than not, is anybody's guess.

When conflict erupts, so do countless peaceful voices, although they might be harder to hear amidst the cacophony. For some, the onset of conflict is already a step too far; for others it is merely the beginning. We necessarily wonder how we can achieve peace, even if we are presently fighting to change some circumstance. The truth is that peace is achieved in one of two ways, that is, by victory or by truce. The former entails a fight until the bitter end. The latter stops somewhat shy of that, at the point where the realisation dawns that what one is fighting over is no longer worth the price of admission. Some things are worth fighting for, clearly. How hard to fight is a question we ask ourselves once we are so engaged. Every time we escalate in an effort to win, the other finds themselves equally motivated. Before we know it, our living conditions might become insufferable. Perhaps for many this is already so, despite our democratic freedoms or perhaps because of them. Be this as it may, we can only do what we can do according to our convictions. And, in fighting for what we consider to be right, we should also be prepared to lose if what we are fighting for is indeed worth the cost.

Where does this leave us with regards to migration and bridging cultural, social and political divides. In a quandary, I would say. There is no magic solution. Just like our hunter–gatherer ancestors, we realise that what we currently have will not do, so we need to move on and search for new solutions. Out of necessity, more than choice. We can certainly say the same about the grand projects that are meant to resolve our predicament, religious, national, cultural, or other. The bottom line is that none of them has delivered what it promised. Perhaps it is time to wake up to that fact. Perhaps it is time to realise that we are all potentially good and we are all potentially bad. We are all terrorists to one another when we fight, we are all heroes when we help our own kind.

Milgram's point is that it all boils down to conscientious choice, as noted. Considering the grounds we have covered in this volume, this is contentious to say the least. We have seen that we cannot simply stop and let others run all over us. Let us take a moment and go back to where we started. Let us revisit for a moment the social contract once again. This is where we agreed to do some things for others so they could do some things for us. It is in this way that we banded together and thrived in our evolutionary history. All the way to democratic societies that have delivered more by way of health and wellbeing than any other social arrangement that has preceded them. The reason we make one another miserable is because we keep fighting for more, and this is not necessarily a bad thing. Democracies allow for this through political activity. It is not necessary to agree on everything. Democracy allows for disagreement, even discordance. Differences can be settled through a vote. It is dictatorships that aspire for consensus, which often must be forced through obedience and censorship of dissenting voices. So, disagreement is not a problem in itself, a democratic system is designed to handle that. It is only a problem for the party that stands to lose by advocating a less popular option. It becomes a systemic problem when the losing party cannot stand losing and presses on until breaking point for the sake of winning.

In essence, what is ultimately required is strengthening the democratic ties that bind us, to reinforce the rules of the game that force losers to stand down and to re-engage their opponents around the democratic table. Democracy is self-correcting in a way we as individuals are not. When we are wrong, we do not realise it. Others do, and when they point it out to us, sometimes we find it hard to admit. We take refuge in what we believe. In essence, we are all flawed in this way as individuals. To overcome our limitations and rise above our weaknesses, we need to put our faith in systems, not people. Other people, all people, are as flawed as we are. And we as much as them. It is our ability to forge systemic alliances that ensured our evolutionary survival. That condition remains unchanged, we still face the prospect of communion with others however unsavoury we find some of them to be. Who dares wins, but whatever we are fighting for today will still be worth fighting for tomorrow; if there is something left to fight for tomorrow! When we fight too hard today, we risk losing very hard tomorrow. Upping the stakes cuts both ways.

A final point which has not been touched upon relates to how we control the game. Who are the umpires in charge of enforcing the rules of our political tug-of-war? The judiciary, the armed forces, parliament? By the looks of it, we seem to be entering a new era where we are delegating this to artificial intelligence (AI) systems that regulate us; some might say control us. And who designs the AI? Whose interests does that serve? A new utopia, or another dystopia. The story never really ends. But the point I wish to end on is this, whatever your point of view, bring that to the democratic table. This is how the democratic spirit goes. Everything is up for debate, and genuine democratic politics not only permits that but can also handle it. Politicks, on the other hand, is about what one needs to do to win. It is the art of canvassing and soliciting enough support to get oneself over the threshold to win at the polls. And if you can't win the right way, you might have to go left, as Roald Dahl's Big Friendly Giant would put it. Politicks is where politics turns dirty. So, we need to regulate the former to reap the benefits of the latter. Because there really is no other forum that could serve the purpose of bashing our heads together hard enough to forge conciliatory multilateral projects that are yet to be concocted (de Saint-Laurent, Obradović & Carriere, 2018; Nicholson & Howarth, 2018). Any other forum is subject to the whims of man, without a factory reset option that is afforded by a democratic vote, even if that remains no more than a choice between a fascist and a crook.

Appendix

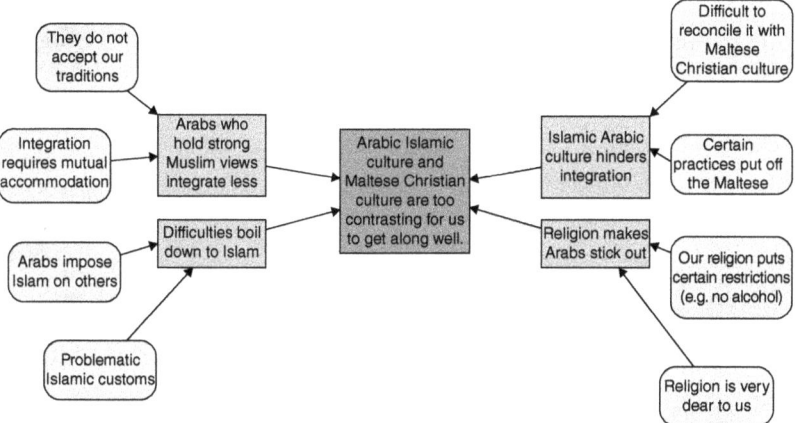

Figure A.1 Argumentation structure: too contrasting

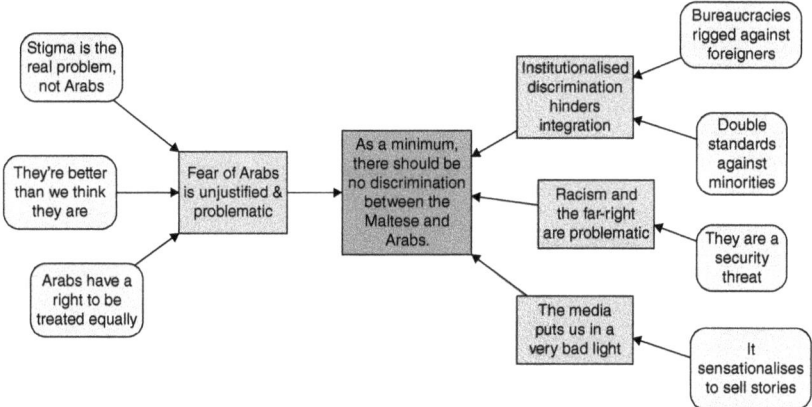

Figure A.2 Argumentation structure: no discrimination

172 *Appendix*

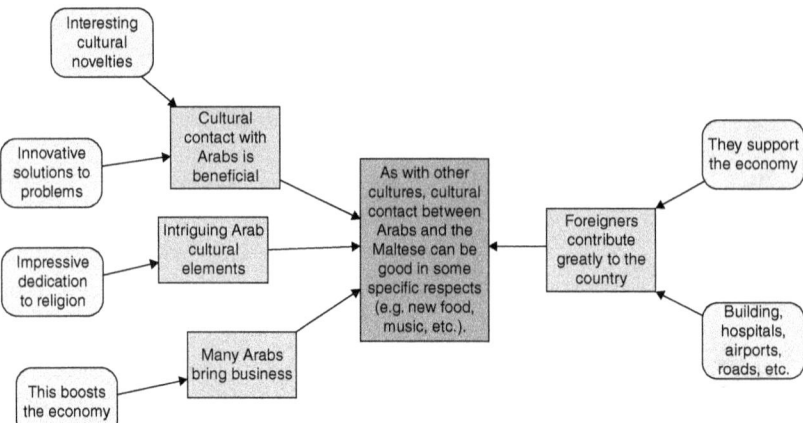

Figure A.3 Argumentation structure: contact can be good

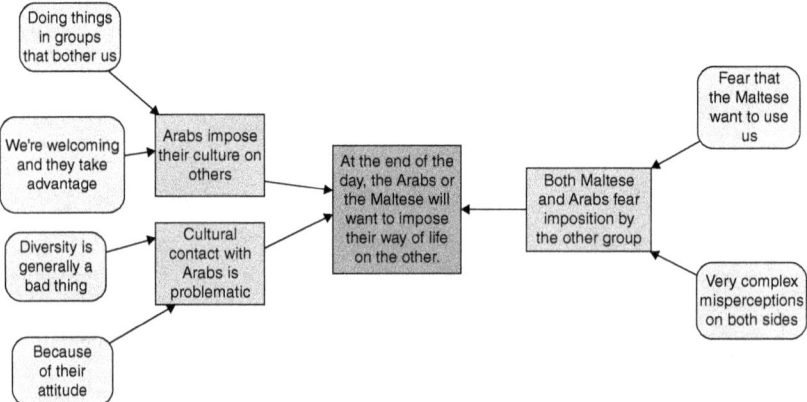

Figure A.4 Argumentation structure: impose ways of life

Appendix

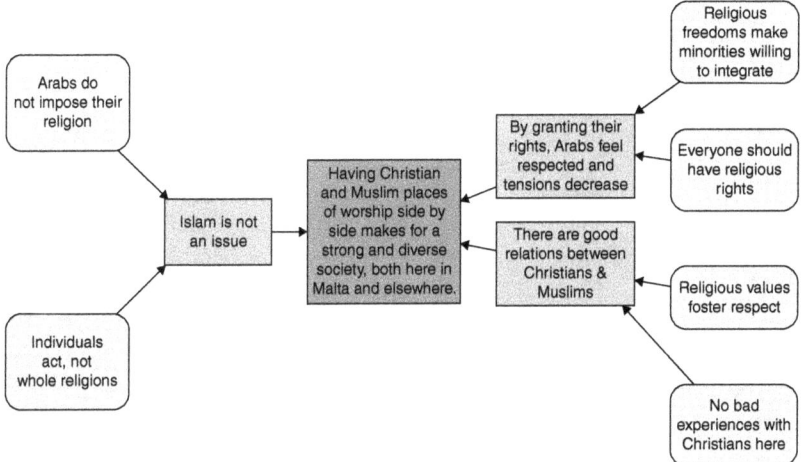

Figure A.5 Argumentation structure: multiple faiths make for a strong society

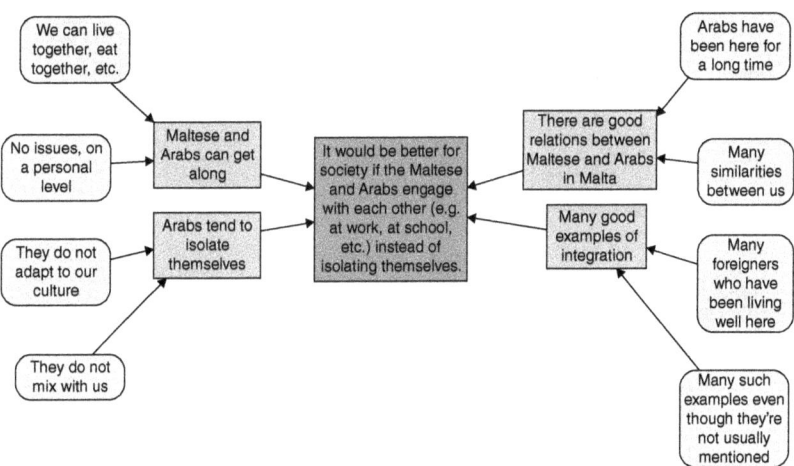

Figure A.6 Argumentation structure: better to engage than isolate

174 *Appendix*

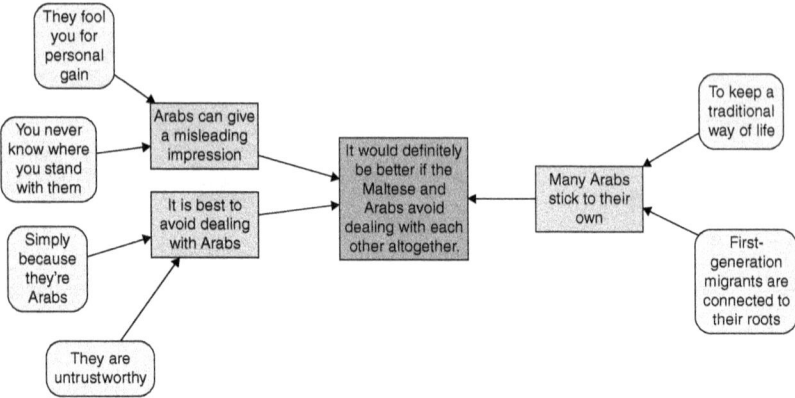

Figure A.7 Argumentation structure: better if Maltese and Arabs avoid each other

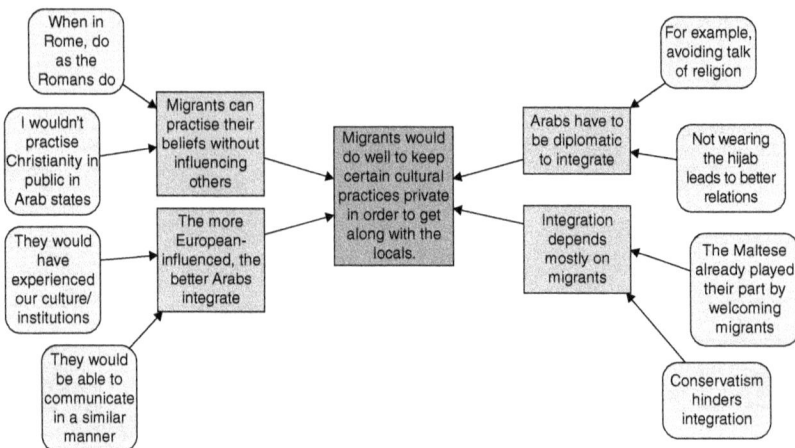

Figure A.8 Argumentation structure: keep cultural practices private to get along

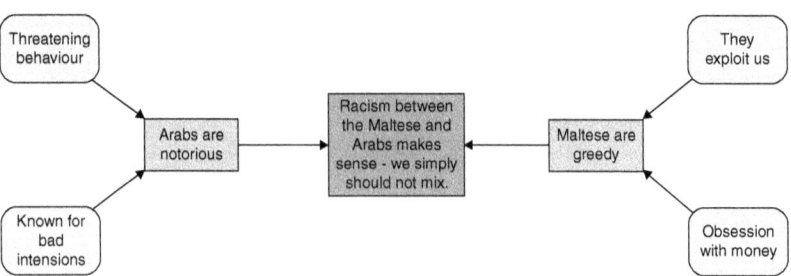

Figure A.9 Argumentation structure: racism makes sense

Appendix

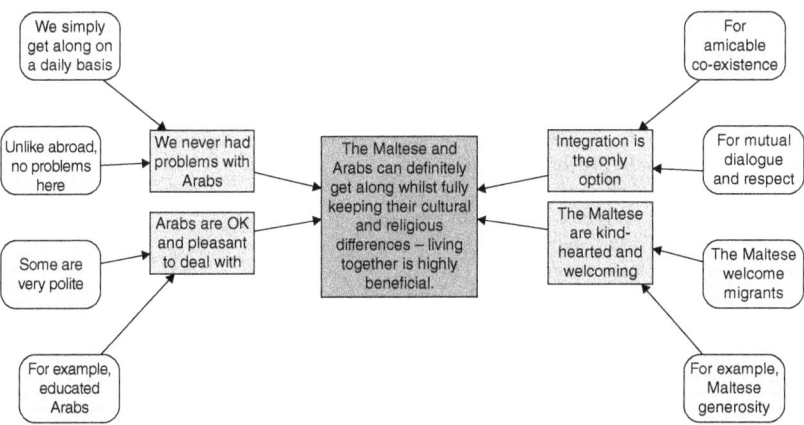

Figure A.10 Argumentation structure: Maltese and Arabs can definitely get along

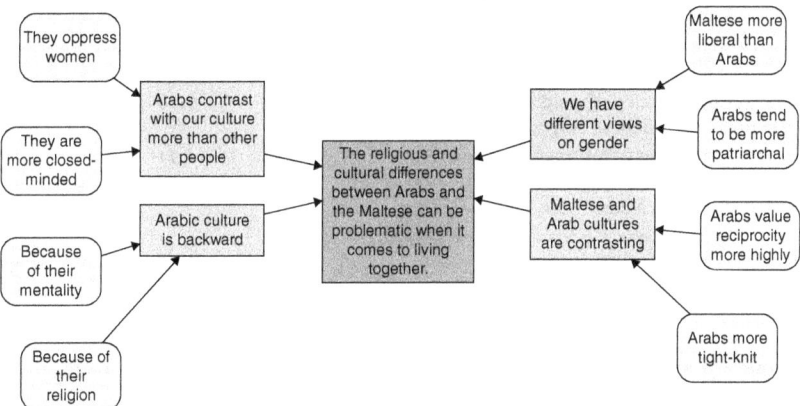

Figure A.11 Argumentation structure: religious and cultural differences can be problematic

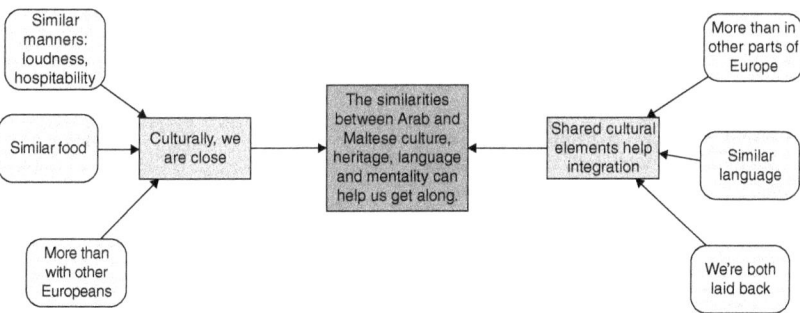

Figure A.12 Argumentation structure: similarities can help us get along

Appendix

Table A1 *Mean responses to ecological integration scale*

OWN VIEWS	Group	Mean	Standard Deviation
Item 1 – Extremely pro-integration The Maltese and Arabs can definitely get along whilst fully keeping their cultural and religious differences – living together is highly beneficial.	Maltese Arab	4.69* 6.15*	1.816 1.343
Item 2 – Highly pro-integration It would be better for society if the Maltese and Arabs engage with each other (e.g. at work, at school, etc.) instead of isolating themselves.	Maltese Arab	5.23* 6.30*	1.751 1.285
Item 3 – Quite pro-integration Having Christian and Muslim places of worship side by side makes for a strong and diverse society, both here in Malta and elsewhere.	Maltese Arab	4.35* 5.70	1.935 1.732
Item 4 – Rather pro-integration The similarities between Arab and Maltese culture, heritage, language and mentality can help us get along.	Maltese Arab	4.24* 5.48*	1.845 1.468
Item 5 – Somewhat pro-integration As a minimum, there should be no discrimination between the Maltese and Arabs.	Maltese Arab	5.35* 6.16*	1.755 1.374
Item 6 – Slightly pro-integration As with other cultures, cultural contact between Arabs and the Maltese can be good in some specific respects (e.g. new food, music, etc.).	Maltese Arab	4.94* 5.76*	1.731 1.362
Item 7 – Slightly anti-integration The religious and cultural differences between Arabs and the Maltese can be problematic when it comes to living together.	Maltese Arab	5.15* 3.09*	1.744 1.830
Item 8 – Somewhat anti-integration Migrants would do well to keep certain cultural practices private in order to get along with the locals.	Maltese Arab	4.76 4.68	1.938 1.863
Item 9 – Rather anti-integration Arabic Islamic culture and Maltese Christian culture are too contrasting for us to get along well.	Maltese Arab	4.24* 2.83*	2.018 1.795
Item 10 – Quite anti-integration At the end of the day, the Arabs or the Maltese will want to impose their way of life on the other.	Maltese Arab	4.74* 3.21*	1.821 1.895
Item 11 – Highly anti-integration It would definitely be better if the Maltese and Arabs avoid dealing with each other altogether.	Maltese Arab	3.29* 1.68*	2.038 1.451
Item 12 – Extremely anti-integration Racism between the Maltese and Arabs makes sense – we simply should not mix.	Maltese Arab	3.12* 1.72*	2.024 1.244

Appendix

Table A1 (cont.)

OWN VIEWS	Group	Mean	Standard Deviation
VIEWS ATTRIBUTED TO OTHER	**Group**	**Mean**	**Standard Deviation**
Item 1 – Extremely pro-integration	Maltese (to Arab)	4.54	1.700
The Maltese and Arabs can definitely get along whilst fully keeping their cultural and religious differences – living together is highly beneficial.	Arab (to Maltese)	4.40	1.752
Item 2 – Highly pro-integration	Maltese (to Arab)	4.82*	1.661
It would be better for society if the Maltese and Arabs engage with each other (e.g. at work, at school, etc.) instead of isolating themselves.	Arab (to Maltese)	4.01*	1.712
Item 3 – Quite pro-integration	Maltese (to Arab)	4.27*	1.879
Having Christian and Muslim places of worship side by side makes for a strong and diverse society, both here in Malta and elsewhere.	Arab (to Maltese)	3.62*	1.767
Item 4 – Rather pro-integration	Maltese (to Arab)	4.33	1.635
The similarities between Arab and Maltese culture, heritage, language and mentality can help us get along.	Arab (to Maltese)	4.20	1.643
Item 5 – Somewhat pro-integration	Maltese (to Arab)	5.49*	1.722
As a minimum, there should be no discrimination between the Maltese and Arabs.	Arab (to Maltese)	3.82*	1.833
Item 6 – Slightly pro-integration	Maltese (to Arab)	4.93	1.509
As with other cultures, cultural contact between Arabs and the Maltese can be good in some specific respects (e.g. new food, music, etc.).	Arab (to Maltese)	4.67	1.536
Item 7 – Slightly anti-integration	Maltese (to Arab)	4.40	1.777
The religious and cultural differences between Arabs and the Maltese can be problematic when it comes to living together.	Arab (to Maltese)	4.11	1.794
Item 8 – Somewhat anti-integration	Maltese (to Arab)	2.97*	1.709
Migrants would do well to keep certain cultural practices private in order to get along with the locals.	Arab (to Maltese)	4.91*	1.676
Item 9 – Rather anti-integration	Maltese (to Arab)	4.18	1.842
Arabic Islamic culture and Maltese Christian culture are too contrasting for us to get along well.	Arab (to Maltese)	3.99	1.800

Table A1 (cont.)

OWN VIEWS	Group	Mean	Standard Deviation
Item 10 – Quite anti-integration	Maltese (to Arab)	4.49*	1.785
At the end of the day, the Arabs or the Maltese will want to impose their way of life on the other.	Arab (to Maltese)	3.85*	1.859
Item 11 – Highly anti-integration	Maltese (to Arab)	2.99	1.732
It would definitely be better if the Maltese and Arabs avoid dealing with each other altogether.	Arab (to Maltese)	3.14	1.706
Item 12 – Extremely anti-integration	Maltese (to Arab)	2.87*	1.667
Racism between the Maltese and Arabs makes sense – we simply should not mix.	Arab (to Maltese)	3.61*	1.811

* $P < 0.05$.

References

Abrams, D. & Hogg, M. A. (1988). Comments on the Motivational Status of Self-esteem in Social Identity and Intergroup Discrimination. *European Journal of Social Psychology*, *18*(4), 317–334.
  (eds.) (1990). *Social Identity Theory: Constructive and Critical Advances*. New York: Springer-Verlag Publishing.
Achen, C. H. & Bartels, L.M. (2016). *Democracy for Realists: Why Elections Do Not Produce Responsive Government*. Princeton, NJ: Princeton University Press.
Adorno, T. W., Frenkel-Brunswik, E., Levinson, D. J. & Sanford, R. N. (1950). *The Authoritarian Personality*. New York: Harper and Row.
Alexander, I. & Moore, M. (2021). Deontological Ethics. In E. N. Zalta (ed.), *The Stanford Encyclopedia of Philosophy* (Winter 2021 ed.). Stanford University. https://plato.stanford/edu/archives/win2021/entries/ethics-deontological.
Altemeyer, B. (1981). *Right-Wing Authoritarianism*. Winnipeg, MB: University of Manitoba Press.
Andreouli, E., Greenland, K. & Figgou, L. (2020). Lay Discourses about Brexit and Prejudice: 'Ideological Creativity' and Its Limits in Brexit Debates. *European Journal of Social Psychology*, *50*, 309–322.
Anduiza, E., Gallego, A. & Muñoz, J. (2013). Turning a Blind Eye: Experimental Evidence of Partisan Bias in Attitudes toward Corruption. *Comparative Political Studies*, *46*(12), 1664–1692.
Asch, S. E. (1952). *Social Psychology*. New York: Prentice-Hall.
Bang, H. P. (2009). 'Yes We Can': Identity Politics and Project Politics for a Late-modern World. *Urban Research & Practice*, *2*(2), 117–137. https:doi.org/10.1080/17535060902979022
Benhabib, S. (2002). *The Claims of Culture: Equality and Diversity in the Global Era*. Princeton, NJ: Princeton University Press.
Berlin, I. (1969). *Four Essays on Liberty*. Oxford: Oxford University Press.
Berry, J. W. (1997). Immigration, Acculturation, and Adaptation. *Applied Psychology*, *46*(1), 5–34. https://doi.org/10.1111/j.1464-0597.1997.tb01087.x
  (2011). Integration and Multiculturalism: Ways towards Social Solidarity. *Papers on Social Representations*, *20*(1), 2.1–2.21.

(ed.). (2017). *Mutual Intercultural Relations*. Cambridge: Cambridge University Press.

Berry, J. W., Lepshokova, Z., MIRIPS Collaboration & Grigoryev, D. (2023). How Shall We All Live Together?: Meta-analytical Review of the Mutual Intercultural Relations in Plural Societies Project. *Applied Psychology: An International Review*. https://doi.org/10.1111/apps.12332 (Member of MIRIPS Collaboration).

Besta, T., Akbas, G., Renström, E. A., Kosakowska-Berezecka, N. & Vazquez, A. (2019). Liking Low-status? Contextual and Individual Differences in Attributional Biases of Low-status Outgroup Members. *Journal of Social and Political Psychology*, *7*(1), 192–212. https://doi.org/10.5964/jspp.v7i1.951

Bourdieu, P. (1986). The Forms of Capital. In J. G. Richardson (ed.), *Handbook of Theory and Research for the Sociology of Education* (pp. 241–248). New York: Greenwood Press.

Brown, R. (1995). *Prejudice: Its Social Psychology*. Oxford: Blackwell Publishing.

Buhagiar, L. J. & Sammut, G. (2020). 'Social Re-presentation for . . .': An Action-oriented Formula for Intergroup Relations Research. *Frontiers in Psychology*, *11*, doi.org/10.3389/fpsyg.2020.00352.

  (2023a). The Minimal Model of Argumentation: Qualitative Data Analysis for Epistemic Speech, Text and Policy. *Journal for the Theory of Social Behaviour*, *53*(4), 535–559. doi: 10.1111/jtsb.12382.

  (2023b). Minority Arguments on Integration: Arabs in the Southern European State of Malta. *Journal of Community and Applied Social Psychology*, *33*(6), 1381–1397. https://doi.org/10.1002/casp.2741.

  (2025). The PASS Method: Ecologically Valid Scaling for Intergroup Relations Research. *Asian Journal of Social Psychology*, *28*, e70001. https://doi.org/10.1111/ajsp.70001

Buhagiar, L. J., Sammut, G., Rochira, A. & Salvatore, S. (2018). There's No Such Thing as a Good Arab: Cultural Essentialism and Its Functions Concerning the Integration of Arabs in Europe. *Culture & Psychology*, *24*(4), 560–576.

Buller, D. J. (2005). Evolutionary Psychology: The Emperor's New Paradigm. *Trends in Cognitive Sciences*, *9*(6), 277–283.

Campbell, D. T. (1965). Ethnocentric and Other Altruistic Motives. In D. Levine (ed.), *Nebraska Symposium on Motivation* (Vol. 13, pp. 283–311). Lincoln: University of Nebraska Press.

Carlson, E. (2015). Ethnic Voting and Accountability in Africa: A Choice Experiment in Uganda. *World Politics*, *67*(2), 353–385.

Castro, P., Seixas, E., Neca, P. and Bettencourt, L. (2018). Successfully Contesting the Policy Sphere: Examining through the Press a Case of Local Protests Changing New Ecological Laws. *Political Psychology*, *39*(1), 107–123. https://doi.org/10.1111/pops.12388

Chryssides, A., Dashtipour, P., Keshet, S., Righi, C., Sammut, G. & Sartawi, M. (2009). We Don't Share! The Social Representation Approach, Enactivism and the Fundamental Incompatibilities between the Two. *Culture & Psychology*, *15*(1), 83–95.

Cialdini, R. B. (2007). *Influence: The Psychology of Persuasion*. New York: Harper Collins.
Clark, K. & Clark, M. (1939). The Development of Consciousness of Self and the Emergence of Racial Identification in Negro Preschool Children. *Journal of Social Psychology*, *10*(4), 591–599. https:doi.org/10.1080/00224545.1939.9713394.
Cohen, D. & Nisbett, R. E. (1994). Self-protection and the Culture of Honor: Explaining Southern Violence. *Personality and Social Psychology Bulletin*, *20*(5), 551–567.
  (1997). Field Experiments Examining the Culture of Honor: The Role of Institutions in Perpetuating Norms about Violence. *Personality and Social Psychology Bulletin*, *23*(11), 1188–1199.
Connelly, B. S., Ones, D. S. & Chernyshenko, O. S. (2014). Introducing the Special Section on Openness to Experience: Review of Openness Taxonomies, Measurement, and Nomological Net. *Journal of Personality Assessment*, *96*(1), 1–16. https://doi.org/10.1080/00223891.2013.830620.
Cosmides, L. & Tooby, J. (1989). Evolutionary Psychology and the Generation of Culture, Part II: Case Study: A Computational Theory of Social Exchange. *Ethology and Sociobiology*, *10*, 51–97.
Costa, P. T., Jr. & McCrae, R. R. (1992). *NEO Personality Inventory: Revised (NEO-PI-R) and NEO Five-Factor Inventory (NEO-FFI) Professional Manual*. Odessa, FL: Psychological Assessment Resources.
Crocker, J. & Luhtanen, R. (1990). Collective Self-esteem and Ingroup Bias. *Journal of Personality and Social Psychology*, *58*(1), 60–67. https://psycnet.apa.org/doi/10.1037/0022-3514.58.1.60
Crocker, J. & Major, B. (1989). Social Stigma and Self-esteem: The Self-protective Properties of Stigma. *Psychological Review*, *96*(4), 608–630. https://psycnet.apa.org/doi/10.1037/0033-295X.96.4.608
Crockett, M. J., Kim, J. S. & Soon Shin, Y. (2024). Intuitive Theories and the Cultural Evolution of Morality. *Current Directions in Psychological Science*, *33*(4), 211–219.
Darwin, C. (1871). *The Descent of Man, and Selection in Relation to Sex* (Vol. 1). London: John Murray.
Drasgow, F., Chernyshenko, O. S., & Stark, S. (2010). 75 Years after Likert: Thurstone Was Right! *Industrial and Organizational Psychology: Perspectives on Science and Practice*, *3*(4), 465–476. https://doi.org/10.1111/j.1754-9434.2010.01273.x
Dweck, C. S. & Yeager, D. S. (2019). Mindsets: A View from Two Eras. *Perspectives on Psychological Science*, *14*(3), 481–496. https://doi.org/10.1177/1745691618804166
Eisenberger, N. I., Lieberman, M. D. & Williams, K. D. (2003). Does Rejection Hurt? An fMRI Study of Social Exclusion. *Science*, *302*(5643), 290–292.
Ellemers, N. (1993). The Influence of Socio-structural Variables on Identity Management Strategies. *European Review of Social Psychology*, *4*(1), 27–57.

EU Observer. (2020). Commissioner: No One Will Like New EU Migration Pact. *EU Observer.* https://euobserver.com/migration/149475.
European Commission. (2020). Communication from the Commission on a New Pact on Migration and Asylum. European Commission. Document 52020DC0609.
European Union. (2020). *Standard Eurobarometer 93: Summer 2020 Public Opinion in the European Union, First Results.* Brussels: European Commission. doi: 10.2775/460239.
Fanon, F. (1965). *The Wretched of the Earth.* New York: Grove.
Fiske, S. T. & Taylor, S. E. (2008). *Social Cognition: From Brains to Culture.* Boston, MA: McGraw-Hill Higher Education.
Fodor, E. M., Wick, D. P., Harsten, K. M., & Preve, R. M. (2007). Right-Wing Authoritarianism in Relation to Proposed Judicial Action, Electromyographic Response, and Affective Attitudes towards a Schizophrenic Mother. *Journal of Applied Social Psychology, 38*(1), 215–233. doi: 10.1111/j.1559-1816.2008.00303.x
Futter, A. (2015). *The Politics of Nuclear Weapons,* 2nd ed. London: Sage.
Gabriel, S. & Schneider, V. (2024). The Need for Social Embeddedness: Human Belonging Goes beyond Dyadic Bonds. *Current Directions in Psychological Science, 33*(4), 247–253.
Gambetta, D. (1993). *The Sicilian Mafia: The Business of Private Protection.* Cambridge, MA: Harvard University Press.
Giddens, A. (1991). *Modernity and Self-identity: Self and Society in the Late Modern Age.* Cambridge: Polity.
Gigerenzer, G., Todd, P. M. & The ABC Research Group. (1999). *Simple Heuristics That Make Us Smart.* Oxford: Oxford University Press.
Gilroy, P. (2005). *Postcolonial Melancholia.* New York: Columbia University Press.
Gittell, R. & Vidal, A. (1998). *Community Organizing: Building Social Capital as a Development Strategy.* California: Sage.
Gladwell, M. (2000). *The Tipping Point.* New York: Little Brown.
Goffman, E. (1963/2009). *Stigma: Notes on the Management of Spoiled Identity.* New York: Simon and Schuster.
Grossman, I. & Eibach, R. E. (2024). Metajudgment: Metatheories and Beliefs about Good Judgment across Societies. *Current Directions in Psychological Science, 33*(4), 261–269.
Habermas, J. (1991). *The Structural Transformation of the Public Sphere: An Inquiry into a Category of Bourgeois Society.* Cambridge, MA: MIT Press.
Haidt, J. (2012). *The Righteous Mind: Why Good People Are Divided by Politics and Religion.* New York: Pantheon Books.
Hardin, G. (1968). The Tragedy of the Commons. *Science, 162*(3859), 1243–1248.
Harré, R. & Sammut, G. (2013). What Lies between? In G. Sammut, P. Daanen & F. M. Moghaddam (eds.), *Understanding the Self and Others: Explorations in Intersubjectivity and Interobjectivity* (pp. 15–30). London: Routledge.

Harré, R. & Secord, P. F. (1972). *The Explanation of Social Behavior*. Oxford: Basil Blackwell.
Harris, E., Pärnamets, P., Sternisko, A., Robertson, C. & Van Bavel, J. J. (2022). The Psychology and Neuroscience of Partisanship. In D. Osborne & C. G. Sibley (eds.), *The Cambridge Handbook of Political Psychology* (pp. 50–67). Cambridge: Cambridge University Press.
Haslam, S. A. & Reicher, S. D. (2012). When Prisoners Take over the Prison: A Social Psychology of Resistance. *Personality and Social Psychology Review*, *16*(2), 154–179.
Hill, J. & Wilson, T. (2003). Identity Politics and the Politics of Identities. *Identities*, *10*(1), 1–8. https:doi.org/10.1080/10702890304336
Hirschfeld, L. A. (1998). Natural Assumptions: Race, Essence and Taxonomies of Human Kinds. *Social Research*, *65*(2), 331–349.
Hobbes, T. (1651). *Leviathan*. Oxford: Oxford University Press.
Hochschild, A. R. (2016). *Strangers in Their Own Land: Anger and Mourning on the American Right*. New York: New Press.
Hofstede, G. (1991). *Cultures and Organizations: Software of the Mind*. London: McGraw-Hill.
Hogg, M. A. (2016). Social Identity Theory. In S. McKeown, R. Haji & N. Ferguson (eds.), *Understanding Peace and Conflict through Social Identity Theory* (pp. 3–17). Peace Psychology Book Series. Cham, Switzerland: Springer.
Hogg, M. A. & Abrams, D. (1988). *Social Identifications: A Social Psychology of Intergroup Relations and Group Processes*. London: Routledge.
Howarth, C. (2002). Identity in Whose Eyes?: The Role of Representations in Identity Construction. *Journal for the Theory of Social Behaviour*, *32*(2), 145–162. https://doi./10.1111/1468-5914.00181
Howarth, C., Wagner, W., Magnusson, N. & Sammut, G. (2014). 'It's Only Other People Who Make Me Feel Black': Acculturation, Identity and Agency in a Multicultural Community. *Political Psychology*, *35*(1), 81–95.
Internal Displacement Monitoring Centre. (2021). *Global Report on Internal Displacement 2021*. Internal Displacement Monitoring Centre. https://internal-displacement.org/global-report/grid2021.
James, O. (2007). *Affluenza: How to Be Successful and Stay Sane*. London: Vermilion.
Joffe, H. (1995). Social Representations of AIDS: Towards Encompassing Issues of Power. *Papers on Social Representations*, *4*(1), 29–40.
Jost, J. T., Glaser, J., Kruglanski, A. W. & Sulloway, F. J. (2003). Political Conservatism as Motivated Social Cognition. *Psychological Bulletin*, *129*(3), 339–375. https://doi.org/10.1037/0033-2909.129.3.339.
Kaufmann, E. (2019). *Whiteshift: Population, Immigration and the Future of White Majorities*. London: Penguin.
Kilmann, R. H. (2023). *Mastering the Thomas-Kilman Conflict Mode Instrument: TKI*. Newport Coast, CA: Kilmann Diagnostics.
Klandermans, B. (1997). *The Social Psychology of Protest*. Oxford: Blackwell.

(2003). Collective Political Action. In D. O. Sears, L. Huddy & R. Jervis (eds.), *Oxford Handbook of Political Psychology* (pp. 670–709). Oxford: Oxford University Press.
Klein, E. (2020). *Why We're Polarized.* New York: Avid Reader Press/Simon & Schuster.
Kohlberg, L. (1981). *Essays on Moral Development, Vol 1. I: The Philosophy of Moral Development.* San Francisco, CA: Harper & Row.
Koltko-Rivera, M. E. (2004). The Psychology of Worldviews. *Review of General Psychology, 8,* 3–58. https://doi.org/10.1037/1089-2680.8.1.3
Krech, D. (1949). Notes towards a Psychological Theory. *Journal of Personality, 18,* 66–87.
Kruglanski, A. W. (1989). *Lay Epistemics and Human Knowledge: Cognitive and Motivational Bases.* New York: Plenum.
(2004). *The Psychology of Closed Mindedness.* New York: Psychology Press.
Kuhn, M. H. (1960). Self-attitudes by Age, Sex and Professional Training. *Sociological Quarterly, 1,* 39–56.
Kuhn, M. H. & McPartland, T. S. (1954). An Empirical Investigation of Self-attitudes. *American Sociological Review, 19*(1), 68–76.
Latour, B. (1996). On Interobjectivity. *Mind, Culture, and Activity, 3*(4), 228–245. https://doi.org/10.1207/s15327884mca0304_2
Lelkes, Y. & Westwood, S. J. (2017). The Limits of Partisan Prejudice. *The Journal of Politics, 79*(2), 485–501.
Leung, K. & Bond, M. H. (eds.) (2009). *Psychological Aspects of Social Axioms: Understanding Global Belief Systems.* New York: Springer-Verlag.
Lippmann, W. (1922). *Public Opinion.* New York: Harcourt Brace.
Liu, J. H. & Hilton, D. J. (2005). How the Past Weighs on the Present: Social Representations of History and Their Role in Identity Politics. *British Journal of Social Psychology, 44*(4), 537–556. https://doi.org/10.1348/014466605X27162
Locke, J. (1690). *An Essay Concerning Human Understanding.* London: Thomas Basset.
Long, K. & Spears, R. (1997). The Self-esteem Hypothesis Revisited: Differentiation and the Disaffected. In R. Spears, P. J. Oakes, N. Ellemers & S. A. Haslam (eds.), *The Social Psychology of Stereotyping and Group Life* (pp. 296–317). Oxford: Blackwell.
Mahendran, K. (2013). 'A Two-Way Process of Accommodation': Public Perceptions of Integration along the Migration–Mobility Continuum. In U. Korkut, G. Bucken-Knapp, A. McGarry, J. Hinnfors & H. Drake (eds.), *The Discourses and Politics of Migration in Europe. Europe in Transition: The NYU European Studies Series.* New York: Palgrave Macmillan. https://doi.org/10.1057/9781137310903_7
(2017). Public Narratives on Human Mobility: Countering Technocratic and Humanitarian Refugee Narratives with a 'One-World' Solidarity Narrative. *Journal of Community Applied Social Psychology, 27,* 147–157. https://doi.org/10.1002/casp.2304

Marinaci, T., Venuleo, C., Infurna, M. R., & Di Maria, F. (2025). What Mafia do We Have in Mind? An Exploratory Study on Mafia Representation among Ordinary People. *Culture & Psychology*. https://doi.org/10.1177/1354067X251315738

Marques, J. M., Yzerbyt, V. Y. & Leyens, J. P. (1988). The 'Black Sheep Effect': Extremity of Judgments towards Ingroup Members as a Function of Group Identification. *European Journal of Social Psychology*, *18*(1), 1–16.

Martel, Y. (2014). *The Life of Pi*. Royal Leamington Spa: Mary Glasgow Magazines.

Marx, K. (1977). *A Contribution to the Critique of Political Economy*. Moscow: Progress Publishers.

McConnell, C., Margalit, Y., Malhotra, N. & Levendusky, M. (2018). The Economic Consequences of Partisanship in a Polarized Era. *American Journal of Political Science*, *62*(1), 5–18.

Meeus, W. H. J., & Raaijmakers, Q. A. W. (1995). Obedience in modern society: The Utrecht studies. *Journal of Social Issues*, *51*(3), 155–175. https://doi.org/10.1111/j.1540-4560.1995.tb01339.x

Mercier, H. & Sperber, D. (2011) Why Do Humans Reason? Arguments for an Argumentative Theory. *Behavioral and Brain Sciences*, *34*(2), 57–74.

Mifsud, R. & Sammut, G. (2023). Worldviews and the Role of Social Values that Underlie Them. *PLoS ONE*, *18*(7), e0288451. https://doi.org/10.1371/jounral.pone.0288451.

Milgram, S. & Toch, H. (1969). Collective Behavior: Crowds and Social Movements. In G. Lindzey, D. Gilbert & S. T. Fiske (eds.), *The Handbook of Social Psychology* (Vol. 4, pp. 507–610). Reading, MA: Addison Wesley.

Mitchell, A. (2021). *Beyond a Fringe: Tales from a Reformed Establishment Lackey*. London: Biteback Publishing.

Moghaddam, F. M. (2008). *Multiculturalism and Intergroup Relations: Psychological Implications for Democracy in Global Context*. Washington, DC: American Psychological Association.

  (2013). *The Psychology of Dictatorship*. Washington, DC: American Psychological Association.

  (2016). *The Psychology of Democracy*. Washington, DC: American Psychological Association.

  (2020). Omniculturalism, Diversity, and Human Commonalities [Editorial]. *Peace and Conflict: Journal of Peace Psychology*, *26*(2), 107–109.

Moscovici, S. (1961/1976). *La Psychanalyse, son Imgae et son Public* (2nd ed.). Paris: Presses Universitaires de France.

National Statistics Office. (2023). *Census of Population and Housing 2021: Final Report*. Valletta, Malta: National Statistics Office.

Nesse, R. M. (2019). The Smoke Detector Principle: Signal Detection and Optimal Defense Regulation. *Evolution, Medicine, and Public Health*, *1*, 1. doi.org/10.1093/emph/eoy034.

Nicholson, C. (2019). Working Together, Living Together: Jewish and Palestinian Citizens of Israel Crossing Imagined Group Boundaries. *Journal of Social and Political Psychology*, *7*(2), 959–977.

Nicholson, C. & Howarth, C. (2018). Imagining Collective Identities Beyond Intergroup Conflict. In C. de Saint-Laurent, S. Obradović & K. Carriere (eds.). *Imagining Collective Futures* (pp. 173–196). Palgrave Studies in Creativity and Culture. Cham, Switzerland: Palgrave Macmillan.

Nisbett, R. E. & Cohen, D. (1996). *Culture of Honor: The Psychology of Violence in the South*. Boulder, CO: Westview Press.

Oakes, P. J. (1987). The Salience of Social Categories. In J. C. Turner, M. A. Hogg, P. J. Oakes, S. D. Reicher & M. S. Wetherell (eds.), *Rediscovering the Social Group: A Self-categorization Theory* (pp. 117–141). Oxford: Basil Blackwell.

Obradović, S. (2019). Who Are We and Where Are We Going: From Past Myths to Present Politics. *Integrative Psychological and Behavioral Science*, 53, 57–75. https://doi.org/10.1007/s12124-017-9410-x

Obradović, S., Albayrak-Aydemir, N., Amer, A., Boza, M., & Kışlıoğlu, R. (2024). Power, Meta-perceptions, and Belonging: How Positive Recognition Matters for Group Identification, Identity Compatibility, and Intergroup Attitudes. *Political Psychology*, 1–21. https://doi.org/10.1111/pops.13069

Obradović, S. & Howarth, C. (2016). Everyday Reconciliation. In C. Howarth & E. Andreouli (eds.), *The Social Psychology of Everyday Politics* (pp. 131–145). London: Routledge.

Obradović, S., Power, S. A. & Sheehy-Skeffington, J. (2020). Understanding the Psychological Appeal of Populism. *Current Opinion in Psychology*, 35, 125–131. https://doi.org/10.1016/j.copsyc.2020.06.009.

Paulhus, D. L. (2014). Toward a Taxonomy of Dark Personalities. *Current Directions in Psychological Science*, 23(6), 421–426. https://doi.org/10.1177/0963721414547737

Perner, J., Leekam, S. R. & Wimmer, H. (1987). Three-Year-Olds' Difficulty with False Belief: The Case for a Conceptual Deficit. *British Journal of Developmental Psychology*, 5(2), 125–137. https://doi.org/10.1111/j.2044-835X.1987.tb01048.x

Pew Research Center (2022). Key Facts about US Immigration Policies and Biden's Proposed Changes. www.pewresearch.org/short-reads/2022/01/11/key-facts-about-u-s-immigration-policies-and-bidens-proposed-changes/

Power, S. A., Zittoun, T., Akkerman, S., Wagoner, B., Cabra, M., Cornish, F., Hawlina, H., Heasman, B., Mahendran, K., Psaltis, C., Rajala, A., Veale, A. & Gillespie, A. (2023). Social Psychology of and for World-Making. *Personality and Social Psychology Review*, 27(4), 378–392. https://doi.org/10.1177/10888683221145756

Pratto, F., Sidanius, J., Stallworth, L. M. & Malle, B. F. (1994). Social Dominance Orientation: A Personality Variable Predicting Social and Political Attitudes. *Journal of Personality and Social Psychology*, 67(4), 741–763.

Rawls, J. (1971). *A Theory of Justice*. Cambridge, MA: Harvard University Press.

Rentsch, J. R. & Heffner, T. S. (1994). Assessing Self-concept: Analysis of Gordon's Coding Scheme using 'Who am I?' Responses. *Journal of Social Behavior and Personality*, 9(2), 283–300.

Rios, K. & Ybarra, O. (2009). Symbolic Threat and Social Dominance among Liberals and Conservatives: SDO Reflects Conformity to Political Values. *European Journal of Social Psychology*, *39*(6), 1039–1052.

Roberts, J. S., Laughlin, J. E., & Wedell, D. H. (1999). Validity Issues in the Likert and Thurstone Approaches to Attitude Measurement. *Educational and Psychological Measurement*, *59*(2), 211–233. https://doi.org/10.1177/00131649921969811

Rokeach, M. (1951a). A Method for Studying Individual Differences in 'Narrow-Mindedness'. *Journal of Personality*, *20*, 219–233.

(1951b). 'Narrow-Mindedness' and Personality. *Journal of Personality*, *20*, 234–251.

Ross, L. & Ward, A. (1996). Naive Realism in Everyday Life: Implications for Social Conflict and Misunderstanding. In E. S. Reed, E. Turiel, & T. Brown (eds.), *Values and Knowledge* (pp. 103–135). London: Psychology Press.

Rousseau, J.-J. (1762/2004). *The Social Contract*, trans. M. Cranston London: Penguin Books.

Rubin, M. & Hewstone, M. (1998). Social Identity Theory's Self-esteem Hypothesis: A Review and Some Suggestions for Clarification. *Personality and Social Psychology Review*, *2*(1), 40–62.

Runciman, D. (2018). *How Democracy Ends*. London: Profile Books.

de Saint-Laurent, C., Obradović, S. & Carriere, K. R. (eds.) (2018). *Imagining Collective Futures: Perspectives from Social, Cultural and Political Psychology*. Cham, Switzerland: Palgrave Macmillan.

Salvatore, S., Fini, V., Mannarini, T., Veltri, G. A., Avdi, E., Battaglia, F., et al. (2018). Correction: Symbolic Universes between Present and Future of Europe. First Results of the Map of European Societies' Cultural Milieu. *PLoS ONE*, *13*(6): e0200223. https://doi.org/10.1371/journal.pone.0200223

Sammut, G. (2010). Points of View and the Reconciliation of Identity Oppositions: Examples from the Maltese in Britain. *Papers on Social Representations*, *19*, 9.1–9.22.

(2011). Civic Solidarity: The Negotiation of Identities in Modern Societies. *Papers on Social Representations*, *20*(1), 4.1–4.24.

(2012). The Immigrants' Point of View: Acculturation, Social Judgment, and the Relative Propensity to Take the Perspective of the Other. *Culture and Psychology*, *18*(2), 184–197. https://doi.org/10.1177/1354067X11434837

(2015). Attitudes, Social Representations and Points of View. In G. Sammut, E. Andreouli, G. Gaskell & J. Valisner (eds.), *The Cambridge Handbook of Social Representations* (pp. 96–112). Cambridge: Cambridge University Press.

(2016). Cognition sociale situationelle: l'architecture imbriquée des représentations sociales, des attitudes et des points de vue. In G. Lo Monaco, S. Delouvée & P. Rateau (eds.), *Les representations sociales: Théories, methods et applications* (pp. 473–486). Bruxelles: De Boeck.

(2018). Alternating Dominance: Social Categorization, Group Formation and the Problem of Borders. In B. Wagoner, I. Bresco de Luna & V. Glaveanu (eds.), *The Road to Actualized Democracy: A psychological exploration* (pp. 129–146). Charlotte, NC: Information Age.

(2019). Mentalities and Mind-sets: The Skeleton of Relative Stability in Psychology's Closet. *Europe's Journal of Psychology, 15*(3), 421–430.

Sammut, G. & Bauer, M. W. (2021). *The Psychology of Social Influence: Modes and Modalities of Shifting Common Sense.* Cambridge: Cambridge University Press.

Sammut, G., Bezzina, F. & Sartawi, M. (2015). The Spiral of Conflict: Naïve Realism and the Black Sheep Effect in Attributions of Knowledge and Ignorance. *Peace and Conflict: Journal of Peace Psychology, 21*(2), 289–294.

Sammut, G., Buhagiar, L. J., Mifsud, R., DeGiovanni, K. & Brockdorff, N. (2022). Attitude Polarisation and Closed-mindedness: The Immigration Issue in Malta 2010–2020. In F. M. Moghaddam & M. Hendricks (eds.), *Contemporary Immigration: Psychological Perspectives to Address Challenges and Inform Solutions* (pp. 123–141). Washington, DC: American Psychological Association.

Sammut, G., Daanen, P. & Moghaddam, F. M. (eds.). (2013). *Understanding the Self and Others: Explorations in Intersubjectivity and Interobjectivity.* London: Routledge

Sammut, G., Daanen, P. & Sartawi, M. (2010). Interobjectivity: Representations and Artefacts in Cultural Psychology. *Culture & Psychology, 16*(4), 451–463.

Sammut, G. & Gaskell, G. (2010). Points of View, Social Positioning and Intercultural Relations. *Journal for the Theory of Social Behaviour, 40*(1), 47–64.

Sammut, G. & Howarth, C. (2014). Social Representations. In T. Teo (ed.), *Encyclopedia of Critical Psychology* (pp. 1799–1802). New York: Springer.

Sammut, G., Jovchelovitch, S., Buhagiar, L. J., Veltri, G. A., Redd, R. & Salvatore, S. (2018). Arabs in Europe: Arguments for and against Integration. *Peace and Conflict: Journal of Peace Psychology, 24*(4), 398–406.

Sammut, G. & Lauri, M. A. (2017). Intercultural Relations in Malta. In J. W. Berry (ed.), *Mutual Intercultural Relations* (pp. 231–248). Cambridge: Cambridge University Press.

Sammut, G., Mifsud, R. & Brockdorff, N. (2021a). Introspective Projection: Prototypical Representations of Policing in the Service of Rule of Law. *Integrative Psychological and Behavioral Science.* https://doi.org/10.1007/s12124-021-09632-w.

(2021b). *Societal Debates,* Vol. III. Msida, Malta: University of Malta. doi: 10.13140/RG.2.2.12228.96646.

(2022). The Role of Worldviews in Predicting Support for Recreational Cannabis. *Frontiers in Psychology.* https://doi.org/10.3389/fpsyg.2022.880537

Sammut, G. & Sartawi, M. (2012). Perspective-taking and the Attribution of Ignorance. *Journal for the Theory of Social Behavior, 42*(2), 181–200.

Sammut, G., Sartawi, M., Bauer, M. W. & Mifsud, R. (2024). Worldviews, Attitudes to Science and Science Policy in Kuwait: The Engagement and Mobilisation Effects. *Research & Politics, 11*(4). https://doi.org/10.1177/20531680241297669

Sammut, G., Tsirogianni, S. & Moghaddam, F. M. (2013). Interobjective Social Values. In G. Sammut, P. Daanen & F. M. Moghaddam (eds.), *Understanding the Self and Others: Explorations in Intersubjectivity and Interobjectivity* (pp. 161–174). London: Routledge.
Sammut, G., Tsirogianni, S. & Wagoner, B. (2012). Representations from the Past: Social Relations and the Devolution of Social Representations. *Integrative Psychological and Behavioral Science, 46*(4), 493–511.
de Saussure, F. (1915/1959). *Course in General Linguistics*. Glasgow: William Collins.
Schwartz, S. H. (1992). Universals in the Content and Structure of Values: Theoretical Advances and Empirical Tests in 20 Countries. *Advances in Experimental Social Psychology, 25*, 1–65. https://doi.org/10.1016/S0065-2601(08)60281-6
Seabright, P., Stieglitz, J. & Van der Straeten, K. (2021). Evaluating Social Contract Theory in Light of Evolutionary Social Science. *Evolutionary Human Sciences, 3*, e20. doi: 10.1017/ehs.2021.4
Shafik, M. (2022). *What We Owe Each Other: A New Social Contract*. London: Bodley Head.
Sidanius, J. & Pratto, F. (1999). *Social Dominance: An Intergroup Theory of Social Hierarchy and Oppression*. New York: Cambridge University Press.
  (2003). Social Dominance Theory and the Dynamics of Inequality: A Reply to Schmitt, Branscombe, & Kappen and Wilson & Liu. *British Journal of Social Psychology, 42*(2), 207–213.
Simon, H. A. (1956). Rational Choice and the Structure of the Environment. *Psychological Review, 63*(2), 129–138.
Stephan, W. G. & Renfro, C. L. (2002). The Role of Threat in Intergroup Relations. In D. M. Mackie & E. R. Smith (eds.), *From Prejudice to Intergroup Emotions: Differentiated Reactions to Social Groups* (pp. 191–207). New York: Psychology Press.
Stephan, W. G. & Stephan, C. W. (2000). An Integrated Threat Theory of Prejudice. In S. Oskamp (ed.), *Reducing Prejudice and Discrimination* (pp. 23–45). Mahwah, NJ: Lawrence Erlbaum Associates.
Stroebe, W. & Frey, B. S. (1982). Self-interest and Collective Action: The Economics and Psychology of Public Goods. *British Journal of Social Psychology, 21*, 121–137.
Sunstein, C. R. (2016). *The Ethics of Influence: Government in the Age of Behavioral Science*. New York: Cambridge University Press.
Tajfel, H. (1982). Social Psychology of Intergroup Relations. *Annual Review of Psychology, 33*(1), 1–39.
Tajfel, H., Billig, M. G., Bundy, R. P. & Flament, C. (1971). Social Categorization and Intergroup Behaviour. *European Journal of Social Psychology, 1*(2), 149–178.
Tajfel, H. & Turner, J. C. (1979). An Integrative Theory of Intergroup Conflict. In M.J. Hatch & M. Schultz (Eds.), *Organizational Identity: A Reader* (pp. 56-65). Oxford, UK: Oxford University Press.

(2004). The Social Identity Theory of Intergroup Behavior. In J. T. Jost & J. Sidanius (eds.), *Political Psychology* (pp. 276–293). London: Psychology Press.

Taylor, D. M. & McKirnan, D. J. (1984). Theoretical Contributions: A Five-stage Model of Intergroup Relations. *British Journal of Social Psychology*, 23(4), 291–300.

Thaler, R. H. & Sunstein, C. R. (2021). *Nudge: The Final Edition*. New Haven, CT: Yale University Press.

Thomas, E. F., Louis, W. R. & McGarty, C. (2020). Collective Action for Social Change: Individual, Group, and Contextual Factors Shaping Collective Action and Its Outcomes. In D. Osborne & C. G. Sibley (eds.), *The Cambridge Handbook of Political Psychology* (pp. 492–507). Cambridge: Cambridge University Press.

Thomas, W. I. & Znaniecki, F. (1918–1920). *The Polish Peasant in Europe and America*, 5 volumes. Boston: Gorham Press.

Tomasello, M. (2014). *A Natural History of Human Thinking*. Cambridge, MA: Harvard University Press.

(2022). *The Evolution of Agency: Behavioral Organization from Lizards to Humans*. Cambridge, MA: MIT Press.

Tomasello, M. & Carpenter, M. (2007). Shared Intentionality. *Developmental Science*, 10(1), 121–125. https://doi.org/10.1111/j.1467-7687.2007.00573.x

Tooby, J. & DeVore, I. (1987). The Reconstruction of Hominid Behavioral Evolution through Strategic Modeling. In W. G. Kinzey (ed.), *The Evolution of Human Behavior: Primate Models* (pp. 183–237). Albany, NY: SUNY Press.

Topaloglu, S. (2019). Smarties Task, The. In: T. Shackelford & V. Weekes-Shackelford (eds.), *Encyclopedia of Evolutionary Psychological Science*. Cham: Springer. https://doi.org/10.1007/978-3-319-16999-6_3121-1

Tsirogianni, S., Kostas, M. & Sammut, G. (2021). Social Values and Good Living. In F. Maggino (ed.), *Encyclopedia of Quality of Life and Well-Being Research*. Cham: Springer. https://doi.org/10.1007/978-3-319-69909-7_3666-2

Turner, J. C. (2010). Social Categorization and the Self-concept: A Social Cognitive Theory of Group Behavior. In T. Postmes & N. R. Branscombe (eds.), *Rediscovering Social Identity* (pp. 243–272). London: Psychology Press.

Turner, J. C., Hogg, M. A., Oakes, P. J., Reicher, S. D. & Wetherell, M. S. (1987). *Rediscovering the Social Group: A Self-categorization Theory*. Oxford: Basil Blackwell.

Tyler, T. R. & Smith, H. J. (1998). Social Justice and Social Movements. In D. T. Gilbert, S. T. Fiske & G. Lindzey (eds.), *The Handbook of Social Psychology* (pp. 595–629). Boston, MA: McGraw-Hill.

Van Hear, N., Bakewell, O. & Long, K. (2018). Push–Pull Plus: Reconsidering the Drivers of Migration. *Journal of Ethnic and Migration Studies*, 44(6), 927–944.

Wagner, W., Holz, P. & Kashima, Y. (2009). Construction and Deconstruction of Essence in Representing Social Groups: Identity Projects, Stereotyping, and Racism. *Journal for the Theory of Social Behaviour, 39*(3), 363–383.

Westra, E. & Carruthers, P. (2017). Pragmatic Development Explains the Theory-of-Mind Scale. *Cognition, 158*, 165–176.

Whiten, A. & Byrne, R. (1988). Tactical deception in primates. *Behavioral and Brain Sciences, 11*(2), 233-244. Doi:10.1017/S0140525X00049682

Williams, K. D. & Nida, S. A. (2011). Ostracism: Consequences and Coping. *Current Directions in Psychological Science, 20*(2), 71–75.

World Health Organisation. (2020). *Novel Coronavirus (2019-nCoV): Situation Report – 1, 21 January 2020*. Geneva: World Health Organisation. https://apps.who.int/iris/handle/10665/330760.

van Zomeren, M., Kutlaca, M. & Turner-Zwinkels, F. (2018). Integrating Who 'We' Are with What 'We' (will Not) Stand For: A Further Extension of the Social Identity Model of Collective Action. *European Review of Social Psychology, 29*(1), 122–160.

Index

Please not that a page number in bold indicates a table, while those in *italics* denotes a figure.

accounts, 116, 118
acculturation, 76, 80–81, 89, 123
   definition, 75
   expectations, *79*
Achen, C.H., 102–103, 105
activism, 152–154, **156**
Adorno, T.W., 83
affiliation, 18, 63, 133
Afghanistan, 58, 63
Africa, 3–4, 7, 32, 74, 109
ageism, 48–49
agency, 133–134, 166, 168
AIDS, 48
Altemeyer, B., 83
Anduiza, E., 50
Appendix, 176
Arabs, 30, 33, 82, 119–127, 129
argumentation
   deconstructing conflict, 116–120
   qualitative data (types), 118
Aristotle, 135
   Politics, 14
armed forces, 99–100, 170
artificial intelligence, 170
Asch, S., 72
assimilation, 8, 10, 73, 75, 77, 80–81, 85, 120
   bonding social capital, 78
   case for, 74
   identity-based cultural, 94
association, 53, 78
asylum-seekers, 2–3, 8, 104
attire, 8, 37
attunment triangle, *87*
authoritarianism, 10, 83
authority, 56, 65, 97, 99, 105, 108, 139, **140**, 166

Babylon (building bridge), 112–128
Bartels, L.M., 102–103, 105
Bauer, M.W., x, 36

Beatles: *All You Need Is Love* (1967), 112
being together, 51, 53
Belfort, J., 24
belief theories (intuitive), **140**
Berlin, I., 93
Berlusconi, S., 148
Berry, J.W., 76
Besta, T., 84
Biden, J.R., 101
black letter law, 42, 106, 142
Black Lives Matter, 49
black sheep effect, 34, 50
Bolsonaro, J., 163
Boney M: *Rivers of Babylon* (1978), 112, 127
bonobos, 18, 135
Bourdieu, P., 78
Brexit, 2, 50
bridging divides, 168
bridging strategy, 11
Brixton riots (1980s), 49
Brockdorff, N., x
Brown, R., 29
Buhagiar, L.J., x, 33
   publications, 180, 188
Buller, D.J., 18
bullying, 30, 107, 110, 149
burden-sharing, 2

Campbell, D.T., 36
cancer, 129, 158
cannabis, 87, 115, 140, 145–147
Carlson, E., 51
Carpenter, M., 16
Castro, P., 65
categorical thinking, 145–146
Catholics, 29, 37, 55, 59–60, 110, 115, **140**
cheating, 20, 28, 38, 68, 72, 99, **140**
   adaptive, 67
cheats, 18, 23, 112

Index

detection, 21, 25
identification, 25
socio-cognitive counter-action, 22
childcare, 56, 132
chimpanzees, 18, 135, 167
China, 105, 141
Chirac, J., 162
Christianity, 71, 119, 136
Churchill, W., 96, 101
Cialdini, R.B., 64
citizens, 2, 13, 98–99, 105, 108, 145, *See also* host citizens
'prone to irritability', 101
second-class, 9
training in democratic skills, 107
citizenship, 8, 22, 41, 98
civil war, 70, 101, 104
claims, 118, 121
ecological scale, 121–127
ranking procedure, 121
Clark, K., 49
Clark, M., 49
climate change, 114, 142, 160
Clinton, W.J., 100
closed-mindedness, 10, 89
coalitions for action, 143–144
cognition, 94, 102, 113
phenotype switching, 141
situated view, 136–138
substantive, 138–142
summary, 141–142
cognitive bias, 10, 32, 34, 109
cognitive closure, 86–87, 89
cognitive dissonance (Festinger), 87
cognitive heuristics, 10, 31–34, 109
accuracy versus usefulness, 31–32
race, 32
cognitive miser theory, 31
cognitive representations: versus 'social representations', 59
cognitive science, 131, 138
Cohen, D., 6–8, 12–13
collaboration, 25, 40, 112
not with just anyone, 25
collective action, 51, 65
collective representations (Durkheim), 58
colonialism, 49
common sense, 30–31, 34, 36, 60
communicative action, 64
structural conditions (Habermas), 64
community, 82–83
community policing, 67
conciliation, 94, 112, 125
confession, 59–60
confirmation bias, 33

conflict, 2, 7, *See also* spiral of conflict
conflict (deconstruction), 10, 128
argumentation, 116–120
bridging intergroup divide, 120–127
conclusion, 127–128
projects, 114–116
conflict-resolution styles, 139
conscience, 150, 167
consensus, 94, 96, 152, 169
conservation, 142, 145
conservatism, 84, 143
conspiracy theories, 161
Constant, B., 102
contact hypothesis (Allport), 151
conversation, 39–40, 148
cooperation, 20–22, 136
cooperatives, 19
corruption, 51, 149, 162
Cosmides, L., 18, 21–22, 25
COVID-19 pandemic, 1–2, 112, 130
cowboys, 12–13, 15, 21
crime, 55
criminal law, 130
critical thinking, 105
Crockett, M.J., 131, 136
Cronbach's alpha, 155
cultural capital, 78
cultural contexts, 94, 131
cultural dimensions (Hofstede), 137
culture, 33, 85–86, 91, 119, 121, 125
Hofstede, 137
culture clash, 111
culture of honour, 6, 12–13
culture of science, x, 145–146

Dahl, R., 170
Darwin, C.R., 18
decision-making, 87, 98, 105, 135, 142
deconstructing conflict, 114–128
deep stories, 138, **140**
profiles, 139
Defoe, D., 14
democracy
actualised, 10, 103–104
'becomes province of self', 106
benefits (Moghaddam), 103
conclusion, 110–111
folk theory, 102
functioning, 16
ideal versus reality, 102–103
'impossible dream', 96–111
politics, 97–103
politics (manner of doing), 100–101
'proxy for civil war', 101
psychology, 106–108

democracy (cont.)
  'self-correcting', 97, 101, 169
  sociology, 104–106
democratic citizens, 101, 108
democratic creed, 108–110
democratic manner, 100
  nine criteria, 105
democratic skills, 107
democratic societies, 108, 161, 169
democratic systems, 10, 94, 111
demographics, 8, 81, 84, 91, 141
deontological ethics, 131, 144
Deuteronomy: promised land, 1
deviance, 62, 94
dictatorships, 65, 96, 104, 169
discord (patching up), 112–128
discrimination, 33, 47–48, 50, 120, 122, 126
displacements, 1, 70
dissent, 34, 93–94, 96, 107, 169
distrust, *See* trust
diversity, 10, 38, 73, 92–93
division of labour, 16, 132
dolls experiment, 49
Donne, John, 14
duels of honour, 14
Durkheim, É., 58–59
dynamic systems model (Krech), 85

educational system, 5, 105
efficiency, 103, 136
engagement effects (political activity), 144–148
equilibration (Heider and Simmel), 87
essentialisation, 33, 35
ethics: 'deontological' versus 'utilitarian' (*qqv*), 131
ethics-politics, 129–149
  conclusion, 148
  moral compass, 11, 142–144, 165
  normative rationality, 131–136
  political activity (engagement and mobilisation effects), 144–148
  worldviews, 136–142
ethnic groups, 82, 92, 94, 119, 121
  internal dissent (silencing), 93
ethno-traditional nationalism, 92–94
European Union, 2–3, 104
everyday extremism, 165
  incremental behavioural scale, 152–155, **157**, 160–162, 164, 167
  Maltese responses, **163**
  ranked items, **156**
  themes and actions, **154**
everyday life, 8, 10, 52–53, 92, 167
evidence, 86, 108–109, 118–119
evolution, 38, 107

evolutionary history, 15–16, 32, 41, 56, 110, 132, 169
exclusion, 77, 94, *See also* social exclusion
  mechanisms, 41
exile, x, 41, 127
exploitation, 6, 28, 38, 149
export, 19–20
extremism in everyday, 152
extremism: breeds counter-extremism, 69

false beliefs: smarties test, 26–27
familiarity heuristic, 31
family, 74, 115
  dual-earner, 56
  extended, 115, 132
far right, 4, 104
farmers, 12, 15, 82
fascism scale (F-Scale), 83
feminism, 49, *See* also gender
Fiske, S.T., 31
folk theories, 131–132, 136, 138
  'build solidarity amongst ingroup strangers', 136
  key feature, 131
France, 4, 58–59, 104, 115
fraud, 24
free speech, 105–106, 161, 164
  'requires psychological skills', 107
free-riding, 21, 72, 75, 131
Frey, B.S., 21
fundamentalism, 29, 62, 104

Gambetta, D., 13, 117
gaslighting, **156–157**, 160–161, **163**
gender, 43–44, 48, 56–57, 63, 104, *See also* women
Giddens, A., 115
Gigerenzer, G., 31
Gittel, R, 78
Goffman, E., 48
government, 16, 35, 51, 63, 96–97, 101, 103
grand projects, 55, 169
grand theories, 10, 131
Greece, 97–98, 100, 154
group cohesion, 34, 42
group membership, 35, 42, 44–47, 94
guns, 63, 101, 110

Habermas, J., 64
Hardin, G., 20
Harré, R., 116
Harris, E., 50
Harris, K., 148
health, 2, 5, 35, 70, 145, 169
Heffner, T.S., 42
HeForShe (feminist males), 48

Heinz's tale, 129–136, 148, 150–151, 155–161
herding economies, 6, 12
Hiroshima and Nagasaki, 113
Hirschfeld, L.A., 32
Hobbes, T., 16–17
Hofstede, G.: cultural dimensions, 137
Homo sapiens, 32
Horizon Europe programme (EU), 152
host citizens, 77
    attitudes, 76
Howarth, C., 44, 49
human nature, 7, 9, 11, 52, 67–68, 108, 112–113
    social-psychological manifestation, 10
human rights, 3, 103, 105–106, 108
hunter-gatherers, 7, 16, 18, 168

identification (friend from foe), 41, 57, 84
identity, 49–51, 93
    negotiation, 47–49
    personal and social, 42–43
    political, 50, 93–94
ideologies, 72, 85, 105, 110
ignorance (attribution), 116, 118, 127
imagination, 8, 14–15, 19–20, 25, 30, 39–40, 60, 67, 69–71, 117, 126
incremental behavioural scale, *See* everyday extremism
individual differences, 5, 12, 81, 137
individuals, 14, 16, 18, 30–31, 41, 48, 57, 84, 87, 148, 169
inequality, 49, 164
influencer, 152
ingroup, 34, 38, 42, 111, 167
ingroup strangers, 133, 136
institutional trust, 164–165
institutions, 40–41, 68, 99, 102
    social, 7
integration, 10, 71–75, 80–81, 85, 89, 119–120, 123
    'affords bonding and bridging social capital', 79
    Arab and Maltese views, *124–125*
    case for, 75–79
    domains, 72
    investment (rather than expense), 74
    Malta (2010, 2019), **91**
    points of view (closed-minded, dialogical, open-minded), **90**
    vignettes, **90**
    win/win solution, 79
intercultural differences, 9–10, 45, 77, 129
interests, 53, 72, 114
    competing, 54
    etymology, 51
intergroup competition, 18, 133
intergroup differences, 10, 97, 129

intergroup divide (bridging), 120–127
intergroup relations, 11, 18, 30, 36
Internal Displacement Monitoring Centre, 1
inter-objectivity, 106, 134–135
interpersonal relations, 44–45, 55
introspective projection (Sammut *et al.*), 28, 67, 99
intuitive belief theories, **140**
irregular migration, 2, 37, 98
Islam, 120–121

Jews, 55, 66, 71, 127
Joffe, H., 48
Johansson, Y., 2, 11, 96, 111
Johnson, B., 100
Jost, J.T., 84
judiciary, 103, 105, 117, 170
Just Stop Oil, 161

Kandinsky, W., 46–47
Kaufmann, E., 91–93, 146
Klee, P., 46–47
Klein, E., 93–96
knowledge, 17, 28, 86, 145–146
Kohlberg, L., 129
    moral reasoning (three stages), 129
Koltko-Rivera, M.E., 142
Krech, D., 85
Kruglanski, A.W., 86–87
    derivation of knowledge, 86
    open- and closed-mindedness, 86
Kuhn, M.H., 42
Kuwait, x, 109, 145

law and order, 16, 19, 40, 130
lawcourts, 3, 17, 65, 134
laws, 20–21
leaders, 106, 163
leadership, 65, 105
left-modernists, 91
left-wing, 85, 165
Lelkes, Y., 50
liberty: 'negative' versus 'positive' (Berlin), 93
Likert scales, 141, 162
Lincoln, A., 102
live and let live, 148–149
livestock, 19, 21
lobby groups, 147
localised worldview, 139, 142–146, 165
    definition, 139
Locke, J., 16
loneliness, 41–42, 52

machismo, 58
Macron, E., 148

Mafia, 13, 65, 117
Mahendran, K., x
majority-minority status, 92
Malta, 3, 22, 81, 84, 94, 115, 119, 139, 147, 154, 162
   Arab and Maltese attitudes, *124–125*
   everyday extremism responses, **163**
   growth in GDP (and labour demand), 91
   intergroup divide (conflict deconstruction), 120–127
   migrant integration, 35, 74
   migrant integration (points of view, 2010, 2019), **91**
   National Statistics Office, 91
marginalisation, 77–78
Marques, J.M., 34, 50
marriages, 115
Martel, Y.: *Life of Pi* (2014), 71
Marx, K.H., 103
McConnell, C, 50
McPartland, T.S., 42
media, 65, 100, 154
Meeus, W.H.J., 167
Meloni, G., 3–4, 148
melting pot, 77–78, 80
mental exercise, 39, 44
mental states, 27–28
Mexico, 3, 75
Mifsud, R., x, 139, 142
migrant-host relations, 9, 71, 80–81
migration, 11, 168
   'in pursuit of own projects', 65
   individual needs, 73
   pacts (EU), 96
   policy challenge (accommodation versus assimilation), 73
   populist backlash, 81–95
   problem, 69–71
   psychology, 4–6
   push-pull theory, 5, 7, 91
   remains everywhere 'perennial concern', 2
   'strikes heart of politics', 97–98
Milgram, S., 108
mind: theory, 25–28
minimal group paradigm, 57
minimal groups, 45–47
   matrices, *46*
minimal model of argumentation (MMA), 118–119
misunderstandings, 32, 45, 66, 129, 145
mobilisation effects, 144–148
   explanation, 146
modernists, 146, 164–165
Moghaddam, F.M., ii, x, 62, 73, 106, 108, 110
   'actualised democracy', 103, 105, 107
   psychology of democracy, 109
   ten convictions democrats need to internalise, 108
moral compass, 142–144
   ethics-politics, *144*
moral dilemmas, 134, 149, 167
moral foundations, 139
moral frameworks, **140**
moral reasoning, 130–131, 160
   stages (Kohlberg), 129
morality, 24, 115, 142
Moscovici, S., 58–60, 115
multiculturalism, 104
   acculturation expectations and social capital, *79*
   case for integration, 75–79
   competing policies, 10, 67–81
   conclusion, 80
   integration (or not), 72–75
   points of view (closed-minded, dialogical, open-minded, **90**
   problem of migration, 69–71
   question of policy, 71–72
multilateralism, 151, 170
Muslims, 36, 45, 55, 57, 66, 71, 74, 119–121
Mutual Intercultural Relations in Pluralistic Societies (MIRIPS) project, 85

naïve realism, 33, 167
narrow-mindedness, 85–86
nationalism, 48, 92–94, 102, 104, 110
nation-states, 92, 104, 130
natural disasters, 2, 7, 70
naturalisation, 98
need for cognitive closure, 86–87
Netflix, 24, 167
New York, 7, 141
Nisbett, R.E., 6–8, 12–13
nonverbal communication, 28
normative rationality, 131–136
nuclear weapons, 63, 112
nudge theory, 27, 35, 64

obedience, 130, 161, 169
obedience studies (Milgram), 108, 166–167, 169
objectivity, 116, 149
omniculturalism, 111
Open Science Framework, 153
open-mindedness, **90**, 109
openness to change, 142–143
openness to experience, 137
OppAttune, 152, 161, 164
opposition, 11, 37, 84, 96, 152, 161, 163
Orban, V., 148, 163
organised crime, 13, 65, 117

orthodox worldview, 139–140, 142–147, 165
  definition, 139
other and othering, 8, 44–45, 127
outcasts, 18, 41
outgroup, 34–35, 38, 42, 47, 50, 72, 80, 84, 111

paired samples t-tests, 155
papacy, 110
parliament, 4, 99–101, 162, 164, 170
partisanship, 50
PASS method of reconciliation, 10, 153–154
  project, argumentation, scale, survey, 127
peace, 111, 127, 168
peer-review, 65
Perner, J., 26
personal identity, 42–43
personal interests, 10, 41, 52–53, 68, 143
personality
  Big-Five model, 137
  Dark Tetrad, 137
  models (explanatory failures), 137
  relative instability and stability, 137
  sociological models, 137
personality approach, 82–84
  authoritarianism, 83
  community, 82–83
persuasion: modality of social influence, 64–65
phylogenesis, 7, 9, 17, 21
places of worship, 71
points of view, 87–91
  dialogical, 88
  metalogical, 88
  monological, 88, 94
  on integration (in Malta), **90–91**
polarisation, 90, 92, 94, 96, 107, 119–120
police, 17, 55, 98, 117, 130, 159–160
policy-making, 105, 145
political activity: engagement effects, 144–148
political dynamics: social relations, 11
political participation, 98, 164–165
political process, 49, 98
political voice, 164–166
politicians, 102, 146, 152, 157–158
politics, 11, 54, 62, 69, 170
  'based on our psychology', 95
  democracy, 97–103
  democratic manner, 100–101
  'economic bedrock' (Marx), 103
  etymology, 97
  fundamental question, 161
  ideological outlooks, 85
  ideologies (left-wing, right-wing), 72, 83, 90
  immigration 'strikes right at heart', 97–98
  key (control over violence), 99
  nature, 20

virtues, 99
who dares wins, 149–170
politics (dark side), 149–170
  'all fair in love and war', 160–163
  art of politicking, 163–166
  conclusion, 170
  doing something about something, 151–153
  everyday extremism, 153–155
  fighting fire with fire, 155–160
  future empirical enquiry, 167
  incremental behavioural scaling, 153–155
  political tug-of-war, *166*, 168, 170
Politics and New Challenge of Migration
  'addressed at psychological dimension', 6
  empirical solution advanced, 11
  focus (psychology of migration), 11
  overview, 9–11
  reconciliatory method, 11
politics of identity, 49–51
polygamy, 37
populism, 74, 102, 104, 164
  contemporary, 91–94
  right-wing, 92–93
populist backlash, 10, 81–95
  conclusion, 94–95
  contemporary populism, 91–94
  personality approach, 82–84
  social cognition approach, 84–91
populists, 164–165
  survivor worldview, 148
power, 99
Power, S.A., 138
pragmatist worldview, 139, 143–146, 148, 165
  definition, 139
Pratto, F., 84
predators, 16, 132–133
prejudice, 28–31, 33, 48, 50
  ABC model, 29
  'crucial thing', 29
  definition (Brown), 29
  relational functions, 30
  social-cognitive (crucial point), 32
primates, 18, 135, 167
principal components analysis, 155
prisoner's dilemma, 130
private property, 20
projects, 54, 60, 62–63
  deconstructing conflict, 114–116
promised land, 1–11
  Deuteronomy, 1
prostitution, 140
proverbs, 31
Psalm 19 (verse 14), 112, 127
psychoanalysis, 59–60
psychology, 10–11, 25, 38, 136, 149, 151

psychology (cont.)
  democracy, 106–108
  'individual differences', 5
  social judgement, 85
psychology of migration, 4–6
public sphere, 10, 52–66
  conclusion, 65–66
  social categories, 55–58
  social influence, 62–65
  social representations, 58–62
push-pull theory of migration, 5, 7
Putin, V.V., 110, 152

qualifiers, 118
qualitative data, 118, 153
qualitative differences, 89
qualitative research, 161
quality of life, 7, 66, 74, 114

Raaijmakers, Q.A., 167
race, 33, 84, 111, 119
  social construction, 32
racism, 44, 49, 119–120, 122
Rawls, J., 16
realistic conflict theory, 10
realistic threat, 35–37, 92, 112
  originally proposed by Campbell (1965), 36
reasoning, 67, 75, 109, 116, 118, 128–129, 131,
  See also moral reasoning
reciprocal altruism, 18
recognition, 49, 93, 113
reconciliation, 126–127, 151
recreation, 53
recreational cannabis, 87, 140, 145–146
Reddit, 155
  incremental behavioural scaling, 153–155
Refugee Act (USA, 1980), 2
relational thinking, 145–146
religion, 71, 110, 115
Renfro, C.L., 35
Rentsch, J. R., 42
reputation, 13, 21
'reservations to science', 145
resilience, 109, 142
revolution, 49, 65, 83, 96
revolutionaries, 147, 164–165
reward worldview, 139, 142–143, 145, 165
  definition, 139
  focus, 143
right-wing authoritarianism, 84
  RWA Scale, 83
Rios, K., 85
robbers cave experiments (Sherif), 151
Rokeach, M., 85–86

closed-mindedness (amongst both left and right-wing tendencies), 90
cognitive organisation (three kinds), 85–86, 88–89
Rome, 97
Rousseau, J.J., 16–17
rule of law, 100, 103, 105, 108, 161
rules of game, 101, 104, 163, 169
Runciman, D., 99–102, 110
Russo-Ukrainian War, 1, 3, 97

Salvatore, S., x
Sammut, G., i, 80, 139
  adaptation in human species, 142
  family, v, xi
  human adaptability to situational demands, 141
  ingroup dissenters, 34
  migrant integration (Maltese arguments), 35
  publications, 180, 182–183, 185, 187–190
  social beliefs (typology), 138
  social representations, 87
  social values theory, 142
  symbolic threat, 36
  worldviews (fivefold typology), 139
  worldviews (manner of operation), 141
Sarkozy, N., 148
Sartawi, M., x
satisficing (Simon), 87
Saudi Arabia, 75
Saussure, F. de: *langue* versus *parole* (language versus speech), 59
Schwartz, S.H., 142
science, 97, 145–146, 166
  self-correcting mechanisms, 97
Scotland, 6, 50
Seabright, P., 17
Secord, P.F., 116
security, 13, 16–17, 21, 41, 66, 79, 117, 119
segregation, 77–78, 120
self-determination, 43, 50
self-enhancement, 142–144
self-esteem, 49, 57–58
self-interest, 113, 130, 137, 148
selfishness, 10, 17, 136, 139
self-report, 141
self-transcendence, 142–143
sellers, 13
separation strategy, 77–78
  bonding social capital, 78
sexism, 44, 48
Shafik, M., 16
shared intentionality, 16
Sidanius, J., 84
Silco (in *Arcane*), 149
Simon, H., 87

situated cognition, 136–138, 140
  definition, 138
smarties test (false beliefs), 26–27
smoke detector principle, 30, 32
social axioms, 138, **140**
social beliefs: five-factor typology, 138
social capital, 79, 83
  'bonding' versus 'bridging', 9–10, 78, 80, 82, 121
  definition, 78, 133
social categories, 40, 55–58, 62
  centrality to identity, 42
  relative value, 57
social categorisation, 44–45
  impact on behaviour, 39–40
social cognition, 10, 24–38, 149
  cognitive heuristics, 31–34
  conclusion, 38
  prejudice and stereotyping, 28–31
  theory of mind, 25–28
  xenophobia, 34–38
social cognition approach, 84–91
  attunment triangle, 87
  narrow-mindedness, 85–86
  need for cognitive closure, 86–87
  points of view, 87–91
  social dominance orientation, 84–85
social contract, 10, 12–23, 35, 68, 72, 130, 147, 169
  basis for reciprocation, 17
  conclusion, 21–24
  essence, 17
  experiments, 14, 19
  'leap from private to collective security arrangements', 16
  theory, 19
  tragedy of commons, 19–21
social contract theory, 98–99
social dominance, 10, 49
social dominance orientation (SDO), 84–85, 164–165
social embeddedness, 132, 136, 138
social exchange, 18
social exclusion, 11, 41
social groups, 10, 40, 45, 47, 59–60, 133, 137
social hierarchy, 84
social identity, 10, 39–51, 53, 94, 108, 133, 148
  categories, 42
  conclusion, 51
  crucial point (how we define ourselves for others), 43
  formulation (three-step process), 57
  minimal groups, 45–47
  negotiating identity, 47–49
  politics, 49–51

root process, 84
social categorisation, 44–45
social identity theory, 45, 53, 84
social influence, 62–65
  'gentle nudge', 64
  'other modalities' (Sammut and Bauer), 65
  persuasion, 64
  project legitimation, 65
social interaction, 16, 27–28
social judgement, 85
social media, **156**, 156, 158–160, 164
social movements, 48, 152, 167
social norms, 133, 138–139, 148
  'both descriptive and prescriptive', 138
social relations, 31, 52, 131
  political dynamics, 11
  real dilemma, 160
social representations, 7, 10, 58–62, 65, 114, 118, 151
  'compete with each other in public domain', 61–62
  'conceived in service of projects', 115
  'framing object in line with group's *raison d'être*', 60
  music, 61
  project-serving, 60
  psychoanalysis, 59–60
  Sammut, 87
  systemic conceptions, 59
  systems of construals, 62
  versus 'cognitive representations', 59
socialisation, 55, 84, 109, 137
  abstract concepts, 55
  definition, 56
  gender roles, 56
sociality, 9, 18, 52, 135, 137
sociology: democracy, 104–106
spiral of conflict, 92, 118, 121, 153
  definition, 90
spoiled identity, 48–49
state, 13, 117
state of nature, 15
statistical weighting, 162
Stephan, W.G., 35
stereotypes, 45, 48, 70
  definition, 29
  main point, 30
  relational functions, 30
stereotyping, 28–31, 167
stigma, 8, 31, 48–49, 63, 119
Stroebe, W., 21
subjectivity, 43, 86, 106, 116
subreddits, 153
substantive cognition, 138–142
sunbathing, 114

surplus, 18, 35
survival, 6–7, 16, 32, 38, 41–42, 52, 94, 112, 132, 169
survival of fittest, 107, 110, 168
survivor worldview, 139, **140**, 141–143, 145–146, 165
  definition, 139
  populist politicians, 148
symbolic threat, 36–38
symbolic universes, 139, **140**
Syria, 3, 75, 91, 101, 104

Tajfel, H., 45, 50–51, 57
Taliban, 63–64
Taylor, S.E., 31
technocracy tolerance, 145–146
technocrats, 147, 164–166
terrorism, 29, 63, 69–70, 75, 152
theory of mind, 25–28
  cultural-type, 133
  'evolved psychological mechanism for detecting cheating', 28
  false beliefs, 26–27
  mental states, 27–28
  social extension, 68
  social interaction, 27–28
  street-sellers (purchaser distrust versus FOMO), 25–26
  tenet, 27
Thomas, W.I., 82–83
Thomas-Kilmann conflict mode instrument, 139
threat, 30, 34–38, 74, 85, 100, *See also* xenophobia
Thurstone scaling, 162
tipping point, 102, 150
Todd, P.M., 31
tolerance, **90**, 108, *See also* technocracy tolerance
Tomasello, M., 16, 132–135, 139, 150, 166
  'commonality of experience', 133
Tooby, J., 18, 21–22, 25
tourism, 69
trade, 12, 18
traditionalists, 147, 164–165
tragedy of commons, 19–21, 23, 35–36, 64–65, 98
  'spanner in works of cooperative activity', 20
tribes, 17, 132, 167
Trump, D., 100–101, 148, 152, 163
trust, 25–26, 28, 40, 68
  distrust, 67–68, 111–112, 139
truth, 35, 67, 88, 113, 116
Turner, J.C., 50
twenty statements test (Kuhn and McPartland), 42

United Kingdom, 2, 48, 88, 104, 154
  Maltese migrants, 80
United Nations Security Council, 63
United States, 3, 63, 75, 105
  homicide rates (northern versus southern states), 6–7, 12
  Polish community, 82–83
  presidential election (2024), 4
universities: student tourism, 69
University of Malta, i, x, 152
utilitarian ethics, 131, 143–144, 167

values, 33, 35–36, 71, 74, 108, 114, 134, 137, 142, 144
van Zomeren, M., 51
Vidal, A., 78
violence, 63, 99
virtue, 100–101, 105
von der Leyen, U., 3
voting, 48, 65, 102–103, 105–106

war, 5, 70, 104, 113
warrants, 118
welfare state, 52
wellbeing, 18, 35, 42, 66, 169
Westwood, S.J., 50
Wilcoxon-rank test, 155
Wolf of Wall Street, 24
women, 3, 36, 56, 98, *See also* feminism
  educational value (USA versus Taliban Afghanistan), 58
  suffragette movement, 48
worldviews, 132, 136–142, 164
  fivefold typology (Sammut *et al.*), 139
  further research required, 141
  literature 'remains scant', 138
  localised, orthodox, pragmatist, reward, survivor (*qqv*), 139–148
  situated cognition, 136–138
  substantive cognition, 138–142
  summary, 141
  typology, 142

xenophobia, 4, 10, 34–38, 81
  definition, 37
  realistic threat, 35–36
  symbolic threat, 36–38
Xi, J., 110, 152

Yanukovych, V., 97
Ybarra, O., 85

Znaniecki, F., 82–83

For EU product safety concerns, contact us at Calle de José Abascal, 56–1°,
28003 Madrid, Spain or eugpsr@cambridge.org.